CONTENTS

The P&O liner *Macedonia* and *Ville de la Ciotat* of Messageries Maritimes berthed at Circular Quay East on 25 June 1904.

Migrant Ships to Australia and New Zealand
1900 to 1939

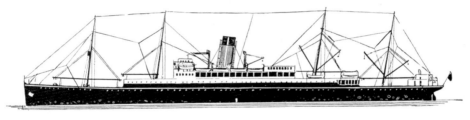

Ceramic

Peter Plowman

ROSENBERG

in association with

transpress NZ

Four migrant ships together at Princes Pier, Port Melbourne, in 1926. Left foreground is *Oronsay*, with *Euripides* berthed behind and *Demosthenes* on the other side of the pier, with *Moreton Bay* berthed ahead. Station Pier is under construction in the background, with Town Pier behind it. (Bobby Brookes collection)

First published in Australia in 2009
by Rosenberg Publishing Pty Ltd
PO Box 6125, Dural Delivery Centre NSW 2158
Phone: 61 2 9654 1502 Fax: 61 2 9654 1338
rosenbergpub@smartchat.net.au
www.rosenbergpub.com.au

Published in New Zealand in 2009
by *transpress* NZ, P.O. Box 10-215
Wellington, NZ
transpress@paradise.net.nz
www.transpressnz.com

The National Library of Australia Cataloguing-in-Publication

Author: Plowman, Peter.

Title: Migrant ships to Australia and New Zealand 1900 to 1939 /
          Peter Plowman.

Edition: 1st ed.

ISBN: 9781877058592 (pbk.) (Australian edition)

ISBN:.....9781877418105 (pbk.) (New Zealand edition)

Notes: Includes index.

Subjects: Passenger ships—Australia—History.
          Passenger ships—New Zealand—History.
          Shipping—Australia—History.
          Shipping—New Zealand—History.
          Immigrants—Australia—History—20th century.
          Immigrants—New Zealand—History—20th century.
          Australia—Emigration and immigration—History—20th century.
          New Zealand—Emigration and immigration—History—20th century.

Dewey Number: 387.243099

Printed in Thailand by Kyodo Nation Printing Services

Introduction

I have frequently been asked for information about ships that brought migrants to both Australia and New Zealand in pre-1939 years. This book is the result of several years of intense research about these ships.

There are numerous differences between the pre-1939 and post-1946 periods with regard to migrant movements. In the years after World War II there was an intensive assisted passage scheme to attract migrants from Britain and several European countries, and also the mass migration of 'displaced persons', under the auspices of the International Refugee Organisation, using specifically designated ships for this role.

In the period covered by this book, there was no regular assisted passage scheme available, though from time to time incentives would be offered by various governments. For the vast majority of migrants, moving to a new country meant paying a full fare, and they mostly travelled on regular passenger liners.

In the early years of the twentieth century companies providing passenger services to Australia included P&O, Orient-PSNC, Aberdeen Line, North German Lloyd and Messageries Maritimes, while Shaw Savill & Albion, White Star Line and the New Zealand Shipping Company were the primary operators to New Zealand. Other companies offered passages to Australia and New Zealand via South Africa in cargo ships providing temporary quarters in their holds for persons unable to afford the fares required by the liner companies.

Domestic servants were in great demand in New Zealand in the early 1900s. In Wellington, middle-class matrons would board immigrant ships to lure any single women into their employ. In Napier in 1906 a 'domestic syndicate' paid the fares of 23 servants.

The first ten years of the new century saw the regular introduction of new and larger tonnage to operate to both Australia and New Zealand. Probably the most notable of these vessels was the Athenic trio built for the entry into the New Zealand passenger trade of the White Star Line, while from 1903 P&O began taking delivery of what would develop into a class of ten liners in their M class for their Australian service.

The newbuildings culminated with the five ships of the Orsova class built for the Orient Line in 1909, while the New Zealand Shipping Company took delivery of three new ships during 1909/10. A year later, the P&O Branch Line took delivery of five vessels specifically designed to bring migrants to Australia in large numbers.

Although the vast majority of migrants arriving in Australia and New Zealand came from Great Britain, there was also a steady flow of settlers from Germany and Italy, as well as a trickle from other countries. From 1910 there was an enormous increase in demand for migrant passages to Australia and New Zealand from Britain, largely at the expense of migration to Canada.

Instead of a bid by the Commonwealth Government to attract migrants to Australia, this was largely left to the individual states. On 23 January 1912 the Victorian Government signed a contract with three shipping lines to bring some 24,000 British assisted migrants to Melbourne at £12 per person over the next three years.

New South Wales was also seeking new settlers, but preferred a scheme of nominated immigrants whose fares would be paid in part or full by relatives or friends already in Australia. A report in the *Sydney Morning Herald* on 14 February 1911 stated:

A declaration of the Government policy with regard to nominated immigrants was made yesterday by Mr Carmichael (the Assistant Treasurer). It has been decided to limit the nomination of adults to agriculturists, domestic servants, artisans, and manual workers, except in the case of near relatives, where there will be no restriction. Among the classes for which nominations will not be received are clerks, shop assistants, and similar occupations.

On Monday, 8 May 1911, the *Sydney Morning*

Gothic, right, berthed alongside *Ruapehu* in Lyttelton.

Herald carried the following story from their London correspondent:

> The steamer *Mamari* has sailed with 640 emigrants for New South Wales. Mr T. A. Coghlan, Agent-General, has arranged for a full complement by the Shaw Savill steamers every two months, in addition to those who will travel by the regular liners.
>
> The emigrants who have received assisted passages, and those who have been nominated for Western Australia, since the New Year, number 2,600. Sir Newton Moore, the Agent-General, has arranged that besides the Orient steamers taking 450 monthly the White Star Line will take 400 each trip in September, October and December. The nominated passages average 130 weekly.

To meet the increase in demand for migrant passages to Australia and New Zealand, several shipping companies built large cargo ships which could be fitted with temporary quarters for a thousand or more passengers on the outward voyage. One such ship was *Port Lincoln*, which departed London in August 1912 on its maiden voyage to Australia. The ship's doctor for the voyage, Bernard Dawson, later recalled that he 'had to look after the crew and 700 migrants, including 150 children, who were accommodated in cramped eight and sixteen-berth dormitories, hedged with flimsy walls and lined with wooden bunks scarcely softened by straw mattresses and pillows'.

The voyage had barely started before bad weather was encountered and the passengers went to their bunks. In those days there were no effective drugs to combat seasickness, so Dr Dawson gave the suffering passengers doses of potassium bromide laced with tincture of ginger. Fresh water was always in short supply and severely rationed, and there was one bathroom that had constant hot seawater provided for a shower.

The arrival of ships carrying large numbers of migrants was occasionally reported. On 21 February 1913 the following small item appeared in the *Sydney Morning Herald* from their Melbourne correspondent:

> The Tyser liner *Hawkes Bay* arrived from London today, having on board 531 newcomers for Victoria. On Saturday the Aberdeen steamer *Norseman* is due at Melbourne. She has on board 551 passengers, including landseekers with capital of £6,370.

The high cost of a passage to New Zealand had discouraged migration, but numbers rose with the introduction in 1904 of government assistance for the fare, and boomed in the six years before the First World War, reaching a peak of 12,000 net migration in 1913.

Migrants considered suitable were not the down-and-out, but, as Prime Minister W. F. Massey said, 'people of the right class — steady, industrious and respectable people'. They had to provide evidence of some capital, and a certificate as to health and character. New Zealanders could also nominate friends and relatives for assistance; about half of the 36,563 assisted immigrants of 1904–15 came out to New Zealand in this way.

The outbreak of war brought the transportation of migrants to Australia and New Zealand to almost a complete halt, with many ships being taken up for military duty, leaving a skeleton service which gradually reduced to almost nothing as the war progressed.

The end of the war brought about another boom in demand by migrants for passages, as for the first time the British government subsidised migration. This started with a scheme in 1919 to assist the migration of ex-servicemen to Australia, New Zealand and other British possessions, and was followed by the *Empire Settlement Act* of 1922, which provided support for family emigration to the dominions.

As a result, the early 1920s saw a major increase in the number of new ships being introduced onto the migrant trades. During 1922 alone no less than fifteen liners joined the Australian migrant trade.

The early 1920s also saw one of New Zealand's major immigration flows. There was much that was familiar about the character of the migrants — women and children were well represented, craftsmen and builders were common among the men, domestic servants among the women. For the first time industry workers figured prominently.

One unusual immigration scheme brought out juveniles to New Zealand farms. Funded by New Zealand sheep farmers, it was known as the Flock House scheme, after the property in the Manawatu where the young people were trained as farmers, and was intended as a debt of gratitude to British seamen. The 635 boys and 128 girls who came out were the children of seamen killed or wounded in World War I.

During the early 1920s the number of migrants arriving in Australia from Italy began to increase quite dramatically. It was stated the reason for the sudden influx of such a large number of Italians was that American immigration regulations had been tightened up and very few Italians were going from Italy to the United States, and Australia was now regarded as the most likely place to make their future.

According to the Consul-General for Italy in Australia, 'all the immigrants paid their own fares, and the fee for the visa of their passports by the British Consuls at Italian ports'.

The influx of migrants from Italy to Australia continued through the 1920s, a situation that did not always sit comfortably with many Australians of British background, who wanted more settlers to be encouraged to migrate from the mother country. On 8 April 1925 an announcement was made that over the next ten years the British and Australian governments would provide funds to enable about 450,000 men and women to migrate from Britain to Australia, and help them buy stock, equipment and the materials required to build houses for themselves.

An economic downturn hit New Zealand in 1927 and became a full depression from 1929. The country was no longer an attractive destination for migrants, and government assistance tailed off before being abandoned in all but name in 1931. The Department of Immigration was shut down in 1932. From that year until 1935, 10,000 more people left New Zealand than arrived. In 1935 there was only one assisted migrant.

With the deepening effects of the worldwide depression, the number of migrants seeking passages to Australia also began to drop off during the 1930s. In order to try and attract migrants, in March 1938 the Australian Government decided to reintroduce an assisted migration scheme from Britain, and by the end of that year almost 5,000 persons had taken advantage of the new scheme, and it was hoped that number would be exceeded in 1939. However, with the outbreak of war in September 1939 the movement of migrants to Australia and New Zealand came to a complete halt.

Acknowledgments

When I decided to write this book, I had a look through my photograph collection to see if I had enough pictures to form the basis of what would be needed to bring the text to life. Over the years I have been the recipient of many photographs from the collections of several friends who have since passed away, in particular Bob Tompkins, Dennis Brook, Fred Roderick and Peter Britz, and these contained a vast array of material that I have used in the following pages.

When it came to putting the text and pictures together, I found a number of gaps, but have been very grateful to various sources who have supplied me with the photographs I needed to make this book as complete as possible. Thanks are extended to Martin Navarro, Ian Farquhar, David Finch and John Bennett.

In this regard I am particularly grateful to John Bone, President of the Victoria Branch of the World Ship Society, for giving me permission to use pictures contained in their collection, and to Glen Stuart for sending them to me. I am also very grateful to Michael Gregg of the Western Australia Maritime Museum for supplying material from the McKenna Collection, and to Rob Henderson, the P&O historian, for his generous assistance with both voyage details and photographs.

The written material in this book has been compiled from notes I have made over many years complemented with new material gathered from extensive research in the newspapers of the day. All dates shown are taken directly from newspapers.

While I have made every endeavour for accuracy in the text, any errors, omissions or misinterpretations included in this book are entirely my own responsibility.

ORIENT

Built: 1879 by John Elder, Glasgow
Gross tonnage: 5,386
Dimensions: 446 x 46 ft/135.9 x 14.1 m
Service speed: 15 knots
Propulsion: Compound inverted/single propeller

The first vessel to be built for the Orient Line, *Orient* was launched on 6 June 1879, and attracted enormous interest in Britain and Australia on completion, as she was the largest vessel then operating on the route to Australia, and far superior to the vessels being operated by the P&O Line. *Orient* provided accommodation for 120 first class, 130 second class and 300 third class passengers.

Orient left London on 3 November 1879 on her maiden voyage to Australia, going by way of Cape Town to make her first port of call at Adelaide on 12 December, continuing to Melbourne and Sydney, the voyage taking 39 days. At that time the third class fare from London to Australia was 18 guineas, while first class fares started at 50 guineas. From 1881 the Orient Line began routing some voyages through the Suez Canal, though in July 1882 that had to be abandoned due to unrest in Egypt. *Orient* was scheduled to depart from London on 24 August 1882 for Australia, but was taken over by the Admiralty to carry troops to Egypt instead. The Egyptian crisis was settled within a few months, and *Orient* was soon back in her owners' service. The Suez transits resumed on alternate sailings, and from

November 1883 all voyages used the canal.

In 1884 electric lighting was installed in *Orient*, and during the latter part of 1897 the vessel was taken out of service for an extensive refit. The original machinery was removed and triple expansion engines installed, and also new boilers. Externally her appearance was drastically altered by the removal of two masts, while the original two funnels were replaced by a single stack of great height. This brought her appearance and machinery into line with the newer ships of the fleet.

One of the first vessels to be called up for trooping duties when the Boer War started was *Orient*, which was requisitioned in November 1899, becoming Transport No. 24, and for the next four years served in this capacity, making many voyages between Britain and South Africa. It was not until June 1903 that *Orient* was released from Government service, and after a refit resumed her former service to Australia with a departure from London on 17 July. By this time *Orient* was the oldest vessel in the Orient Line fleet, and much smaller than the more recent additions.

During 1909 the Orient Line took delivery of five new liners, and with the arrival of the last of these in November 1909, *Orient* was no longer required. Her final departure from London was on 23 July 1909, and on her return to Britain she was laid up pending disposal. The following year the vessel was sold to shipbreakers in Italy, being renamed *Oric* for her final voyage from London to the breakers' yard.

Orient after rebuilding in 1897.

AUSTRAL

Built: 1881 by John Elder & Co., Glasgow
Gross tonnage: 5,524
Dimensions: 456 x 48 ft/139 x 14.6 m
Service speed: 16 knots
Propulsion: Compound inverted/single propeller

Austral was the second ship built for the Orient Line, being an enlarged and improved version of *Orient*. Accommodation was provided for 120 first class, 130 second class and 300 third class passengers. Launched on 24 December 1881 and delivered to the Orient Line in April 1882, *Austral* sailed from London on 19 May 1882 on her maiden voyage to Australia, travelling by way of Cape Town to Adelaide, Melbourne and Sydney.

On her second voyage from London, departing on 7 September 1882, *Austral* was delayed a week at Cape Town by a smallpox epidemic. While steaming across the Indian Ocean she was afflicted by engine problems, and sails were rigged to maintain her progress until repairs could be effected. *Austral* arrived in Sydney on 9 November 1882, and the following day moved to Neutral Bay to take on coal for the return voyage.

A coal barge was secured to the starboard side of the vessel, as it was normal practice to load one side completely before moving to the other side. As the mass in the bunkers grew the ship developed a list to starboard, and during the early hours of 11 November the lowest portholes went beneath the surface of the water. As the portholes were all open, the result was a sudden deluge of water rushing into the ship, and within a few minutes she had gone to the bottom of the harbour, fortunately upright, and with some of her superstructure remaining above the water. At the time there were about eighty officers and crew on board, most of them asleep. Nearly all were able to scramble to safety, but the purser, refrigeration engineer and three Lascar seamen were drowned.

Austral was refloated on 28 February 1883 and towed to Cockatoo Dock for temporary repairs. Once the vessel was seaworthy again, she left for Britain without any passengers, going via Auckland and Cape Horn. *Austral* went to the Clyde for an extensive refit, which lasted almost a year. During the course of the work the accommodation was improved and the funnels were heightened by 16 ft/4.88 m, though the extra sections were of a smaller diameter than the original funnels, which gave the ship a rather odd appearance.

Ready for service in April 1884, *Austral* did not return immediately to the Australian trade, but instead was chartered for six months to the Allan Line to run between Liverpool and New York. *Austral* resumed her place on the Australian service with a departure from London on 11 November 1884. From now on all her voyages were via the Suez Canal in both directions.

On 9 February 1900, *Austral* was chartered by the British Government to carry troops to South Africa, but she was handed back to the Orient Line on 26 April 1900, and returned to the Australian trade. *Austral* made her final departure from Tilbury for Australia on 21 November 1902, and was sold on 8 May 1903 to shipbreakers from Genoa.

Austral with heightened funnels.

ROME

Built: 1881 by Caird & Co., Greenock
Gross tonnage: 5,545 gross
Dimensions: 449 x 44 ft/136.8 x 13.4 m
Service speed: 16 knots.
Propulsion: Triple expansion/single propeller

P&O took delivery of their first steel-hulled vessel, *Ravenna,* in 1880, but owing to a shortage of this new material their next two new liners were built with iron hulls. Designed to operate on either the Australian or Indian trades, the two ships were named *Rome* and *Carthage,* and were completed almost together.

Each ship provided berths for 187 first-class and 146 second-class passengers, the standard of accommodation being the highest yet installed on any P&O liner, and they were powered by a compound inverted steam engine.

Rome was the first to enter service, departing London on 5 October 1881, with *Carthage* following on 28 October. The departure of *Rome* was the first by a P&O vessel from Tilbury docks, which was to remain the P&O base for over 90 years. *Rome* called at Bombay on her maiden voyage, while *Carthage* stopped at Ceylon.

In 1887 *Rome* damaged her rudder in the Bay of Biscay when steaming through flotsam while outward bound for Australia, but her captain decided to continue the voyage though her steering was affected. While passing through the Suez Canal the vessel ran aground, doing more damage to the rudder and sternpost, so the passengers were offloaded and the ship returned to Britain for repairs.

In 1892 P&O decided to upgrade the two liners. *Rome* was taken out of service first and given an extensive refit, during which she was lengthened 19ft/5.7m, and the third mast was restepped closer to the after funnel. The original machinery was replaced by more modern triple expansion engines that raised her service speed to 16 knots.

The refit proved so expensive that plans to alter *Carthage* in a similar fashion were dropped, and she was transferred to the Indian service, her final voyage on the Australian trade departing London on 1 September 1892.

For the next ten years *Rome* remained on the Australian trade, but in 1903 P&O took delivery of the first of a new series of liners to replace their older tonnage on the Australian route, some of which were transferred to the Indian trade. During 1903 *Carthage* was withdrawn from service and sold to shipbreakers, and on 7 August that year *Rome* left London on her final voyage to Australia.

Following another refit, during which *Rome*'s accommodation was altered to carry 150 passengers in first class only, she was renamed *Vectis,* and entered service as the first P&O full-time cruise ship. Over the next eight years she made numerous cruises from Britain to Scandinavia in summer and the Atlantic islands in winter. When withdrawn from this service in 1912, she was sold to the French Government for conversion into a hospital ship, but this plan was abandoned, and in 1913 she was sold to shipbreakers in Italy.

Rome

IONIC / SOPHOCLES

Built: 1883 by Harland & Wolff, Belfast
Gross tonnage: 4,753
Dimensions: 440 x 44 ft/134.1 x 13.4 m
Service speed: 13 knots
Propulsion: Compound inverted/single propeller

Launched on 11 January 1883, *Ionic* was completed in less than three months, being handed over to White Star Line on 28 March. *Ionic* was the first of a pair of large cargo ships, the second, *Doric*, being launched on 10 March 1883, and completed on 4 July that year. These ships were intended to operate on the Atlantic trade, but by the time they were nearing completion there was insufficient business for them, and both vessels were chartered to the New Zealand Shipping Company. Accommodation was originally installed for only 70 first class passengers, but on being chartered by NZSC temporary quarters for migrants were installed in the holds for the outward voyage.

Ionic left London on 25 April 1883 on her maiden voyage via South Africa to New Zealand, taking 43 days 22 hours five minutes to reach Wellington, a new record for the route. Altogether *Ionic* was to make four round trips for NZSC, being joined on 26 July by *Doric*, which also made four round trips.

When the NZSC charter ended late in 1884, Shaw Savill Line arranged to charter both ships, and *Ionic* left London on 3 December 1884, followed by *Doric* on 5 January 1885, again voyaging around South Africa to New Zealand.

On 8 February 1893 *Ionic* lost her propeller north of Cape Town, but was fortunate to be found three days later by the Castle Line steamer *Hawarden Castle*, and towed to Cape Town.

During 1895 *Ionic* had quadruple expansion machinery installed, while *Doric* received a triple expansion engine, though by then *Doric* had made her final sailing to New Zealand, leaving London on 21 March 1895, after which she was returned to White Star Line.

Ionic remained in the Shaw Savill fleet until 1899, making her final departure from London on 21 December that year. She was then used briefly to carry troops to the Boer War before being sold in September 1900 to the Aberdeen Line, to replace their vessel *Thermopylae*, which had been wrecked. Renamed *Sophocles*, and repainted in Aberdeen Line colours, dark green hull and yellow funnel, *Sophocles* left London on 23 October 1900 on her first voyage to Australia, going by way of Cape Town to Melbourne and Sydney, and made four round trips a year on this route.

In 1905 the Aberdeen Line became a public company, White Star Line and Shaw Savill & Albion becoming the majority shareholders in the firm, thus bringing the career of this vessel full circle. On 21 August 1906 *Sophocles* left London on her final voyage to Australia, then was laid up as reserve ship. The building of *Pericles* in 1908 meant *Sophocles* was no longer needed, and on 4 April 1908 she was sold to shipbreakers at Morecambe.

Ionic as *Sophocles*.

ABERDEEN, AUSTRALASIAN and DAMASCUS

Built: 1882/84/87 by Robert Napier & Sons, Glasgow, 1890 by
  Hall Russell, Aberdeen
Gross tonnage: 3,684/3,662/3,726
Dimensions: 362 x 44 ft/110.3 x 13.4 m
Service speed: 12 knots
Propulsion: Triple expansion/single propeller

George Thompson & Co. is better remembered as the Aberdeen Line, under which name they operated a fleet of sailing ships to Australia for over forty years and then switched to steamships. The Aberdeen Line sailing ships were all given dark green hulls, and had a good reputation for comfort and regularity of service.

The opening of the Suez Canal was to bring about great changes in the Australian trade, and while the Aberdeen Line continued to send their sailing ships around the Cape of Good Hope, other companies were building steamers and utilising the shorter route through the new waterway, and in the process taking all the passengers and cargo that had previously been carried by the sailing ships. However, in those early days the steam engine was still not fully reliable, so the Aberdeen Line bided their time until it was essential for to change to steam propulsion if they were to survive.

Their first steamer had an iron hull and triple expansion machinery, the first time this type of engine was installed in an ocean-going ship. Launched in December 1881, and named *Aberdeen*, accommodation was installed for 45 first class and 650 emigrants, though the first class cabins were situated right aft in sailing ship fashion. The ship was also given the famous dark green hull of the sailing ships, with pale cream upperworks and a light yellow funnel.

On 24 March 1882 *Aberdeen* left London on her maiden voyage, with only one stop at Cape Town for coal, reaching Melbourne in 42 days. In order to take advantage of the steady winds that blew in the roaring forties, all three masts were rigged to carry sail, and after leaving Cape Town the ship headed far south to catch the prevailing wind, and raised sail as well as being propelled by the engine, thus increasing speed considerably. On the return voyage, *Aberdeen* was routed through the Suez Canal, and made the entire trip on engine propulsion. For several years the only Australian ports visited were Melbourne and Sydney.

The successful introduction of a steam vessel led the Aberdeen Line to order a second vessel, which was named *Australasian* when launched on 10 April 1884. She was virtually a repeat of *Aberdeen*, although only the foremast was rigged to carry sail. *Australasian* left London on 2 July 1884 on her maiden voyage, carrying 640 migrants, and following the same route out and back as *Aberdeen*.

In February 1885, *Australasian* was one of two ships, the other being *Iberia* of PSNC, requisitioned by the New South Wales Government to carry troops to the Sudan, the first time Australian troops had officially been sent overseas. The force comprised an infantry battalion of 522 men, with 24 horses for officers, and two artillery batteries numbering 212 men and 172 horses. The hulls of both ships were repainted white, with *Iberia* being given the number 1NSW while *Australasian* had the pennant number 2NSW painted on the bow.

On 3 March the troops marched from Victoria Barracks to Circular Quay, where the two ships were berthed. The majority of the artillery men went on board the *Australasian*, where the officers used the first class cabins, while other ranks were allocated the accommodation used by migrants on the voyage from Britain to Australia. Also on board the *Australasian* were 218 horses, which were put into specially constructed stalls in the holds.

The two ships disembarked their troops at the Red Sea port of Suakin, where *Iberia* arrived on 29 March, and *Australasian* the next day. Both ships then continued to Britain, where the hull of *Australasian* was again painted green, and the vessel resumed its place on the trade to Australia.

Over the next four years the company was content to operate just these two steamships, while still maintaining some of their sailing ships on the route as well. However, the days of sail were drawing to a close and the company was forced to order another steamship to remain competitive.

The new ship was another repeat of the *Aberdeen* design, but built with a steel hull. Launched on 31 October 1887 and named *Damascus*, the vessel left London on 17 January 1888 on its maiden voyage, going out to Australia around the Cape, calling only at Melbourne and Sydney, then returning through the Suez Canal.

In 1890 a fourth vessel of the same design was ordered from the Hall Russell shipyard at Aberdeen and when launched on 19 September 1891 it was named *Thermopylae* after the most famous of all the Aberdeen Line clipper ships. On 24 November 1891 this vessel made her maiden departure from London, arriving in Melbourne on 12 January 1892.

With the entry into service of *Thermopylae* the Aberdeen Line withdrew the last of their sailing ships from the Australian trade. Now able to operate a monthly service with their four steamships, the company enjoyed considerable success.

In 1895 the route from Australia to Britain was changed, with the Suez Canal transit being dropped, and the ships returning by way of Durban and Cape Town, and also Teneriffe. Up to this time the company had enjoyed a monopoly on the emigrant trade via South Africa, but in 1896 the Blue Anchor Line began

Damascus

placing passenger ships on the route and in 1899 the White Star Line also entered the trade with four large liners that were a great improvement on the Aberdeen Line ships.

During 1899 two more ships were added to the Aberdeen Line fleet, though they were only half the size of the White Star ships. The same year also brought the first loss for the company, as on 11 September 1899 *Thermopylae* ran aground on Green Point as she was approaching Cape Town on a voyage back to Britain, and became a total loss. Fortunately no lives were lost, and the valuable cargo of gold being carried from Australia was salvaged before the ship broke up where she lay.

It was also at this time that the ports of Albany and Adelaide were added to the Aberdeen Line outbound schedule, with Fremantle being visited on the return trip only. Over the next few years the three surviving original ships were completely overshadowed by their competitors' vessels, and orders were placed for two new ships, which came out in 1903 as *Miltiades* and 1904 as *Marathon*. The introduction of these vessels meant that the two oldest ships could be withdrawn, *Australasian* making her final departure from London on 16 January 1904. *Aberdeen* was also withdrawn in 1904, but kept ready for use as a reserve ship, and in 1905 made two further voyages to Australia, the last of which departed London on 19 December 1905. By this time both ships were up for sale, being purchased by the Turkish Government

in 1906, with *Aberdeen* being renamed *Halep*, while *Australasian* became *Scham*.

Of the original quartet, only *Damascus* now remained in the Aberdeen Line fleet, and in 1907 her first class accommodation was removed, though emigrants were still catered for. By now the Aberdeen Line was under the joint control of the White Star Line and Shaw Savill, with the result that new and much larger ships were being ordered, the first of which was due to enter service in mid-1908. In anticipation of this *Damascus* made her final departure from London on 18 February 1908, and on her return was laid up. In 1909 she was sold to N. G. Pittaluga, of Italy, and on 2 June 1910 arrived in Genoa to be broken up.

This left the former *Aberdeen* and *Australasian* still afloat, under Turkish ownership. When war came in 1914, Turkey sided with Germany, and their ships were prey for British submarines. One of these was the *E11*, which was sent to patrol the Sea of Marmora in August 1915. On 6 August *E11* torpedoed *Scham* off Constantinople, but the vessel was able to survive the damage inflicted and was beached, though she would not return to service again during the war. Less than three weeks later, on 25 August, *E11* came upon *Halep*, and hit her with a torpedo too, but once again the ship was able to be beached. *Halep* was later refloated and sold for breaking up, while *Scham* was refloated during 1918, converted into a coal hulk, and served in this capacity until being sold to shipbreakers at Savona, arriving there on 1 August 1955.

ORIZABA and OROYA

Built: 1886 by Barrow Shipbuilding Co., Barrow
Gross tonnage: 6,057/6,077 gross
Dimensions: 460 x 50 ft/140.2 x 15.2 m
Service speed: 16 knots
Propulsion: Triple expansion/single screw.

The Pacific Steam Navigation Company became involved in the Australian trade as a result of heavy losses they were incurring on the route from Liverpool to the west coast of South America. In 1874 they were forced to lay up eleven steamers, and in 1877 three of them were chartered by the Orient Line to commence their service to Australia. These vessels plus one other were later purchased by the Orient Line, but as a result of their relationship in 1879 a joint service to be operated by ships of both companies to Australia came into effect. Initially the PSNC utilised ships that had been built for their South American route, but in 1885 they placed an order for two new ships designed for the Australian route.

The first to be completed was *Orizaba*, launched on 6 May 1886, which left London on her maiden voyage on 30 September 1886, calling at Naples before passing through the Suez Canal on her way to Melbourne and Sydney, where she arrived on 19 November. Next day the *Sydney Morning Herald* reported:

The *Orizaba* is the largest mail steamer that has yet visited Australian waters. She is fitted for 126 first class passengers, and 154 second class passengers, in staterooms which extend along nearly the whole range of the main deck, and she also has accommodation for about 400 steerage passengers in the 'tween decks below. Forward of the machinery and boiler compartments on the main deck is situated the first class saloon, a spacious apartment 32 feet long, communicating by a handsome staircase with an elegant drawing room and a comfortable smoking room in a broad deckhouse overhead. The second class saloon, which is aft, is about 28 feet long, and like that of first class, extends the whole breadth of the vessel. There is a handsome smoking room above, and in point of comfort and fulfilment of the wants of intending voyagers, no pains have been spared to make the after cabin, no less than the forward one, as desirable a place of abode as the watery foundation of a vessel will permit. The saloons, staterooms and passages are well lighted and ventilated by handsome skylights, decklights, and very large sidelights, and by means of Green's system of artificial ventilation, which is applied to the whole of the cabin accommodation, a current of cool air may be set up at will even when running before the wind in the tropics. The *Orizaba* left London with a total of 761 passengers, of whom 13 were for Naples, 26 for Adelaide, 313 for Melbourne and 337 for Sydney.

The *Orizaba* proved herself to be a splendid seaboat in the heavy weather which was encountered, and though in the opinion of many scarcely so attractive or well-finished a boat as the Clyde-built ships, yet she is undoubtedly a magnificent craft, and a marvellous testimony to the increasing importance of the trade between London and the Australian colonies.

The second vessel was named *Oroya* when launched on 31 August 1886, and was handed over to PSNC in January 1887. *Oroya* departed London on 17 February on her maiden voyage to Australia. Both ships provided accommodation for 126 first class, 154 second class and 400 third class passengers and were similar in appearance to the current Orient liners, having two black funnels and four masts.

Oroya entered service just two weeks after the latest Orient Line vessel, *Ormuz*, had made her maiden departure for Australia. With the addition of these three vessels the Orient-PSNC joint fleet was far superior to the contemporary vessels being operated by the P&O Line.

On 22 February 1895, *Oroya* departed London on a voyage to Australia, arriving at Naples on 3 March. Shortly after departing, that night *Oroya* ran aground in the Bay of Naples in very stormy weather. It was decided to evacuate the 260 passengers on board, but after 70 had been taken ashore one of the lifeboats capsized while being launched, and three members of the crew were drowned. It was then decided not to take any more passengers ashore until the weather eased. A report from London that appeared in the *Sydney Morning Herald* on 7 March stated:

Further particulars in regard to the grounding of the RMS *Oroya* in the Bay of Naples show that the vessel lies with a list to seaward, about 300 yards from the shore. The *Oroya* took the ground in trying to turn during the heavy gale which was blowing at the time. The waves broke over the decks and stove in some portholes. The vessel was severely strained in bumping, and nearly touched some jagged rocks in close proximity to the spot where she grounded.

In consequence of the heavy gale blowing, the landing of the passengers was effected with some difficulty and amidst a scene of considerable excitement on board.

The ship remained hard aground, and it was decided to remove the cargo to lighten her, but bad weather continued to hamper salvage attempts. By 8 March the gale had begun to abate, and unloading cargo from *Oroya* was able to proceed, but on 12 March another gale hit the region, bringing salvage work to a stop, while the ship itself was driven further towards the shore. Once this storm passed, salvage work was able to recommence. A Court of Inquiry was convened at Naples, and the master of *Oroya*, Captain Reginald Routh, was blamed for the grounding, and had his

Orizaba

certificate suspended for three months.

On 22 April *Oroya* was refloated, and after basic repairs had been completed, the vessel steamed to Belfast, where full repairs were carried out. The vessel departed London again on 1 November, but due to heavy fog did not clear the mouth of the River Thames until the next day.

Having been fortunate to survive, *Oroya* settled back into regular service again with her sister, but ten years later disaster struck *Orizaba*. On 17 February 1905 *Orizaba* was approaching Fremantle on an outward voyage from Britain, her last port of call having been Colombo. In the pre-dawn darkness the officers on the bridge found themselves unsure of their position as the coastline was obscured by a thick smoke haze caused by bushfires burning on the coast of Western Australia. They had expected to see the beam of the lighthouse on Rottnest Island, but as daylight came there was no sign of the light.

As the day dawned it was realised that the vessel was in very shallow waters, meaning she had passed to the west of Rottnest Island, and was in great danger. The captain turned his ship west to head out to sea again, as he realised they were crossing the treacherous Five Fathom Bank. Unfortunately his course to safety took him over an area that was only three fathoms deep, and *Orizaba* drove hard aground on a rocky bottom.

All attempts to refloat the vessel failed, so the passengers were removed by tugs and other small craft and carried to Fremantle, along with their baggage and a large percentage of the ship's cargo. Salvage attempts continued for some time, but to no avail, and eventually the vessel was abandoned to the underwriters. *Orizaba* began to break up where she lay, and ultimately was totally destroyed.

This disaster happened one year before the PSNC decided to withdraw from the Australian trade, and in February 1906 they sold their interest in the route and their four surviving vessels to the Royal Mail Line. *Oroya* was one of the ships included in the deal, and after the change of ownership her mainmast was removed and the funnels painted yellow in the traditional Royal Mail Line colours, and she resumed her place on the Australian trade. Unfortunately the Royal Mail Line and Orient Line did not enjoy a good partnership, and in 1907 Royal Mail gave notice of their intention to withdraw from the joint service in 1909.

The Royal Mail Line were primarily involved in the trade from Britain to North and South America, and on 5 February 1908 *Oroya* made her first departure from Southampton on a voyage to the West Indies and on to New York, returning by the same route. After this one trip the vessel returned to the Australian trade, and made her final departure from London on 16 April 1909, being withdrawn on her return. Being twenty three years old, she was sold to shipbreakers in Italy, and was renamed *Oro* for her delivery voyage to Genoa, where she arrived on 15 November 1909.

ORMUZ

Built: 1887 by Fairfield SB & E Co., Glasgow.
Gross tonnage: 6,387
Dimensions: 482 x 52 ft/146.9 x 15.8 m
Service speed: 17 knots
Propulsion: Triple expansion/single screw

Ormuz was the third ship built by the Orient Line for their Australian service, and the first to be fitted with triple expansion machinery. It was similar in design to the earlier *Orient* and *Austral*, having two funnels and four masts, though of larger dimensions and tonnage. It was also in 1887 that the PSNC introduced two new steamers to bolster their section of the joint fleet, *Oroya* and *Orizaba*, and this trio was an adequate response to the four new vessels of the Jubilee class then being introduced by the P&O Line.

Ormuz was built to comply with Admiralty requirements for rapid conversion to an armed merchant cruiser in times of emergency, so was given extensive subdividing and an almost full-length double bottom. Launched on 29 September 1886, *Ormuz* was completed in January 1887, at which time it was the largest and fastest ship on the Australian service, a title she would hold for four years until surpassed by *Ophir*. There was accommodation for 166 first class, 170 second class and 300 third class passengers, and four cargo holds.

In January 1887 the Orient Line moved their London terminal to the newly completed dock complex at Tilbury, and when *Ormuz* berthed there on 11 January it became the largest ship yet to enter the Port of London. *Ormuz* left Tilbury on its maiden voyage on 3 February 1887, calling at Plymouth the next day, Naples on 12 February, Aden and Colombo, then direct to Adelaide, arriving on 15 March, reaching Melbourne three days later, and creating a new record for the voyage by arriving in Sydney on 20 March.

On 26 February a lengthy description of the vessel appeared in the *Sydney Morning Herald*, which included the following:

The comfort of the residents in the ship has been studied to the point of luxury. The dining saloon, or coffee room as it is called, is a work of art. The panels are of rosewood inlaid with satinwood, and a large square window alternates with a mirror the whole length of the saloon. These are divided by pairs of mahogany columns carved with grotesque figures and supported by brackets carved as birds or animals of the East. From the ceiling of white and gold depend electric lamps in opal globes; the skirting is made of mahogany, and the carved mahogany chairs turn on an eccentric, so that in revolving they approach nearer the table. It is not intended that the passengers should breakfast or dine all at the same time. In this matter they are to please themselves. They will be at liberty to choose a small or large table,

and will most probably make up parties among themselves for any hour they fancy. The dining being spread over a longer time, the strain on the kitchen and the service will be less severe, and the passengers will be relieved of the necessity of cultivating an appetite to order. Contrary to the usual practice, the dining saloon of the *Ormuz* is placed on the upper deck and above the library and drawing room, an arrangement that places the kitchen on a level with the dining room and prevents the drawing room being made the receptacle for the odours of dinner.

The drawing room is panelled with maple and decorated with original paintings by Pettie, Colin Hunter, M'Whirter and others; the library adjoining is similar in design, but with leather instead of velvet seats; and the two together can be used as a theatre. But the chief attraction of the ship is the magnificent promenade on the uppermost deck, extending on both sides a distance of 240 feet, and wide enough for six to walk abreast. At the stern end of this is the first class smoking room, and at the fore part is a large saloon, placed immediately under the bridge. It is most luxuriously furnished, and being 30 feet above the sea level, with windows on three sides, it will be a favourite place at all times, and especially in fair weather. The windows in its rounded front afford a look out only inferior to that of the bridge itself.

The marble baths, capable of being filled with hot or cold water in five minutes, the barber's shop, where a shave or a shampoo can be had at any hour, and the bar presided over by an expert in American drinks, and where one can have anything from a 'nignog' to 'a bosom consoler', will contribute to the personal comfort of the most exacting. Among the smaller items of consideration may be mentioned a series of small cupboards along the side of the coffee room, where residents may have stored their unfinished bottles of wine with their cards pinned on to them, after the Continental fashion.

On the day *Ormuz* arrived in Sydney, a reporter from the *Sydney Morning Herald* was among those who swarmed aboard to inspect the new ship, and part of his report, published the next day, stated:

The description of the *Ormuz*, which was published in this journal some three weeks ago, in no way exaggerated the merits of the vessel; in fact the reality comes as a surprise. Her accommodation is really magnificent, the first saloon being marvels of art, down to the smallest detail, and every other part of the ship being in keeping therewith. The visitor cannot fail to be struck with the luxuriousness of the interior fittings and decorations, and at the same time note the harmony of the colours, the exquisite taste, and the marvellous workmanship displayed throughout. The *Ormuz* is a wonderful ship, and her enterprising owners, in placing her on the line, are doing more than keeping faith with the Australian public. Over 300 passengers arrived by

Ormuz (Robert Henderson collection)

the *Ormuz*, including a large number of returned colonists, who speak in the highest terms of her.

Ormuz remained in the Australian service with little interruption for most of its career, but in June 1887 was withdrawn for one voyage to represent the Orient Line at the Naval Review at Spithead held on 3 August. *Ormuz* became the first Orient Line vessel to call at Fremantle, in August 1900, on the way back to Britain.

Ormuz gave solid and unspectacular service to the Orient Line for twenty-five years, apart from a collision in Port Phillip Bay on 12 December 1900. *Ormuz* had just entered the bay when it collided with the outbound cargo vessel *Ismaila*. Both ships suffered serious damage, but were able to reach Melbourne safely. *Ormuz* spent eight weeks in drydock undergoing repairs, and did not leave Melbourne until February 1901.

In 1906 *Ormuz* was the first of the Orient Line fleet to be given yellow funnels following the merger with Royal Mail Line when they bought out the PSNC interests in the Australian trade. In 1909 Royal Mail Line pulled out of the Australian trade, and Orient Line introduced a class of five new liners of 12,000 tons. Several of the older vessels were withdrawn at the same time, leaving *Ormuz* as the oldest vessel in the fleet.

In November 1911 a slightly larger version of the 1909 vessels, *Orama*, was scheduled to enter service, so on 18 August 1911 *Ormuz* left London on its final voyage for the Orient Line, and on returning to Britain was put up for sale.

At twenty five years of age it seemed the vessel was headed for the breakers' yard, but in 1912 *Ormuz* was purchased by a newly formed French concern, Compagnie Sud Atlantique, who were taking over the South American services of Messageries Maritimes, and bought several old ships to commence their operation.

Renamed *Divona*, the accommodation was altered to carry 108 first, 89 second, 54 intermediate and 330 third class passengers, while the funnels were raised 13 ft/3.96 m and painted buff with a black top and narrow black band, above which was a red cockerel. The tonnage rose to 6,812 gross, and the old vessel was still credited with a speed of 16.5 knots.

Divona entered service under the French flag in September 1912, operating to ports in the River Plate estuary, and was meant to be merely a stopgap until two new vessels were completed for the route, which occurred in 1913. *Divona* would probably have been broken up shortly afterwards, but when war broke out in 1914 the vessel was taken over by the French Government for service as a hospital ship, serving in this capacity throughout the war years.

During the war one of the new liners built for Cie Sud Atlantique, *Gallia*, was lost, so in 1919 when *Divona* was released by the French Government it returned to the River Plate trade until another new ship, *Massalia*, was completed in 1920. Once the new liner was settled into service, the ageing *Divona* was withdrawn, and sold in 1922 to French shipbreakers.

THE P&O JUBILEES

VICTORIA & BRITANNIA
Built: 1887 by Caird & Co., Greenock
Gross tonnage: 6,091/6,061 gross
Dimensions: 466 x 52 ft/141.9 x 15.8 m
Service speed: 15 knots
Propulsion: Triple expansion/single propeller

OCEANA & ARCADIA
Built: 1888 by Harland & Wolff, Belfast.
Gross tonnage: 6,188 gross
Dimensions: 468 x 52 ft/142.7 x 15.8 m
Service speed: 15 knots
Propulsion: Triple expansion/single propeller

These four ships were designed for service on both the Australian and Indian trades, and were built to Admiralty requirements to be converted into armed merchant cruisers in the event of war. As 1887 was the golden jubilee of Queen Victoria, the new ships were known as the Jubilees.

First to be completed was *Victoria,* launched on 9 May 1887 and achieving 17.5 knots on trials. Her maiden voyage was delayed so that she could represent P&O at the Jubilee Naval Review off Portsmouth, and on 1 October she left London on a special voyage to Bombay, breaking the previous record for the trip.

Britannia was launched on 18 August 1887, being handed over to P&O on 16 October. On 18 October, while entering the River Thames, she ran aground, being refloated after twelve hours without having suffered any damage. On 5 November *Britannia* left on her maiden voyage to Australia. On 31 December

Victoria left London on her first voyage to Australia.

Oceana was launched on 17 September 1887 and handed over to P&O on 26 February 1888. On 19 March she left London on her maiden voyage to Australia. *Arcadia* was the last of the group, being launched on 17 December 1887 and completed on 12 May 1888, making her first departure from London for Australia on 1 June. At that time *Oceana* and *Arcadia* were the largest and fastest ships on the Australian trade.

Each vessel had accommodation for 230 first class and 160 second class passengers, which was of a very high standard for that era. They also had a considerable cargo capacity. In service the four ships proved to be very fast, capable of bursts of 17 knots when required.

In 1894 *Britannia* and *Victoria* were taken by the British Government on six-month charter as troopships. Painted white with yellow funnels, they carried troops between Britain and India, and returned to the Australian trade in 1895

In January 1897 *Oceana* loaded £5 million worth of gold in Sydney, then proceeded to Melbourne where more gold was taken on board. On 23 January it was discovered that the strongroom holding the gold had been broken into while the ship was in Melbourne, and a box containing 5,000 gold sovereigns stolen.

In 1898 P&O won a new mail contract from the British Government, which required them to introduce an accelerated schedule with a reduction of four days in each direction. The company withdrew four of their older ships that could not maintain the new schedule, which left the four Jubilees as the

Victoria

Arcadia

oldest of the nine P&O vessels on the Australian service.

Arcadia left London on 24 December 1904 for her final voyage to Australia, then was transferred to the Bombay service. *Oceana* made her final departure from London on 12 May 1905, and joined *Arcadia* on the service from London to Bombay. Towards the end of 1905 *Victoria* and *Britannia* were also transferred to the service from London to Bombay. *Victoria* was modernised prior to moving to this route, but *Britannia* was not.

However, both *Victoria* and *Britannia* continued to make an occasional appearance on the Australian service. *Britannia* left London on her final voyage to Australia on 14 August 1908, and *Victoria* departed from London on her final voyage on the route on 27 March 1909. The departure of *Victoria* from Sydney on 22 May marked the last time a four-masted P&O vessel would be seen in the port.

Later in 1909 both *Victoria* and *Britannia* were purchased by Cerruti Bros, who steamed them to Genoa where *Britannia* arrived on 22 August and *Victoria* the next day, and they were broken up side by side.

In 1911, *Oceana* and *Arcadia* were transferred to the long route from Britain to the Far East and China. On 16 March 1912 *Oceana* was outward bound from London, passing through the Straits

of Dover, when she came into collision with the French sailing barque *Pisagua*. *Oceana* suffered enormous bow damage and began to sink. All passengers and crew were ordered away in the lifeboats, one of which overturned while being launched with the loss of fourteen lives. Six hours after the collision *Oceana* sank in fifteen fathoms off Beachy Head, sitting upright with the tops of her masts protruding above the water.

Salvage work began at once, but had to be abandoned because of the strong tidal flows in the area, though £750,000 worth of bullion being carried in her strongroom was recovered. The wreck had to be blown up as it was a menace to other shipping.

Arcadia remained on the Far East trade, and was in Bombay when war broke out in August 1914. She continued on her scheduled voyage to Shanghai, and there was requisitioned for service as a troop transport. Following conversion, she steamed to Chinwangtao to embark a battalion of the Gloucester Regiment, whom she carried to Southampton, arriving on 8 November 1914.

Considered too old to be of use in the war, *Arcadia* was laid up by P&O, and sold to Esafji Tajbhoy Borah, an Indian shipbreaker, in January 1915. The old ship arrived at Bombay in March 1915, and was soon broken up.

OROTAVA and ORUBA

Built: 1889 by Barrow Shipbuilding Co., Barrow
Gross tonnage: 5,857/5,852
Dimensions: 430 x 49 ft/131.1 x 14.9 m
Service speed: 16 knots.
Propulsion: Triple expansion/single screw

In 1888 the Pacific Steam Navigation Company ordered two new vessels for their long-established service from Liverpool to Valpariso in Chile, the first of which was launched on 20 March 1889 and named *Oruba*, being followed by *Orotava* which was launched on 15 June 1889. *Orotava* and *Oruba* were each provided with accommodation for 126 first class, 120 second class and 300 third class passengers. On completion both vessels entered the South American trade, but only made two voyages each on the route before being transferred to the Australian trade, on the joint service operated in conjunction with the Orient Line.

This pair was smaller than their predecessors built for the route, *Orizaba* and *Oroya*, but had an extra deck amidships. They also had two funnels, painted black, and four masts, their nomenclature fitted in with that of the vessels on the joint service, and they appear to have fitted into the Australian trade well as they were to spend almost all of their careers on this route. *Orotava* was the first to depart, commencing her voyage from London on 6 June 1890, with *Oruba* following on 4 July. *Orotava* arrived in Sydney for the first time on 19 July, and two days later the *Sydney Morning Herald* carried a report on the liner, which included the following :

The entrance to the saloon from the promenade deck is very spacious, and the first apartment that attracts attention is the drawing-room, which is decorated with carved cabinet work, and polished woods, chiefly sycamore and walnut. The upholstery is of blue material, which contrasts with the polished woods. The smoking room is handsomely fitted up in oak and Hungarian ash, and the arm chairs are upholstered in morocco. The dining-room is on the upper deck, is very elegantly decorated with elaborately carved oak, and the upholstery is in rich maroon Genoa velvet. The passenger berthing space is planned for 130 in the saloon, 93 in the second saloon, and 620 in the third class.

For several years they gave excellent service without untoward incident until *Orotava* was involved in an incident that was almost a carbon copy of the accident that sent *Austral* to the bottom of Sydney Harbour in 1882. Whilst coaling at her berth in Tilbury on 14 December 1896 in preparation for her next voyage to Australia, due to depart on 24 December, *Orotava* suddenly took a heavy list to starboard, and sank, with five men losing their lives. As had happened with the *Austral*, *Orotava* went down in shallow water, so only part of the hull was submerged, with the superstructure above water, leaning against the wharf.

On the first attempt to raise the vessel on 19 December, a rope broke and left the vessel in a worse position than before. *Orotava* was finally refloated on 21 December, and as extensive repairs were needed, the 24 December departure was taken by *Oroya*. After repairs, *Orotava* was able to resume her place in the Australian trade

Orotava as built.

with a departure from Tilbury on 5 February 1897.

For the next two years *Orotava* continued in regular service, but the outbreak of the Boer War in October 1898 was to result in the British Government requisitioning many vessels to carry troops to South Africa. In February 1899 *Orotava* was taken over, and served as a troopship between Britain and South Africa for the next four years. On her final voyage from South Africa in January 1903, *Orotava* brought Lord Kitchener back to Britain. The vessel was then handed back to her owners, and it was about this time that the funnels of both ships were raised by 10 ft/3.3 m. On 13 March 1903 *Orotava* departed from Tilbury on her first voyage to Australia for the PSNC in four years.

In February 1906 PSNC sold out their Australian interests to the Royal Mail Line, with *Orotava* and *Oruba* being included in the sale. Under the new ownership both ships lost their mainmasts and had their funnels painted yellow, but they remained on the Australian trade in partnership with the Orient Line vessels. Unfortunately the new partners did not get along, and in 1909 Royal Mail withdrew their ships from the Australian trade altogether. *Oruba* made her final departure from Tilbury on 16 October 1908, while the last voyage of *Orotava* commenced on 5 March 1909.

Oruba was transferred to the Royal Mail Line service from Southampton to the West Indies and on to New York, making her first departure from the British port on 14 April 1909. *Orotava* was temporarily surplus to requirements, and it was not until April 1911 that she

was placed on the same service. It was about this time that the vessels lost their mizzenmasts, reducing them to two masts only, and the accommodation was altered to cater for 250 passengers in two classes only. They proved quite popular on the trade, but in April 1914 *Orotava* was laid up. *Oruba* remained in service a few months longer, and on 10 August 1914 made her final voyage from Southampton.

By the time she returned Britain was at war, and both *Orotava* and *Oruba* were requisitioned, then bought outright by the Admiralty. *Oruba* was converted to a dummy battleship of the *Orion* class, but when this experiment was abandoned she was taken to Mudros in 1915 and scuttled on 1 January 1916 at Kephalo Bay to form part of a breakwater.

Orotava was fitted out as an armed merchant cruiser, commissioned in December 1914, and joined the 10th Cruiser Squadron, which was composed solely of converted merchantmen and patrolled the waters north of Scotland. Her war career was unspectacular, though in December 1915 her steering gear was disabled during a gale. The engineers were able to repair the fault before the ship got into any difficulties. In January 1916 the wheelhouse and bridge were destroyed by heavy seas in another gale, forcing the vessel to run before the storm. Late in 1917 *Orotava* was refitted and sent south for service as a convoy escort on the Atlantic, where she remained until the end of the war. In the final months of 1921 *Orotava* was sold by the Admiralty to shipbreakers in Glasgow.

Oruba with heightened funnels after 1903.

EARLY MESSAGERIES MARITIMES VESSELS

AUSTRALIEN POLYNESIEN ARMAND BEHIC VILLE DE LA CIOTAT
Built: 1890/1891/1892/1892 by Ch Navals de La Ciotat, La Ciotat
Gross tonnage: 6,365/6,363/6,397/6,378
Dimensions: 482 x 49 ft/146.9 x 15 m
Service speed: 14 knots
Propulsion: Triple expansion/single propeller

Messageries Maritimes opened their service from Marseilles to Australia in 1882 using eight ships, and in 1888 placed orders for four larger vessels with their own shipyard at La Ciotat. These ships were required to meet the challenge posed by new ships being placed in service by the P&O and Orient Lines, and they were to be given names in accord with the route they would operate: *Australien*, *Polynesien*, *Malasien* and *Tasmanien*. In design the ships would be enlarged versions of the group of seven built for the opening of the Australian service, having two thin funnels, three barque-rigged masts and a single propeller, but with enlarged accommodation for 170 first class, 70 second class and 112 third class passengers.

The first of the quartet to be built was *Australien*, which was launched on 26 May 1889, and on trials reached a speed of 17.6 knots. On 3 March 1890 the vessel left Marseilles on her maiden voyage, which took her through the Suez Canal and on to Mahe in India, then to the French Indian Ocean islands of Reunion and Mauritius before calling at Australian ports and continuing on to Noumea. The second vessel to be completed was *Polynesien*, launched on 18 April 1890, which sailed on her maiden voyage from Marseilles on 3 January 1891.

The third and fourth ships had been laid down under their intended names, but during construction they were renamed, and the third vessel was launched on 26 April 1891 as *Armand Behic*, after a long-time president of Messageries Maritimes who had recently died. This vessel entered service with a departure from Marseilles on 3 February 1892, and on 10 April 1892 the final ship of the group was launched as *Ville de la Ciotat*, being named in honour of the company shipyard. When she entered service on 3 December 1892 the company was able to offer an improved and faster schedule.

As seven ships were required to maintain a regular sailing schedule, three of the older ships remained on the route, and in 1894–95 they were given new engines to improve their speed. It was shortly afterwards that the Indian Ocean islands were dropped from the itinerary, and the ships instead called at Bombay and Colombo then went directly to Fremantle and other Australian ports, still terminating in Noumea as before.

These four ships remained on the Australian service for ten years, the only incident of note concerning

Polynesien

Ville de la Ciotat

them occurring in February 1891, when *Australien* came upon the disabled Austrian steamer *Apis* in the Mediterranean, and towed it to safety at Ajaccio. In 1903 two steamers formerly on the South American trade were transferred to the Australian service, and from that time the four ships in this class also made some voyages on the Far East route.

September 1903 was to be a bad month for the ships, as on 14 September *Polynesien* was being towed into Marseilles when the tow ropes parted, and the ship drifted aground under Fort St Jean. It took four days to refloat the vessel, as a rocky ledge had to be removed by explosives first, and *Polynesien* returned to service after repairs on 29 November. On 27 September *Australien* ran aground on Umashima Island in Japan, being pulled free by the cruisers *Montcalm* and *Bugeaud* and having to enter drydock at Nagasaki for repairs.

Polynesien made her final appearance on the Australian trade with a departure from Marseilles on 26 June 1913, while *Armand Behic* made its final sailing from Marseilles on 10 December 1913. On 7 January 1914 *Ville de la Ciotat* began its final Australian passage, so it was left to the pioneer ship of the group, *Australien*, to make their final trip on the Australian

trade when it left Marseilles on 27 May 1914.

As 1914 progressed it was clear that war would break out some time soon in Europe, and that France would be involved, so the French Government began taking over various vessels and converting them into troopships. As soon as war was declared all four ships began serving their country as troop transports. Three of them would be lost before the conflict ended.

The first to be sunk was *Ville de la Ciotat*, torpedoed by *U34* west of Crete on 24 December 1915 and going down in twenty minutes. It was almost three years before the next was lost, when *Australien* was torpedoed on 19 July 1918 while in a convoy passing through the Mediterranean. The explosion started a fire which burned for thirteen hours until the ship sank. Less than a month later, on 10 August 1918, *Polynesien* either struck a mine or was torpedoed while in the Malta dredged channel, and sank.

This left only *Armand Behic* surviving when the war ended, and it was used by Messageries Maritimes on various routes for several years, but did not return to Australia. In October 1924 *Armand Behic* was sold to shipbreakers at Marseilles.

KAISER WILHELM II

Built: 1889 by Vulcan, Stettin
Gross tonnage: 6,661
Dimensions: 449 x 51 ft/136.9 x 15.5 m
Service speed: 16 knots
Propulsion: Triple expansion/single propeller

Launched on 23 April 1889 for North German Lloyd, *Kaiser Wilhelm II* was a most impressive vessel for the era, having a white hull, four masts, two funnels, and accommodation for 120 first class, 80 second class and 1,000 third class passengers.

On 2 October 1889 *Kaiser Wilhelm II* departed Bremen on its maiden voyage to Australia, with a call at Antwerp, Southampton and Genoa to embark more passengers, arriving in Adelaide on 16 November, Melbourne on 23 November and Sydney Harbour two days later, first going to anchor at Neutral Bay before docking at Circular Quay. The largest vessel yet seen in Australian waters, the *Sydney Morning Herald* of 26 November headlined its report on the new liner 'A Floating Palace.'

The state cabins are rooms, in a liberal acceptation of the term, and as there are only three occupants allowed to each, the comfort is manifest. The feature of the *Kaiser Wilhelm II*, however, is the saloon accommodation. The upholstering of the saloon is of blue leather and blue damask silk; the cabinet work is of various fine dark woods, and the portholes, which are unusually large, run round three sides.

The second saloon has its own smoking and music room, and nothing has been left undone to render it attractive. For third class passengers there is berthing space for 600, and no overcrowding is permitted. There are baths, washhouses, lavatories etc provided for them, and the ventilation of this portion of the ship, as well as the ventilation all over, has been made a thorough study. Provision is made for the expulsion of foul air and for an unintermittent supply of fresh air, and in tropical weather it was found most beneficial. There is plenty of light as well as ventilation on board, and the darkest corners are lit up with the electric system.

Over the next few years *Kaiser Wilhelm II* made more trips to Australia, though was never a regular feature on the trade. In February 1893, the vessel departed Bremen for Australia, but sank alongside the pier at Genoa. After being refloated she returned to Germany for repairs, during which two masts were removed, quite changing her appearance.

Over the next eight years *Kaiser Wilhelm II* continued to make voyages to Australia on an irregular basis, though being surpassed by newer and larger vessels by the late 1890s. She departed Bremen on 28 October 1901, called at Antwerp, Southampton and Genoa to embark more passengers, arriving in Sydney on 17 December, the last time she visited Australia. On returning to Germany the vessel was renamed *Hohenzollern*, to free the original name for a large new liner being built for the company. *Hohenzollern* was placed on a service from Genoa and other Mediterranean ports to New York. On 9 April 1908 the vessel ran aground on the coast of Sardinia at Alghero. Although refloated, the damage was so severe that *Hohenzollern* was sold to shipbreakers in Italy.

Kaiser Wilhelm II

AUSTRALIA and HIMALAYA

Built: 1892 by Caird & Co., Greenock
Gross tonnage: 6,898/6,901
Dimensions: 482 x 56 ft/146.9 x 15.9 m
Service speed: 16 knots
Propulsion: Triple expansion/single propeller

Himalaya and *Australia* were built to meet Admiralty requirements for conversion to armed merchant cruisers in time of emergency, the pair being subsidised by the Admiralty, which held eight 4.7 inch guns in reserve for them at all times.

Himalaya was launched on 27 February 1892, and left London in July on her maiden voyage, to India. *Australia*, launched on 29 July 1892, left London on 25 November 1892 on her maiden voyage, to Australia. They had accommodation for 265 passengers in first class and 144 second class.

Himalaya left London on 6 January 1893 on her first voyage to Australia. In May 1893 *Australia* made a passage from London to Adelaide in 26 days 16 hours, but the next month *Himalaya* reduced this time by almost ten hours, a record that was to stand for many years.

In the early morning hours of 20 June 1904, *Australia* was approaching the entrance to Port Phillip Bay, and ran aground on a submerged reef that runs between Point Nepean and Corsair Rock. All passengers and crew were removed, but salvage was found to be impossible, and shortly afterwards the vessel was

swept by fire to complete her destruction. The wreck was sold at auction for £290. *Australia* was the only P&O vessel to be lost in Australian waters throughout their long connection with the trade.

Himalaya remained on the Australian trade, but on 9 October 1908 she left London on her final regular voyage in the trade, returning to Britain in January 1909. She was then placed on the Indian service, and on occasion continued on to the Far East and Shanghai. On 14 June 1912, *Himalaya* departed London on a voyage to Australia, replacing *Mongolia* for the single round trip.

When war broke out in August 1914, *Himalaya* was outward bound crossing the Indian Ocean to Penang, from where she was ordered to Hong Kong. There she was converted into an armed merchant cruiser, with eight 4.7 inch guns fitted, and then commissioned as HMS *Himalaya* with a Royal Navy captain. Following patrols around the Philippines, she was sent to Aden in January 1915, and in September 1915 returned to Britain for refitting and rearming with 6 inch guns, being purchased outright by the Admiralty at this time.

Himalaya served as a gunnery spotting ship off German East Africa, and finished the war as a troopship, then returned to Britain and was bought back by P&O in 1919. After a refit at Southampton *Himalaya* returned to the Indian trade, but in 1922 was withdrawn and sold to shipbreakers at Bremen, arriving there on 11 May 1922.

Australia

OPHIR

Built: 1891 by Robert Napier & Sons, Glasgow
Gross tonnage: 6,814
Dimensions: 465 x 53 ft/141.7 x 16.3 m
Service speed: 18 knots
Propulsion: Triple expansion/twin propellers

The first Orient Line vessel to be equipped with twin screws, *Ophir* was launched on 11 April 1891, and on trials six months later a maximum speed of 18.8 knots was attained. In appearance *Ophir* was totally unlike any previous Orient Line vessel, as the two funnels were 100 ft/33m apart. This was caused by Admiralty requirements that the engines be positioned between the two boiler rooms.

Accommodation was provided for 220 first class passengers in opulent luxury, 150 second class passengers and 520 in third class. *Ophir* departed London for Australia on 6 November 1891, with a call at Plymouth the next day.

While crossing the Bay of Biscay condenser problems arose in one engine, which had to be stopped, but the ship was able to keep going for fifteen hours on the other engine, which later was stopped for ten hours for similar repairs. *Ophir* arrived in Sydney for the first time on 21 December, and the *Sydney Morning Herald* reported:

> There arrived yesterday on her maiden voyage from London the latest and most remarkable development of the great Australian liner. It is, however, the features of this new ship that possess the greatest interest to Australians. She has twin screws, worked by entirely independent sets of engines, so as to be free from the possibility of having to use sails as a means of motion. At her launch on the Clyde she attracted no little attention, and some of the comments made there were repeated here yesterday, namely, that she has the appearance of being too much built up amidships for gracefulness of appearance, and that her two tremendous funnels are remarkably wide apart, while her two masts are little better than apologies. These peculiar features are accounted for with the best of reasons, and all agree that, while she is a departure from some accepted ideas, the *Ophir* is a remarkable ship.

> The first class dining saloon, on the upper deck, is right in the centre of the ship, in fact it and the stairway from which is the entrance to the saloon lie between the two funnels, which are 100 feet apart. It is a grand room, richly panelled in satin-wood and rosewood, is well lighted from the sides with large square windows, and from above with an arch-shaped dome 20 ft in height, 27 ft long by 20 ft 6 ins wide, filled with painted glass, giving the saloon a height which has hitherto been wanting.

> The lower deck is given up to third-class passengers, for whom the accommodation is of a superior character, special features being the subdivision into compartments, thus securing greater privacy, the convenient arrangement of cabins of different sizes for married couples and families, completely furnished, the separate apartment for women travelling alone, and the unusually ample bathroom and lavatory accommodation. Bedding and all requisites for the voyage are provided for third-class as for other passengers. A large space on the upper deck is at the disposal of third-class passengers for fresh air and exercise, in part protected from sun and rain by the poop and promenade decks.

In 1892 *Ophir* voyaged from Albany to London in 24 days 2 hours, beating the previous record by some four

Ophir

Ophir as a Royal Yacht in 1901.

days. Unfortunately the ship had a very healthy appetite for coal and limited cargo spaces, making her rather an uneconomical proposition to operate. Eventually it was found necessary to lay the ship up during the slack season of each year. In 1899 *Ophir* was sent cruising, departing London on 14 July and visiting Norway and Iceland.

In November 1900 *Ophir* was chartered by the Admiralty as a Royal Yacht to carry the Duke and Duchess of York, later King George V and Queen Mary, to Australia to officiate at the opening of the first Commonwealth Parliament in May 1901, which included repainting the ship white with a blue riband and yellow funnels.

Leaving Portsmouth in March 1901, the first stop was at Ceylon, then the vessel continued to Australia, arriving in Melbourne on 6 May 1901. Once the royal visitors had completed their engagements in Australia, *Ophir* took them to New Zealand, then west to South Africa, followed by Canada, with *Ophir* going to Quebec where the Royal party disembarked. They rejoined the ship at Halifax for the journey back to England, returning to Portsmouth on 1 November 1901.

Ophir was returned to her owners, and given a refit before returning to her regular service, once more with black hull and funnels. However, some of the Royal apartments were retained, and became very popular with wealthy travellers.

On 20 June 1913 the vessel left Tilbury on what was intended to be her final voyage to Australia, as she was then laid up in reserve off Southend. Within a few weeks of war breaking out in August 1914, Orient Line vessels were being requisitioned for military duty by both the British and Australian governments, so *Ophir* was reactivated and departed London on 23 October, her voyage back leaving Sydney on 19 December.

This was the last commercial voyage to be operated by *Ophir*, as the vessel was taken over by the Admiralty, converted into an armed merchant cruiser, and attached to the Ninth Cruiser Squadron. Armed with eight 6 inch guns, she was sent to patrol between Sierra Leone and the Azores.

Ophir served in this capacity for the next three years, and in 1918 the Admiralty purchased the ship outright. Converted into a hospital ship, *Ophir* was based in Hong Kong for the remainder of the war. After the Armistices she returned to Britain and was laid up in the Thames, later being moved to the Clyde in February 1919.

The Admiralty had no further use for the old ship, so in February 1920 she was offered at auction, the highest bid being £45,000, which was below the reserve price set, so she was withdrawn from sale, and remained idle. Further attempts to sell the ship also failed, as the asking price was too high. Eventually the vessel was sold to shipbreakers in September 1922 for a mere £6,000 and broken up at Troon.

THE NDL OLDENBURG CLASS

KARLSRUHE STUTTGART DARMSTADT GERA
OLDENBURG WEIMAR
Built: 1889 - 1891 by Fairfield SB & E Co., Govan
Gross tonnage: 5,057/5,048/5,012/5,005/5,006/4,996
Dimensions: 415 x 48 ft/126 x 14.6m
Service speed: 13 knots
Propulsion: Triple expansion/single propeller

North German Lloyd had opened their Australian service in July 1886 using five vessels that had been transferred from the South American trade. From 1888 the company began building ships with a view to their being used on any of the routes they operated, North Atlantic, South America, Far East or Australia, and from 1889 they began taking delivery of a class of six vessels of this type, the Oldenburg class.

The first to be launched, on 31 August 1889, was named *Karlsruhe*, being handed over two months later, and departing Bremen on 10 November on its maiden voyage, to Montevideo and Buenos Aires. It was closely followed by *Stuttgart*, launched on 26 October 1889, which entered service on 10 January 1890 on the South American trade.

Three more vessels of the class were launched during 1890, the first being *Darmstadt* on 27 September, which was placed on a service across the North Atlantic, followed by *Gera* on 11 November 1890 and *Oldenburg* on 13 December 1890, both of which initially operated to South America. The last to be built, *Weimar*, was launched on 9 February 1891, and entered service in April on the route between Bremen and Baltimore.

The original vessels placed on the Australian trade by North German Lloyd had carried only first and third class passengers, but with this new class being designed for a variety of services, they were given accommodation for 49 first class, 36 second class and 1,900 third class passengers. At that time the major passenger flow on the North Atlantic, South American and Australian trade was emigrants, and much of the third class accommodation was of a temporary nature erected in the holds and 'tween decks for the outward passage, with the same areas being used for the carriage of cargo on the return trip to Germany.

The first of these ships to appear on the Australian trade was *Oldenburg*, which left Bremen on 2 September 1891, with calls at Southampton and Genoa before passing through the Suez Canal. The first port of call in Australia was Adelaide, on 19 October, then Melbourne two days later, reaching Sydney on 25 October. Next day the *Sydney Morning Herald* reported:

A large and powerful new steel screw steamer, the *Oldenburg*...arrived yesterday from the home port in the Imperial German mail line. She is constructed entirely of steel, with a double bottom, and is fitted with water-tight compartments.

The first saloon, which is capable of accommodating 44 passengers, is very commodious, and is solidly and elegantly built with all the most modern conveniences, and is fitted with a well-stocked library and piano. The furniture is upholstered in terra-cotta, and the effect is pleasing and artistic.

The first saloon is situated in the middle of the ship, and the second saloon is aft, providing accommodation for 40 persons. Special apartments are appropriated as smoking rooms for first and second class passengers, and there are also first and second class retiring rooms for ladies.

The steerage accommodation is superior to that usually

Darmstadt

Gera

found in ocean-going steamers, and particular care has been given to the matter of ventilation. The vessel is supplied throughout with electric light worked by three engines, and all the arrangements are on the most complete scale.

The next vessel to be sent to Australia, *Karlsruhe*, departed Bremen on 30 September 1891 and reached Sydney on 24 November. Late in 1892 *Karlsruhe* and *Oldenburg* each made another voyage to Australia, and continued to be seen occasionally in local waters. *Gera* departed Bremerhaven on 22 November 1893 on its first voyage to Australia, calling at Antwerp and Southampton for more passengers. The first Australian port of call was Adelaide on 9 January 1894, then Melbourne, and Sydney on 15 January.

Gera returned to Australia again in 1895, while the same year *Darmstadt* arrived in Sydney for the first time, on 18 October. The next of the class to make a first voyage to Australia was *Stuttgart*, which sailed from Bremerhaven on 6 July 1896, but it was not until June 1897 that *Weimar* departed on her first voyage to Australia. By 1900 all six vessels were making an occasional voyage to Australia, though none was permanently assigned to the trade, and this continued into the new century.

Stuttgart departed Bremen on 16 July 1904 on its final voyage to Australia. The other five vessels all continued to appear on the route for another two years, but from September 1906 North German Lloyd began operating an accelerated schedule to Australia using only twin propeller vessels.

Darmstadt made its final departure from Bremen for Australia on 21 March 1906, followed by *Oldenburg* on 21 April, *Karlsruhe* on 19 May, *Weimar* on 16 June, and *Gera* on 11 August. When the vessels returned to Germany they were placed on other routes, but by then they were some of the oldest units in the North German Lloyd fleet.

In May 1908 *Stuttgart* was sold to shipbreakers at Lemwerder, and in August *Karlsruhe* was also sold for breaking up. *Gera* and *Weimar* were sold during 1908 to an Italian company, Lloyd del PacifiCo., with *Gera* being renamed *Valparaiso* while *Weimar* became *Santiago*. However, in 1909 *Santiago* was sold to a Chilean company and renamed *Armonia*.

Both these vessels were torpedoed and sunk towards the end of World War I, *Valparaiso* by a German submarine off the coast of Libya near Marsa Susa on 14 October 1917. *Armonia* was taken over by Canadian authorities in 1917, but not renamed, and torpedoed by a German submarine near Porquerolles Island, France, on 15 March 1918, with the loss of seven lives.

Oldenburg and *Darmstadt* were sold at the end of 1910 to a Turkish operator. *Oldenburg* was renamed *Ak Deniz*; *Darmstadt* became *Kara Deniz*. This pair survived the war, in 1923 being sold to Italian shipbreakers at Savona.

GOTHIC

Built: 1893 by Harland & Wolff, Belfast
Gross tonnage: 7,755
Dimensions: 491 x 53 ft/149.6 x 16.2 m
Service speed: 14 knots
Propulsion: Triple expansion/twin propellers

When new, *Gothic* was the most outstanding vessel on the trade between Britain and New Zealand, which White Star Line operated jointly with Shaw Savill Line, though the latter company managed all the ships. *Gothic* was launched on 28 June 1893, and handed over to White Star Line on 28 November. Accommodation was provided for 104 first class and 114 third class passengers, the standard of comfort being a great improvement on previous ships on the trade, and comparable to the best liners then being operated across the Atlantic by the White Star Line. In addition the vessel had a large refrigerated hold capacity for carrying dairy produce and up to 71,000 carcasses of mutton.

Gothic was much larger than the existing ships on the route, and the largest vessel operating out of London, from where it departed on 28 December 1893 on its maiden voyage, stopping first at Plymouth to embark more passengers. On 16 January 1894 a report on the ship appeared in the *Sydney Morning Herald*, which said in part:

The *Gothic* is the largest passenger steamer or combined passenger and cargo steamer now in the Australasian trade. She has been specially designed for the New Zealand service, and was despatched from London by the Shaw, Savill and Albion Company on her first voyage, via Plymouth, Teneriffe, Cape Town, Hobart and Wellington on the outward passage, and Rio de Janeiro and Teneriffe on the homeward journey. The distance traversed on the round voyage exceeds 26,000 miles.

Unrivalled accommodation of the highest class, similar in character to that of the *Teutonic* and *Majestic*, is provided for 104 saloon passengers amidships, the dining saloon and many of the superior staterooms being above the main deck, so that the ventilation is as complete as possible, and in the control of passengers themselves. In the quarter-deck aft there is accommodation of a unique character for 114 steerage passengers.

Probably the most notable advance with *Gothic* was the provision of twin propellers, the first to be fitted to a ship on the New Zealand service. At the same time the inclusion of yard arms on the masts for emergency sail was abandoned. Later in 1894 *Gothic* made a record voyage, arriving in Wellington in 37 days, 10 hours and 16 minutes from Plymouth, at an average speed of 14.16 knots, although experience showed the vessel was rather tender, and rolled badly.

During the Boer War, *Gothic* transported New Zealand troops to and from South Africa in the course of her regular voyages. In 1901 the three much larger vessels of the Athenic class (*Athenic, Corinthic,* and *Ionic*) were added to the New Zealand service alongside *Gothic*.

Gothic (Ian Farquhar collection)

On 3 June 1906 *Gothic* was in the North Atlantic on the last leg of a voyage from New Zealand to London via Cape Horn and Montevideo when a fire broke out in the cargo of wool and flax in No. 4 hold. After three days the crew was able to quell the fire, but on the evening of 6 June another fire was discovered burning in No. 3 hold, directly beneath the first class dining room. Next day the ship reached Plymouth, and the passengers were sent ashore by tender. The fire was still blazing, and eventually the vessel had to be run aground near Plymouth, with a heavy list to port. The fire was finally extinguished on the morning of 8 June, but not before the first class accommodation had been extensively damaged.

After being refloated, *Gothic* spent many months being repaired, but the former first class accommodation was replaced by enlarged migrant quarters. At the same time the poop deck aft was extended forward, and additional lifeboats fitted, as the ship would in future be able to carry about 1,500 third class passengers.

Gothic made only two more sailings to New Zealand, the last departing London on 2 May 1907, its thirty-fourth voyage on the route. Upon returning to Britain, the vessel was transferred to the Belgian flag under the ownership of another company in the International Mercantile Marine group, Red Star Line.

Renamed *Gothland*, it was used on their Atlantic migrant service between Antwerp and Philadelphia, making its first departure from Antwerp on 11 July 1907. This lasted until 1911 when the vessel returned to the White Star Line fleet, was renamed *Gothic*, and chartered to the Aberdeen Line, while two of their older vessels, *Marathon* and *Miltiades*, were out of service being lengthened.

Gothic was placed on the route from London via Cape Town to Australian ports, mostly carrying migrants to Melbourne under a contract with the Victorian Government. At that time there was a great demand for migrant passages to Australia, and on the first voyage *Gothic* carried more than 1,400 migrants, arriving in Melbourne on Sunday, 3 December 1911, and in Sydney on 9 December. On 11 December the *Sydney Morning Herald* reported: The *Gothic*, at one time a favourite Royal Mail steamer, sailing under the Shaw, Savill, and Albion Co's flag between London and New Zealand, is now in Sydney, having brought 1,400 immigrants to Australia, the great majority of whom landed in Melbourne. The vessel sails on or about 14th inst for London, via Suez Canal, and presents an excellent opportunity for travellers to proceed to England via this route in a one-class vessel. As regards the accommodation, this is excellent; the dining room presents a model feature, being on the awning deck, and is fitted with windows instead of portholes, as is usual. In addition, there is on this deck a smoke-room, and social room. The cabins consist of single, two, four and six berth rooms, and the deck space is ample.

Gothic remained under charter to the Aberdeen Line throughout 1912, making two round trips from Britain during the year, passing through Fremantle on 10 April and 6 September. Its final departure for Aberdeen Line from London was on 19 December 1912, with over 1,400 migrants on board. At the time a measles epidemic was sweeping through various parts of Britain, and some of the children who boarded were infected, though still in the incubation stage.

Two days after departing London the first case of measles was detected, while throughout the voyage more children became ill, and five died before the ship reached Australia. There was also one birth, the boy being christened Gothic Moorehouse after the ship and its captain.

When *Gothic* anchored in Gage Roads on 27 January 1913, medical authorities found 42 children with measles, of whom 21 were intended for disembarkation in Fremantle. In all 599 nominated migrants and 413 on assisted passages were due to leave the ship at Fremantle, with the other 400 continuing to the eastern states.

The sick children and their parents were taken ashore to the Woodman Point Quarantine Station, where one child died four days later. The ship was able to berth in Fremantle, but the passengers for the eastern states were not allowed to go ashore during the stopover.

The voyage continued to Melbourne and Sydney, and at each port sick children and their families were put into quarantine until the illness was contained. On 21 February 1913, the *Sydney Morning Herald* noted:

When the steamer *Gothic* arrived here recently 27 passengers were sent to quarantine on account of the existence of measles and scarlet fever on board. Yesterday the last lot of the batch of patients was released from Quarantine.

With the return of *Marathon* to service in April 1913, *Gothic* was no longer needed by the Aberdeen Line. On returning to Britain that month, *Gothic* went back to the Red Star Line fleet, and resumed its former name, *Gothland*. At various times *Gothland* operated between Antwerp and New York or Rotterdam and Montreal.

In June 1914 *Gothland* was returning from Canada when it stranded on the Gunner Rocks off the Scilly Isles, but after three days was refloated. Quite serious damage was sustained, and the ship was out of service for several months undergoing repairs.

During the war years *Gothland* maintained an irregular service between Rotterdam and New York, but in March 1919 began running out of Antwerp again. There were also some special migrant voyages from Danzig, Hamburg and Corunna to North America before *Gothland* resumed a regular service from Antwerp and Southampton to Baltimore in 1920, and in 1921 began operating to New York once more.

Gothland remained in service until the end of 1925, then was sold to shipbreakers at Bo'ness, arriving there on 16 January 1926.

SHIRE LINE VESSELS

PERTHSHIRE BUTESHIRE BANFFSHIRE
MORAYSHIRE
Built: 1893/93/94/98 by Hawthorn Leslie, Newcastle
Gross tonnage:5,550/ 5,574/5,736/5,851
Dimensions: 420 x 54 ft/128 x 16.5 m
Service speed: 11 knots
Propulsion: Triple expansion/single propeller

FIFESHIRE NAIRNSHIRE
Built: 1898/1899 by Clydebank Engineering & Shipbuilding Co.,
Clydebank
Gross tonnage: 5,812/5,747
Dimensions: 420 x 54 ft/128 x 16.5 m
Service speed: 11 knots
Propulsion: Triple expansion/single propeller

AYRSHIRE
Built: 1903 by Hawthorn Leslie, Newcastle
Gross tonnage: 7,749
Dimensions: 460 x 58 ft/ 140.2 x 17.9 m
Service speed: 12 knots
Propulsion: Quadruple expansion/twin propellers

Turnbull, Martin & Co. Ltd, established in Glasgow in 1877, and gradually built up a fleet of small cargo ships trading to Australia and New Zealand. They first became involved in the Australian migrant trade in 1884, when the 2,761 gross ton Elderslie was built, and fitted out with regular accommodation for a small number of first and second class passengers, while migrants were carried in temporary quarters erected in the holds.

Between 1887 and 1890 three ships, named Fifeshire, Nairnshire and Morayshire, were added to the fleet. They were fitted out to carry first and third class passengers. The company began using the title Shire Line for its service in 1893, and at the end of that year began taking delivery of a trio of new and larger ships for the trade.

The first to be completed was Perthshire, launched on 12 August 1893 and completed three months later, quickly followed by Buteshire, launched on 10 October 1893 and entering service two months later. These vessels provided permanent cabins for 12 first class passengers, and could carry up to 320 migrants in more basic quarters. They were joined in 1894 by the slightly larger Banffshire, but it was only fitted out to carry 50 third-class passengers in addition to 12 first-class.

These ships usually voyaged by way of South Africa to Adelaide, Melbourne and Sydney, then crossed the Tasman to various ports in New Zealand. With the Western Australia gold rush of 1893, additional calls were often made at Fremantle and Albany as well, and sometimes Hobart was also included.

The original Fifeshire, Nairnshire and Morayshire were sold in 1898 to the Ducal Line, and renamed Duke of Fife, Duke of Norfolk and Duke of Portland respectively. Under these names the vessels continued to trade to Australia, mostly Queensland ports, and on some voyages did carry passengers, but mostly they were operated as cargo ships. Duke of Fife was sold in 1903 to Japanese buyers, being renamed Itsukishima Maru, and broken up in 1934. The other two had much shorter careers. Duke of Portland was sold to another British company, the Nelson Line, in 1905, and renamed Highland Fling, only to be wrecked near The Lizard in southern England on 7 January 1907. Duke of York was also sold in 1905, to German buyers, being renamed Marcellus, then going under the Swedish flag in 1908 as Johanna. Returned to the German flag in 1914 and renamed Pericles, it foundered off Ushant in a storm on 24 May 1914.

In 1898/99 three more ships were added to the Shire Line fleet. The first was named Morayshire when launched on 1 September 1898, entering service in December. It was quickly followed by Fifeshire, launched on 15 October 1898, and also in service by the end of December. The third vessel, Nairnshire, was launched on 16 December 1898, and joined the first two in February 1899. Each vessel provided permanent accommodation for 12 first class passengers, as well as basic facilities for 150 passengers in third class, though this number could be increased by temporary quarters fitted in the holds on the outward voyage.

In early April 1899 the Perthshire, on a voyage from Britain, departed Sydney bound for Wellington, but failed to arrive on schedule. For eight weeks nothing was heard of the ship, and fears grew it had been lost, but on 3 June the Union Steamship Company vessel Talune happened upon the Perthshire, which had lost its single propeller and had been slowly drifting south. Had the Talune not found her, the ship would almost inevitably have disappeared and become one of the many mysteries of the sea. Instead, Talune was able to pass a line to the disabled vessel, and tow it to safety.

Another new vessel, Ayrshire, was launched on 28 August 1903 and completed at the end of the year. Much larger than the earlier vessels, Ayrshire provided comfortable first class accommodation for 22 passengers, while up to 230 could be carried in improved third class quarters. Ayrshire departed London on 3 January 1904 on its first voyage to Australia and New Zealand, via South Africa, going directly from Cape Town to Adelaide, then Melbourne, arriving in Sydney on 28 February.

In 1904 the Shire Line became involved in a joint service with the Federal Steam Navigation Company and Houlder Bros, the new operation being known as

Nairnshire

the Federal-Houlder-Shire Line. All seven Shire vessels appeared on this service at various times, the route followed being from Liverpool or London to Teneriffe or Las Palmas, Cape Town, Adelaide, Melbourne and Sydney, and then various New Zealand ports.

From 1906, several Shire Line ships, but mostly *Perthshire* and *Banffshire*, also operated in conjunction with British India Line on the trade from London via the Suez Canal to Thursday Island and Queensland ports as far south as Brisbane.

The Shire Line ships would call at numerous ports in New Zealand to load cargo for Britain, including Port Chalmers, where in April 1907 two of their ships encountered problems. Early in the month *Ayrshire* was proceeding down the channel during a very dense fog when it veered off course and ran aground off Ravensbourne. Fortunately the vessel was able to refloat itself quite quickly, and suffered no damage.

On the morning of 19 April *Morayshire*, which had left Liverpool on 2 February with 100 passengers on board for New Zealand, as well as cargo, ran aground at the entrance to the Victoria Channel, just above Kilgour's Point. As the tide was falling at the time it was not possible to quickly refloat the vessel, which was sitting on an even keel on a soft, sandy bottom. After the ballast tanks were pumped out, the vessel was pulled free by a tug, and towed into Port Chalmers, where it was found that no damage had been caused.

In 1910, another British shipping company, the Clan Line Ltd, obtained a controlling interest in Turnbull, Martin & Co., and their seven ships were registered under the ownership of a new company, the Scottish Shire Line. However, none were renamed, nor was

their operation altered in any way, and they continued to carry the same funnel colours as before.

On 7 July 1911, the *Fifeshire* departed Sydney, calling at Melbourne, Adelaide and Albany, departing there on 21 July for Liverpool and London, via the Suez Canal, with 105 persons on board, including about 25 passengers. On the evening of 9 August, *Fifeshire* ran hard aground on sand and coral in bad weather some 20 miles (32 km) south of Cape Guardafui. The vessel stranded broadside on to the heavy swell, and at noon on 10 August Captain Cremer gave the order to abandon ship. Several lifeboats were launched, but some crew remained on board until the next day, when they also abandoned the stricken vessel.

Three boats were picked up by the French steamer *Adour*, and the survivors taken to Aden, but this left two boats unaccounted for, and a search was started. On 18 August the steamer *Ardandearg* found one boat, which only contained five seamen, but despite an intensive search the other boat, containing 8 passengers and 16 crewmen, was never located.

A few days before the loss of the *Fifeshire*, the Scottish Shire Line had placed a new ship in service, *Argyllshire*, which was one of three sisters built for the combined Federal-Houlder-Shire Line operation. (This ship is discussed on page 120.)

In April 1912, Houlder Bros withdrew from the Australian trade, but the joint service continued as the Federal & Shire Line, providing a departure from Liverpool every six weeks. However, over the next two years the participation by Scottish Shire Line ships in the Australian migrant trade was reduced, and eventually ceased altogether.

When war broke out in 1914 the fortunes of the company took a dive, and before the end of that year three ships had been disposed of, with *Banffshire*, *Morayshire* and *Nairnshire* being sold to the Union Cold Storage Co., a subsidiary of Blue Star Line, by whom they were renamed *Brodness*, *Brodliffe* and *Brodholme* respectively. Of their other ships, *Ayrshire* was requisitioned by the Australian Government when it arrived in local waters in November 1914, and as transport A33 embarked troops in Sydney and departed on 20 December for Albany, from where the second convoy of Australian and New Zealand troops to be sent overseas departed on 31 December, arriving at Alexandria on 1 February 1915. *Ayrshire* continued to trade to Australia as a cargo ship for the rest of the war.

Early in 1915, *Perthshire* was sold to the British Admiralty, and used by them for many years as a stores carrier. Also in 1915, *Buteshire* was sold to Houlder Bros, being renamed *Bollington Grange*, but after only a couple of voyages from Britain to the River Plate was transferred to the Furness Houlder Argentine Line, and renamed *Canonesa*.

After the war ended, *Ayrshire* was refitted to carry 30 first class passengers only, and remained on the Australian trade until 28 November 1926, when it caught fire in the Indian Ocean, and had to be abandoned. While being towed to a port, *Ayrshire* sank on 2 December.

Of the vessels that had been sold, *Brodness*, the former *Banffshire*, was torpedoed and sunk in the Mediterranean on 31 March 1917. In 1919 the two other vessels sold to the Union Cold Storage Co. in 1914 were transferred to the parent company, Blue Star Line, and again renamed, the former *Nairnshire* becoming *Gothicstar*, while the former *Morayshire* became *Tuscanstar*. At the same time the former *Buteshire* was bought by Blue Star Line from Furness Houlder, and renamed *Magicstar*.

In 1929 the *Gothicstar* had its name amended to *Gothic Star*, and served under this name until arriving at Savona on 4 July 1938 to be broken up. Also in 1929, *Magicstar* was sold to shipbreakers, while *Tuscanstar* was sold for further trading, and renamed *Fortunstar*, becoming *Semien* in 1936 and *Lugarno* in 1942, surviving World War II and being broken up at Savona towards the end of 1952.

Ayrshire

NINEVEH

Built: 1894 by Robert Napier & Co., Dalmuir
Gross tonnage: 3,808
Dimensions: 365 x 45 ft/111.2 x 13.7m
Service speed: 12 knots
Propulsion: Triple expansion/single propeller

George Thompson & Co., of Aberdeen, better known as the Aberdeen Line, were well known as sailing ship owners long before they placed their first steamships in service. Drawing on their background in sail, their early ships (see page 12) followed the sailing ship practice of having the best accommodation right aft, which in a ship under sail was the best place, but in a propeller driven vessel was where the most vibration could be felt. It took the Aberdeen Line ten years to realise their mistake, and when they ordered a fifth ship for the Australian trade in 1893, it had the first class accommodation amidships.

Launched on 18 August 1894 and named *Nineveh*, the new vessel left London on 31 October 1894 on its maiden voyage via Cape Town to Australia. *Nineveh* carried much the same passenger complement as the earlier ships, 50 first class and about 600 third class, though much of the latter was temporary accommodation erected in the holds and used only by migrants on the outward journey, the same spaces being used for cargo on the return trip.

With five ships on the route the Aberdeen Line was able to offer regular monthly departures from London, and the company prospered over the next few years. In 1905 the Aberdeen Line was reorganised as a public company, with White Star Line and Shaw, Savill & Albion becoming majority shareholders.

This was to bring great changes to the Aberdeen Line, as in 1906 a joint service with the Blue Anchor Line commenced, which meant that some of the older ships could be disposed of, and in 1907 *Nineveh* was sold to the Eastern & Australian Steamship Co., better known as the E&A Line. On 19 November 1906 the E&A vessel *Australian* had been wrecked on the coast of northern Australia, and the company urgently needed a replacement. *Nineveh* was an ideal choice, as it was only thirteen years old, and also larger than the lost ship.

On 14 May 1907 *Nineveh* made its final sailing from London to Australia for the Aberdeen Line, and was handed over to the E&A Line in Sydney. Renamed *Aldenham*, it was placed in service from Australian east coast ports to Manila, Hong Kong and Japan, being partnered by *Eastern* and *Empire*; in 1910 *St Albans* was added to the service. When war came in 1914 these ships remained on their regular route, but trade with the Far East slumped.

In 1916 the Royal Mail Line bought *Aldenham*, which was renamed *Larne*. The vessel served Royal Mail Line for only two years, as in 1918 it was sold again, to the Zurbaran Steam Ship Co., of London, whom it served without being renamed for the next five years. In May 1923 was sold to shipbreakers at Wilhelmshaven in Germany.

Nineveh

PRINZ REGENT LUITPOLD and PRINZ HEINRICH

Built: 1894/95 by Schichau, Danzig
Gross tonnage: 6,288/6,636
Dimensions: 455 x 50 ft/138.8 x 15.6 m
Service speed: 14 knots
Propulsion: Triple expansion/twin propellers

North German Lloyd entered the Australian trade in 1886, transferring five vessels from their South American route to inaugurate the service. These ships were supplemented from time to time by other vessels drawn from the various routes operated by the company, and it was not until 1894 that North German Lloyd built a vessel specially designed for the Australian trade, though it could be used on the Far East route as well if necessary.

The vessel was named *Prinz Regent Luitpold* when launched on 20 March 1894, and ran final sea trials on 19 August. A sister ship, *Prinz Heinrich*, was launched on 20 August 1894, and placed on the Far East trade in 1895.

The first twin-screw vessel to be placed on the Australian trade by North German Lloyd, *Prinz Regent Luitpold* was fitted out with permanent accommodation for 76 first class and 72 second class passengers, but on the outward voyage to Australia a large number of steerage passengers, mostly migrants, could be carried in temporary quarters erected in the holds. When the ship reached Australia these quarters would be disassembled and a full cargo loaded in the holds for the return voyage to Germany.

Prinz Regent Luitpold departed Bremen on 29 August, calling at Antwerp, Southampton, Genoa and Naples before passing through the Suez Canal. After further stops at Aden and Colombo, the vessel went directly to Adelaide, where it arrived on 13 October, reaching Melbourne on 15 October and berthing in Sydney on 18 October. Next day the *Sydney Morning Herald* reported:

All first and second class cabins are on the upper deck. The first class cabins are amidship, and the second class aft. Special attention has been paid to the ventilation of cabins, and, in addition to the usual ports, Utley's patent ventilator has been adopted for use in case of bad weather.

Prinz Regent Luitpold (WSS Victoria)

The alleyways are large and airy. The cabins contain folding berths, patent washstands, wardrobe, and chest of drawers and table. The electric light is installed throughout the ship.

The fittings of the saloon are after the modern English style. The reception and social rooms of the first class are all amidships on the promenade deck. The dining room is so situated that three sides are open to ventilation, which is effected by 20 large square windows, and a dome-shaped skylight. The ladies room and smoking room, the latter extending across the full width of the deck are, as well as the dining room, master works of the decorative art, and are executed after the plans of the eminent architect Poppe, of Bremen, by the world-renowned firm of A. Bembe, who are known to have decorated most of the steamers of the Norddeutsche Lloyd. The promenade deck for first class passengers, which is 200 feet long, is covered by a permanent wooden awning, which makes this deck attractive in all but very severe weather. The second class cabins are also on the upper deck, and attention has been paid to give them every convenience and comfort. The *Prinz Regent Luitpold* has accommodation for 80 passengers in this class, and the second class ladies room and smoking room are also handsomely fitted up and are situated aft. The third class is divided into cabins of two and four berths and family cabins for eight to 13 persons. The engines are of the compound triple expansion class, and the machinery is placed in such a way that vibration and noise are almost done away with.

Prinz Regent Luitpold was considerably larger than the ships that North German Lloyd had used up to that date on the route, though still slightly smaller than the contemporary vessels of the P&O and Orient lines. *Prinz Regent Luitpold* remained on the Australian trade all year, being partnered by a variety of vessels from other trades, the most frequent being ships of the Karlsruhe class built between 1889 and 1891, which consisted of six vessels of about 5,000 gross tons.

In 1896 Norddeutscher Lloyd began sending some of their latest and largest North Atlantic liners to Australia, these being the vessels of the Barbarossa class, all over 10,000 tons. However, these ships made only one or two voyages a year, and it was mainly *Prinz Regent*

Luitpold that maintained the company service. On 23 February 1898 *Prinz Regent Luitpold* became the first mail steamer to berth in Fremantle Harbour, and from then on the vessel made regular calls at the West Australian port.

During 1897 *Prinz Regent Luitpold* was taken off the Australian trade briefly to make a voyage across the North Atlantic, departing Bremen on 1 May, and in both 1898 and 1899 the vessel operated four more voyages to New York, as well as one in 1900, leaving Bremen on 22 December.

Over the next few years a great variety of liners appeared on the Australian route, most for only one or two voyages, but *Prinz Regent Luitpold* remained the only permanent steamer on the trade until 1904, when the vessel was transferred to the Far East trade, joining its sister ship, *Prinz Heinrich*. The first departure by *Prinz Regent Luitpold* to the Far East was on 26 May 1904, though the vessel still made an occasional sailing to Australia as a relief ship.

When North German Lloyd's Bulow class vessel *Kleist* (see page 92) was not delivered from the builders in time in March 1907, *Prinz Heinrich* was brought onto the Australian route for a single voyage. *Prinz Heinrich* departed Bremen on 20 March, calling at Antwerp, Southampton, Genoa and Naples before proceeding through the Suez Canal. From Colombo *Prinz Heinrich* steamed to Fremantle, arriving on 28 April, then Adelaide on 1 May, Melbourne two days later, and Sydney on 8 May. The arrival of this ship caused some confusion to the local newspapers, which referred to it as a brand-new vessel. This was the only time *Prinz Heinrich* visited Australia.

Prinz Regent Luitpold continued to make occasional voyages to Australia for several more years, the final such trip departing Bremerhaven on 16 April 1910, after which she remained in the Far East trade. In 1914 *Prinz Regent Luitpold* sought shelter in Italian waters, but soon after was seized by the Italian Government, and renamed *Pietro Calvi*. In 1920 the vessel was chartered by Transatlantica Italiana, and used on North Atlantic routes until being sold for scrap in 1928. In 1915 *Prinz Heinrich* was seized by the Portuguese Government, renamed *Porto*, and served under this name until being broken up in Italy in 1927.

THE P&O INDIA CLASS

CHINA
Built: 1896 by Harland & Wolff, Belfast
Gross tonnage: 7,899
Dimensions: 500 x 54 ft/152.5 x 16.5 m
Service speed: 16 knots
Propulsion: Triple expansion/single propeller

INDIA   EGYPT   ARABIA   PERSIA
Built: 1896/96/98/1900 by Caird & Co., Greenock
Gross tonnage: 7,911/7,917/7,903/7,951
Dimensions: 500 x 54 ft/152.5 x 16.5 m
Service speed: 16 knots
Propulsion: Triple expansion/single propeller

The five liners of the India class were intended for service to Australia or India, and were the largest yet built for P&O. In design they were a great advance on previous tonnage, and the last P&O passenger liners to be given only a single propeller at a time when most ship owners were opting for two, for both economy of operation and safety.

India was launched on 15 April 1896, completed in September 1896 and placed on the service to Bombay from London. *China*, which was launched on 13 June 1896, left London on 18 December on its maiden voyage to Australia, arriving in Sydney on 28 January 1897. Next day the *Sydney Morning Herald* reported of the new vessel:

Nothing equal to her has been seen in this part of the world in many respects, nothing that money can buy could indeed be seen aboard a ship that is not here for the comfort and enjoyment of the passengers. Still after spending an hour industriously walking along promenades, themselves longer than many steamers, treading through wide hallways, looking into cabins, for four cabins, three, two and single cabins, saloons bewitchingly furnished, ladies' boudoirs whose loveliness seems like a dream, the sense of wealth produced by the grandeur becomes actually bewildering. The deck one first lands on contains more than half the accommodation, then the hurricane deck is all saloon accommodation, and down below are some more second class berths, with a good sized separate dining saloon for children — a really useful and admirable apartment for children. It may be repeated that the *China* is the largest of the P&O fleet, and the most expensively built merchant ship that has ever visited Australia.

Egypt was launched on 15 May 1897, followed by *Arabia* on 10 November 1897 and *Persia* on 13 August 1900. These three ships spent most of their careers on the Indian service. On all these ships accommodation was provided for 314 first class and 212 second class passengers, and a crew of 400 was carried.

On 28 January 1898 *India* left London on its first voyage to Australia. Disaster almost claimed *China* in March 1898 when, homeward bound from Australia, the vessel ran aground on Perim Island in the Red Sea. With severe bow damage, *China* was at

India

38

Egypt

first considered a total loss, but three months later was refloated and taken to England where the bow was rebuilt.

When P&O's *Australia* was wrecked in Port Phillip Bay in June 1904 (see page 25), *Egypt* was sent from Bombay to Australia, arriving in Sydney on 14 July 1904, and departing on 23 July on a voyage to Britain. *Egypt* then returned to the Indian service.

China was departing Tilbury for Australia on 17 December 1909 when it collided with the pier head, causing serious damage to the stern and rudder. The voyage was abandoned, and on 21 December the passengers were sent overland to Marseilles, where they boarded *Persia* for the voyage to Australia. *Persia* had been inbound from Bombay, but terminated that voyage to take the Australian passage. *Persia* followed this with a round trip to Australia from London, departing on 8 April, then returned to the Indian trade.

India made its final voyage to Australia from London on 22 September 1911, but *China* was retained several months longer, making its final voyage from London on 23 March 1912, leaving Sydney on 18 May. Both ships were then transferred to the Indian trade.

On 12 June 1914, *Egypt* departed London on its first full voyage to Australia, and over the next year made two further round trips on the Australian service, two of them after war broke out in August 1914, at which time *China* and *India* were both taken over for Government service. *India* became an armed merchant cruiser attached to the 10th Cruiser Squadron, which patrolled the waters north of Britain, while *China* became a hospital ship.

In 1915 *Egypt* was also requisitioned for duty as a hospital ship, so on 12 June 1915 *Persia* left London on its third voyage to Australia, and *Arabia* left London on 24 July 1915 on its first voyage to Australia. *Arabia* made two more trips to Australia over the next eighteen months, on one trip picking up 97 Maltese migrants, who disembarked in Sydney in September 1916.

On 8 August 1915 *India* was on patrol off Bodo in Norway when hit by a torpedo fired by *U22,* and the vessel sank with the loss of 120 lives.

Persia, still under P&O control and carrying passengers, was torpedoed by the German submarine *U38* some 70 miles south of Crete on 30 December 1915, with the loss of 335 lives.

On 6 November 1916, *Arabia*, returning to Britain from Australia with passengers and cargo, was torpedoed and sunk by a German submarine in the Mediterranean, with 11 fatalities.

China served throughout the war as a hospital ship, being visited by King George V in June 1916, and after the war returned to the P&O Bombay route. *China* made one further trip to Australia, departing London on 5 June 1920, but the rest of its career was on the Indian trade.

Egypt resumed trading to India in 1921. *Egypt* departed Tilbury for Bombay on 19 May 1922, but the next day in a dense fog was involved in a collision with the French steamer *Seine* off Ushant in the English Channel. *Egypt* sank in twenty minutes, with the loss of 15 passengers and 71 crew members. The ship was carrying over £1 million worth of bullion, and over the next ten years divers managed to recover more than half of this treasure from the wreck.

China operated to India until May 1928, then was sold to shipbreakers in Japan, arriving at Osaka on 22 July 1928.

NARRUNG, WAKOOL and WILCANNIA

NARRUNG
Built: 1896 by Doxford, Sunderland
Gross tonnage: 5,078
Dimensions: 400 x 47 ft/121.9 x 14.3 m
Service speed: 13 knots
Propulsion: Quadruple expansion/single propeller

WAKOOL   WILCANNIA
Built: 1898/1899 by Doxford, Sunderland
Gross tonnage: 5,004/4,953
Dimensions: 400 x 47 ft/121.9 x 14.3 m
Service speed: 13 knots
Propulsion: Triple expansion/single propeller

This trio was built for William Lund & Sons, better known as the Blue Anchor Line, to enable them to enter the migrant trade. *Narrung* was launched on 11 July 1896 and delivered two months later. The new vessel was larger than any the company had previously operated, and fitted with accommodation for 50 first class passengers in the superstructure, and 50 in third class at the bow, plus temporary quarters for several hundred migrants in the 'tween decks in the holds. *Narrung* was also the first Blue Anchor ship to dispense with yards on the masts, as the quadruple expansion engine had become very reliable. On 6 October 1896 *Narrung* left London on its maiden voyage, under the command of Captain J. F. Ilbery, going via Cape Town to Adelaide, Melbourne and Sydney, where it arrived on 28 November.

Narrung proved such a useful addition to the fleet that two sister ships were ordered, the first to be launched being *Wakool* on 4 August 1898, which departed London on 5 November 1898 under Captain Thomas, arriving in Sydney on 3 January 1899. It was followed by *Wilcannia*, which was launched on 26 May 1899. These ships were identical to *Narrung* in every aspect except for their triple expansion engines.

Wilcannia departed London on 25 July 1899 on its maiden voyage to Australia, also commanded by Captain Ilbery, the first stop being Las Palmas on 31 July. Cape Town was reached on 17 August, and the vessel then steamed directly to Adelaide, berthing there on 6 September. Leaving the next day, *Wilcannia* docked in Melbourne on 8 September, and after disembarking passengers and discharging cargo, arrived in Sydney for the first time on 12 September 1899, the entire voyage being made in 48 days. The next day the following report appeared in the *Sydney Morning Herald*:

The *Wilcannia* is a sister ship to the steamers *Narrung* and *Wakool*. Her carrying capacity is 6,000 tons, and accommodation is fitted for 50 first and 50 third class. The steamer is built with full poop and topgallant forecastle with a long citadel bridge, at the forward end of which is placed accommodation for first-class passengers. At the after end is the accommodation for officers, engineers, apprentices, purser etc. On the top of this bridge deck a large house is built containing berths for first-class passengers, opening out onto the deck. At the fore end of this house, and forward of the machinery space, is the first-class dining saloon, which is panelled out in two shades of polished oak; handsome mirrors are fitted with carved oak caps, and moulding relieved with gold. There are three dining tables with revolving chairs. This saloon is specially lighted, and ventilated with dome skylights, and large sidelights all around. There are also on this deck a music room and smoking room. Covering all this accommodation is a complete shade deck extending to the sides of the vessel, forming a promenade for the first-class passengers, 120 ft by 48ft, the only erection upon which is the captain's house and navigation room. Accommodation for 50 third class passengers is placed in the topgallant forecastle, and under the fore end of the bridge, whilst the crew are all berthed in the full poop aft.

The only interruption to the Australia service was caused by the outbreak of war in South Africa in October

Wilcannia

Wakool

1899. *Narrung* and *Wilcannia* were used occasionally to carry troops and horses from Britain to Cape Town on the outward voyages, but *Wakool* was taken over for trooping duty for four years, and did not make any voyages to Australia during that time. With the end of the conflict in 1901 the service returned to normal.

In 1902 the larger *Commonwealth* was built, being joined by *Geelong* in 1904 (see page 70), which allowed the company to dispose of its oldest ships, and keep *Narrung* and her sisters plus the two new ships to operate a schedule of four-weekly departures from London.

In May 1902 *Narrung* was crossing the Indian Ocean on a voyage back to Britain, carrying a large number of passengers bound for the coronation of King Edward VII, when it chanced upon the Howard Smith steamer *Boveric*, which had lost its propeller thirty-seven days earlier when bound for Durban from Australia. Despite the urgency of getting his passengers to London in time for the coronation, Captain Bond of *Narrung* had no hesitation in towing *Boveric* back to Fremantle, which took five days. For this effort all involved on *Narrung* received monetary regards from the salvage—court, and the passengers were not inconvenienced, as the coronation was postponed when the king became ill.

On 23 September 1904, *Wilcannia* was departing Sydney when it ran aground at Shark Beach in the harbour, at low tide. Four hours later the vessel floated free, and returned to its wharf, where it was found that several plates had been damaged. *Wilcannia* had to enter Mort's Dock for repairs, and did not leave Sydney until 25 November.

The Blue Anchor Line reached its peak in 1908 with the delivery of *Waratah*, almost twice the size of the *Narrung* trio (see page 98), with *Wakool* being laid up in reserve. On its second voyage *Waratah*

disappeared off South Africa in July 1909, and *Wakool* was brought back into service. The tragedy destroyed the Blue Anchor Line completely, and the company was purchased in January 1910 by the P&O Line, who retained the three ships on their regular service.

The service was renamed the P&O Branch Line in June 1910, and P&O decided to remove the first class accommodation from these three vessels, the first to be altered being *Wakool*, and only third class passengers were carried from then on.

P&O ordered five new ships for the Branch Line, and as they entered service the older ships were sold. The first to be withdrawn was *Narrung*, which left Sydney for the last time on 28 September, followed by *Wakool* on 31 October, on a voyage through the Suez Canal. *Wilcannia* continued to operate for a further year, making her final departure from Sydney on 12 September 1912.

Narrung was sold to Eng Hok Pong Steamship Co., of Hong Kong, but resold in 1913 to the Mexico Steamship Co., and renamed *Mexico City*. On 5 February 1918 she was torpedoed and sunk off Holyhead in the Irish Sea.

Wakool was sold in 1912 to Goshi Kaisha Kishimoto Shokwa of Japan and renamed *Kwanto Maru*. In 1917 they sold her to the French Government, and she was renamed *Le Myre de Villers*. Sold again in 1919 to Brabant & Pruvost, of Marseilles, she was not renamed again, and in 1923 was sold to S. Bertorello of Spezia for scrapping, but not broken up until 1925.

Wilcannia was sold in 1913 to the same Japanese firm, and renamed *Shinkoko Maru*, and was also purchased by the French Government in 1917, being renamed *Dumont d'Urville*. In 1919 they sold the vessel to Messageries Maritimes, but it was not until November 1921 that they renamed the vessel *André Chenier*. She served them until being sold to shipbreakers at Spezia in December 1925.

FRIEDRICH DER GROSSE and BARBAROSSA

FRIEDRICH DER GROSSE
Built: 1896 by Vulcan, Stettin
Gross tonnage: 10,531
Dimensions: 546 x 60 ft/166.4 x 18.3 m
Service speed: 14 knots
Propulsion: Quadruple expansion/twin propellers

BARBAROSSA
Built: 1897 by Blohm & Voss, Hamburg
Gross tonnage: 10,769
Dimensions: 548 x 60 ft/167.1 x 18.3 m
Service speed: 14 knots
Propulsion: Quadruple expansion/twin propellers

Beginning in 1896, North German Lloyd took delivery of seven new liners which were the first German vessels to exceed 10,000 gross tons. The group as a whole was known as the Barbarossa class, and the ship of that name was slightly the larger of the first pair to be completed. They were designed primarily for the North Atlantic service between Bremerhaven and New York, but also to be used on the Australian trade during the northern winter.

The first to be launched, on 1 August 1896, was *Friedrich der Grosse*, and on completion she was despatched on 11 November from Bremerhaven on a voyage to Australia, via the Suez Canal. The arrival of this new liner caused great excitement in Australian ports, as it was the first ship over 10,000 tons to be seen in local waters, and looked very smart with a white hull. *Friedrich der Grosse* arrived in Melbourne on 6 January 1897, and the following day a report on the ship appeared in the *Sydney Morning Herald*, which said in part:

> The cabin arrangements are superb, and provide for berthing 100 first class and 76 second class passengers; and if the whole of the room available for steerage passengers is taken up no less than 2,000 could be accommodated on a single trip. Under ordinary circumstances, however, this is not needed, and on the present trip she carried less than one-tenth of the maximum number. The first saloon is in the fore part of the ship on the upper deck and is 60ft by 36ft. The second saloon is abaft the engines, on the same deck, but it is situated almost amidships, for it is under the promenade deck, which also carries a number of auxiliary apartments. Passing out of the saloon, a spacious companion way leads to the promenade deck, and immediately above the dining room is the music room. In the cabin arrangements this steamer is claimed to excel. There are single-berth, two-berth and three-berth cabins, all large, airy and well-furnished; also a cabin which connects with a private state-room or drawing-room, and also with what are called Pullman cabins, that is cabins fitted on the principles adopted on Pullman cars, in which

> the sleeping berths can be folded up, making it possible to utilise the chamber as a private sitting room. The size of the steamer also makes it possible for a greater space than usual to be set apart for promenade.

Friedrich der Grosse continued to Sydney, berthing at Circular Quay East on the morning of Sunday, 10 January, where it again created great interest. As was usual at that time, the liner remained in port for over two weeks, during which time it was opened for public inspection at various times, and also hosted a special concert. *Friedrich der Grosse* departed Sydney on 27 January on the return voyage to Germany.

Barbarossa had been launched on 5 September 1896, being handed over to North German Lloyd on 3 January 1897, and on 8 January left Bremerhaven on her maiden voyage, to Australia. Although the ships were very similar externally, their internal design differed, as *Friedrich der Grosse* had berths for 216 first class, 243 second class and 1,964 third class while *Barbarossa* carried 230 first class, 227 second class and 1,935 third class passengers.

After each vessel had made the one voyage to Australia they were transferred to the North Atlantic service. For this trade the hull of *Friedrich der Grosse* was repainted black, and remained that colour for the rest of its career under the German flag. On the North Atlantic these vessels operated a secondary route from Bremerhaven and Southampton to New York, as the main service was operated by several larger steamers that were delivered from 1897 onwards.

When the 1897 North Atlantic summer season ended, *Friedrich der Grosse* and *Barbarossa* returned to the Australian trade again, each making one voyage, and this pattern was followed during the summers of 1899/1900 and 1900/1901. Over the next dozen years *Friedrich der Grosse* and *Barbarossa* continued to make one or two voyages each year to Australia.

Barbarossa departed Germany in January 1911 on a voyage to Australia, calling in to Italian ports along the way to pick up more passengers. As the vessel was crossing the Indian Ocean a fire broke out in a cargo hold, as reported in the *Sydney Morning Herald* on Thursday, 2 February:

> When the German mail steamer *Barbarossa*, which arrived in Fremantle late last night, was about 400 miles from Fremantle a fire was discovered by the baggage master, who on going to the baggage room adjoining the hold found some stanchions almost red hot. Steam was at once turned into the hold. After about two hours the fire was subdued. Subsequently water was pumped into the hold.
>
> Although the outbreak was almost adjoining the steerage quarters there was no panic, but some Italian passengers showed some signs of nervousness and attached

Barbarossa

themselves to lifebuoys. The damage to the cargo has not been ascertained.

A message from Fremantle, received by the Sydney Marine Underwriters' and Salvage Association last night, was to the following effect: 'Barbarossa arrived today. Had fire No. 4 orlop deck two days since. Fire originated in Melbourne cargo. Steam first used, subsequently water, to extinguish. Cargo for Fremantle, Adelaide, Melbourne and Sydney damaged by water. Plates buckled by heat. Cause of fire unknown.'

Fortunately the damage was not serious enough to delay the ship, which completed its voyage as scheduled. On 24 December 1912 *Barbarossa* left Bremerhaven on what was to be her final voyage to Australia. *Friedrich der Grosse* remained on the route for the following season, with her departure from Bremerhaven on 21 January 1914 turning out to be her final appearance in Australia, as the outbreak of war later that year was to bring the North German Lloyd services to Australia to a complete halt.

Barbarossa was berthed in New York when war was declared, being immediately interned by the American authorities, as was *Friedrich der Grosse* upon its arrival at the same port a few days later.

For almost three years they lay idle, until America came into the war on the Allied side. On 6 April 1917 both ships were seized by the United States Government for service with the US Navy. *Friedrich der Grosse* was renamed *Huron*, and *Barbarossa* became *Mercury*. They served as troop transports until 1919, when they were taken over by the US Shipping Board.

Huron was converted to oil firing at Brooklyn, and then chartered in 1922 to the Los Angeles Steamship Co., being renamed *City of Honolulu*. The ship was placed in service between Los Angeles and Hawaii, but on 12 October 1922 caught fire some 400 miles west of Los Angeles and had to be abandoned. The burning ship drifted for five days, and then on 17 October was deliberately sunk.

The former *Barbarossa*, under her new name of *Mercury*, was chartered in July 1920 to the Baltic Steamship Corporation of America for a planned service between New York and Danzig, but this did not eventuate as that company went into liquidation before *Mercury* made a voyage. As a result the vessel was laid up in the reserve fleet, where it remained idle for a further three years, and then in 1924 was sold to shipbreakers in America.

KÖNIGIN LUISE and BREMEN

KÖNIGIN LUISE
Built: 1897 by Vulcan, Stettin
Gross tonnage: 10,566
Dimensions: 552 x 60 ft/168.3 x 18.3 m
Service speed: 14 knots
Propulsion: Quadruple expansion/twin propellers

BREMEN
Built: 1897 by Schichau, Danzig
Gross tonnage: 10,552
Dimensions: 550 x 60 ft/167.6 x 18.4 m
Service speed: 14 knots
Propulsion: Quadruple expansion/twin propellers

The second pair of liners of the Barbarossa class of North German Lloyd were designed for a secondary service between Bremerhaven and New York, and voyages to Australia in the off-season. *Königin Luise* was launched on 17 October 1896 and completed in March 1897, leaving Bremerhaven on 22 March on her maiden voyage to New York. *Bremen* was launched on 14 November 1896, being completed in May 1897, departing Bremerhaven on 5 June on her maiden voyage to New York.

Königin Luise could carry 216 first class, 243 second class and 1,964 third class passengers, while *Bremen* carried 230 first class, 250 second class and 1,850 third class passengers.

Bremen departed Bremerhaven on 20 October 1897 for Adelaide, Melbourne and Sydney, and on 12 November *Königin Luise* left Bremerhaven on its first voyage to Australia. Each ship made only the one return trip to Australia, and also made one trip to Australia in the season 1898/99 and again in 1899-1900.

On 30 June 1900 *Bremen* was docked in New York, along with three other North German Lloyd liners, when a fire broke out in bales of cotton stored in a shed on the wharf. The blaze quickly spread and set fire to the ships. Tugs came racing to tow the berthed ships away from the danger, but by the time *Bremen* was pulled clear her superstructure was burning and the ship had a heavy list to port.

Bremen was run aground and the fire extinguished, but twelve crewmen had died, and the midships area was very badly damaged, much of the superstructure being gutted and buckled. *Bremen* returned empty to Stettin for repairs, which lasted a year. During this period the ship was lengthened by 25ft/7.7m, new boilers were installed and the poop extended forward to the mainmast. As a result of these changes her tonnage rose to 11,540 gross, and speed was also increased.

Bremen returned to the Australian trade again at the end of 1901, and with *Königin Luise* made regular annual voyages on the route. From 1904 until 1910 *Königin Luise* spent most of the year on a service from Mediterranean ports to New York, though still visiting Australia once a year as well. In September 1905 *Bremen* broke its starboard propeller shaft one day after leaving New York for Bremerhaven, and had to be towed to Halifax. In December 1908, while on an Australian voyage, *Bremen* was in the Mediterranean when Mount Etna erupted, and the vessel made a stop

Bremen

at Messina to carry 600 evacuees to safety in Naples.

Bremen left Bremerhaven on its last voyage to Australia on 1 October 1911 and *Königin Luise* made its final departure for Australia on 29 October 1911, after which both ships remained all year on the North Atlantic route.

Both ships remained in Bremerhaven throughout World War I, and in April 1919 they were awarded to the British Government as war prizes, with *Königin Luise* being placed under the management of the Orient Line, and *Bremen* being managed by P&O Line.

Bremen was used to repatriate Australian soldiers from Europe, making several voyages until 1921, when the vessel was sold to the Byron Steam Navigation Co. of London. Renamed *Constantinople*, and with accommodation for 345 first class, 314 second class and 1,700 third class passengers, it entered service from Mediterranean ports to New York.

Königin Luise was also used to repatriate Australian soldiers, arriving in Sydney for the first time in this role on 16 August 1919. On one of its visits to Sydney that year the vessel was loading a cargo of copra when a fire broke out in the hold, causing some damage to the ship. Its British Government service to Australia continued into 1920, but was again interrupted by an accident, this time a fractured tail shaft that resulted in one of the after holds being flooded.

During this same period the Orient Line had been trying to re-establish their service between Britain and Australia, and from September 1919 was able to operate a limited schedule using five vessels, but more were needed to meet the demand for passages. Orient Line chartered *Königin Luise*, which left London on 4 September 1920, having accommodation for 170 first class and 757 third class passengers. The Orient Line purchased the ship outright from the British Government in January 1921, following which it was renamed *Omar*, and on 21 January left London for Australia under that name.

Omar would prove to be a bad buy for the Orient Line, as it could only manage 13 knots when a service speed of at least 18 knots was required by the mail steamers. *Omar* left London on its final voyage to Australia on 9 February 1924.

In July 1924 *Omar* was sold to the Byron Steamship Co. of London, renamed *Edison*, and placed in service between Piraeus and New York, having been refitted to carry 226 first class, 255 second class and 1,500 third class passengers. The Byron Steamship Co. already owned the former *Bremen*, which had been renamed *Constantinople*. In 1924 that vessel was renamed *King Alexander*, still under the same ownership, and remained on their New York service until 1926, when it was withdrawn and sold to Italian shipbreakers.

In 1929 *Edison* was transferred to the ownership of the National Steam Navigation Co. of Greece, a Byron subsidiary, and registered under the Greek flag. By that time the Byron concern was winding down their passenger operation, until only *Edison* was left, and in 1935 it was withdrawn from service, and sold to shipbreakers in Italy.

Omar

DELPHIC

Built: 1897 by Harland & Wolff, Belfast
Gross tonnage: 8,273
Dimensions: 476 x 55 ft/145.1 x 16.8 m
Service speed: 12 knots
Propulsion: Triple expansion/twin propellers

Built for White Star Line as a cargo ship with basic accommodation for third class passengers to operate on the New Zealand trade, *Delphic* was launched on 5 January 1897 and completed on 15 May.

Instead of being placed immediately on the New Zealand trade, *Delphic* departed Liverpool on 17 June 1897 on its maiden voyage to New York, followed by a voyage from London to New York.

In August 1897 *Delphic* was transferred to the New Zealand trade, becoming the first White Star vessel to operate on a joint service with Shaw Savill Line. Some cabins for third class passengers were installed, along with temporary accommodation in the 'tween decks and holds for about 1,000 migrants on the voyage out to New Zealand. The vessel returned to Britain with a full cargo of New Zealand produce.

On 30 September 1897 *Delphic* departed London on its first voyage to New Zealand. The outward voyage took the vessel around South Africa, and sometimes included a call at Hobart or other Australian ports, while the voyage back to Britain was around Cape Horn. For several years *Delphic* was the largest vessel engaged in the New Zealand trade.

Delphic carried a contingent of the Imperial Yeomanry from Britain to South Africa for the Boer War in the course of a regular voyage to New Zealand in March 1900. In April 1901 another contingent of troops was embarked at Queenstown, in Ireland, to be transported to South Africa.

Delphic remained on the combined main line service of White Star and Shaw Savill until 1902, its departure from London on 8 May being the last in this role, and subsequently it primarily operated as a cargo ship, sometimes carrying migrants. In November 1905 the vessel called at Australian ports on its way back to Britain from New Zealand, and made similar visits several times between 1907 and 1912.

It appears *Delphic* made only one voyage to Australia with migrants, departing Liverpool in late November 1912 and arriving in Melbourne on 11 January 1913 and Sydney six days later.

In World War I *Delphic* remained on the New Zealand trade until 10 March 1917, when it was taken over by the British Government under the Liner Requisition Scheme, being used as a cargo ship only.

Delphic was attacked by a German submarine off the south-west coast of Ireland on 16 February 1917, but the torpedo missed.

The reprieve was only temporary, as on 17 August 1917 *Delphic* was at the start of a voyage from Cardiff to Montevideo with a cargo of coal when it was torpedoed by the German submarine *UC72* 135 miles from Bishop's Rock, and sank with the loss of five lives.

Delphic (WSS Victoria)

MORAVIAN and SALAMIS

MORAVIAN
Built: 1899 by Robert Napier & Co., Glasgow
Gross tonnage: 4,573
Dimensions: 391 x 47 ft/119 x 14.3 m
Service speed: 13 knots
Propulsion: Triple expansion/single propulsion

SALAMIS
Built: 1899 by Hall, Russell & Co., Aberdeen
Gross tonnage: 4,508
Dimensions: 391 x 47 ft/119 x 14.3 m
Service speed: 13 knots
Propulsion: Triple expansion/single propeller

Built for the Aberdeen Line at two yards, the Napier ship was the first launched, on 30 September 1898, and named *Moravian*. Leaving London on 14 February 1899 on its maiden voyage to Australia, via Cape Town, *Moravian* went only to Melbourne and Sydney. The second ship, *Salamis*, was launched on 11 April 1899, and followed the same route, departing London on 8 August 1899.

Moravian and *Salamis* had accommodation for 50 first class passengers and about 600 emigrants. However, the Aberdeen pair was completely outclassed by the three 10,000 ton ships placed on the same route during 1899 by the White Star Line.

For ten years *Moravian* and *Salamis* operated a regular schedule of voyages to Australia, but with the pending arrival of two new vessels in 1911, it was not necessary to retain both of them. The final voyage by *Salamis* departed London on 1 October 1910, and was anything but comfortable for the passengers, as shown in this report on its arrival in Melbourne on 18 November that appeared next day in the *Sydney Morning Herald*:

The late arrival of the steamer *Salamis* from London this afternoon was due to several causes. She left London on October 1, and was delayed 16 hours in the English Channel by a strong south-westerly gale. Las Palmas was reached on October 8, and the day being observed as a holiday on the island coaling work was not started till the following afternoon. A few hours after leaving Capetown a breakdown occurred in the machinery, and the steamer was hove-to for nearly a day while repairs were effected. Further trouble was experienced with the machinery, and led to a stoppage of several hours.

On returning to Britain in January 1911 *Salamis* was held in reserve until the new ships were settled into service. When offered for sale, *Salamis* was purchased by the Bank Line in March 1912, but they did not change her name.

At the same time *Moravian* had its first class accommodation removed, but continued to carry migrants. On 7 October 1913 *Moravian* left London on its final voyage to Australia, departing Sydney for the last time on 13 December. In 1914 the vessel was purchased by the Bombay & Persia Steamship Co., more generally known as the Mogul Line, which was involved in the Indian and Persian Gulf coastal trade, and also carrying pilgrims to Mecca. The vessel was renamed *Akbar*, and served under this name until September 1923, when it was sold to Italian shipbreakers and scrapped at Genoa.

Salamis lasted one year longer, having been sold in 1919 by the Bank Line to Canada Steamship Co. and renamed *Kamarima*. It served under this name for five years, and arrived at Savona in Italy on 8 August 1924 to be broken up.

Salamis

PAPANUI and *PAPAROA*

Built: 1898/99 by Wm Denny & Bros, Dumbarton
Gross tonnage: 6,582/6,563
Dimensions: 430 x 54 ft/131.1 x 16.4 m
Service speed: 13 knots
Propulsion: Triple expansion/single-twin propellers

Although externally this pair were almost identical, *Papanui* was the last single-screw liner to be built for the New Zealand Shipping Company, while *Paparoa* was their first vessel to be fitted with twin propellers. When completed they carried yards on the foremast on which sail could be rigged when a following wind was blowing to increase speed, but this practice was abandoned within a few years.

Papanui was launched on 1 November 1898 and completed on 26 December. The vessel departed London on her maiden voyage on 12 January 1899, proceeding around the Cape of Good Hope to pass south of Australia, calling at Hobart before visiting several ports in New Zealand. The return trip continued eastabout to pass around Cape Horn and across the Atlantic to Britain. *Paparoa* was launched on 23 August 1899, and handed over to the NZSC on 19 October, leaving London on 19 November 1899 on its maiden voyage, following the same route as *Papanui*.

Accommodation on both ships consisted of cabins for 35 first class and 45 second class passengers, with more humble temporary arrangements in the holds for up to 250 steerage passengers, mostly emigrants.

Between 1900 and 1902 the NZSC took delivery of four new passenger ships, all of which had twin propellers, and from 1905 *Papanui* was relegated to a cargo service, but on some outward voyages carried large numbers of migrants.

In 1909 *Paparoa* joined *Papanui* on the cargo service, but from time to time *Paparoa* carried migrants to both Australia and New Zealand.

When *Papanui* was departing Hobart on 14 December 1909 it struck an uncharted rock, which inflicted serious bottom damage. After temporary repairs in Tasmania the ship limped across Bass Strait to Melbourne, arriving on 19 January 1910 and being put into drydock.

The NZSC decided the cost of repairing the ship was not justified, so they offered her for sale at auction in Melbourne in her damaged state on 23 May 1910. Mr H. A. Visbord purchased the ship, but then the deal fell through. The NZSC reclaimed *Papanui* in July, and it was auctioned a second time on 12 October.

This time the buyer was James Paterson, but he found the cost of repairs in Australia too great, and port authorities

Papanui

Paparoa

refused to allow the ship to sail in its damaged state. To get around these problems the ship was transferred to Nicaraguan registry on 21 November, and on 5 December slipped out of Melbourne without a pilot, and steamed to Nagasaki, arriving on 3 January 1911.

Repairs were completed there, and on 5 March *Papanui* left Nagasaki, returning to Melbourne on 31 March. On 21 April the ship was re-registered in Melbourne under the ownership of a syndicate headed by local shipping identity H. C. Sleigh and placed under the management of his company, the Australian Shipping Company.

At the time there were many Australians wishing to travel to London for the coronation of King George V in June, and on 10 May *Papanui* left Melbourne with a full load of passengers, bound for Liverpool. The vessel then steamed to London to load cargo and also embark 364 emigrants going to Australia.

On 25 August *Papanui* left London, reportedly without a Bill of Health clearance. The route was to take the ship down the South Atlantic to round the Cape of Good Hope, and thence to Australia, but on 5 September bunker coal stored in No. 3 hold was found to be smouldering.

For five days the crew battled to control the dangerous situation, but to no avail, and the captain reluctantly headed *Papanui* for the island of St Helena, anchoring there on 11 September in James Bay. All passengers and crew were removed and soon after a fire broke out and the next day the entire ship was ablaze, being totally destroyed in a matter of hours. The charred hulk was later scuttled in James Bay.

In 1911 the accommodation on *Paparoa* was regraded to cater for third class only. After war broke out in 1914 the vessel was kept on her regular trade, but only as a cargo ship. During the conflict the New Zealand Shipping Co. suffered several losses, and by the time peace returned, they had only five passenger ships left, one of which was *Paparoa*. The old liner was refitted to carry cabin class and third class passengers, and on 26 May 1921 left London for New Zealand on the main line service again, which now went out and back through the Panama Canal.

For the next two years *Paparoa* remained on this route, but in 1923 *Rotorua* entered the service, and once again *Paparoa* was relegated to the migrant trade. This was operated on the original route followed by the ship, going out to New Zealand around South Africa and returning around Cape Horn, since speed was of no importance.

In March 1926 *Paparoa* was steaming south from Britain, heading for the Cape of Good Hope, but when the ship was in the area of St Helena a fire broke out on board that quickly raged out of control. Radio calls for assistance brought the P&O Branch Line vessel *Barrabool* to the scene, and it took off all the passengers and crew, leaving the blazing ship to its fate.

Later the cruiser HMS *Birmingham* arrived on the scene and managed to get a firefighting party onto *Paparoa*, but they were unable to quell the blaze. In the end it was decided to scuttle the ship, so the boarding party opened the sea cocks, and on 17 March 1926 *Paparoa* went to the bottom.

WAIWERA and KUMARA

WAIWERA
Built: 1898 by Wm Denny & Bros, Dumbarton
Tonnage: 6,237
Dimensions: 425 x 54 ft/129.7 x 16.5 m
Service speed: 12 knots
Propulsion: Triple expansion/single propeller

KUMARA
Built: 1899 by Swan & Hunter, Wallsend
Tonnage: 6,034 gross
Dimensions: 425 x 54 ft/129.7 x 16.5 m
Service speed: 12 knots
Propulsion: Triple expansion/single propeller

These two vessels were basically designed as cargo ships, but fitted out to carry 12 first class passengers and 200 third class, mainly intended for migrants, and employed by Shaw Savill on their main line service from Britain to Australia and New Zealand until new ships were built.

Waiwera was launched on 15 December 1898, being handed over to Shaw Savill Line in February 1899 and departing London the following month on its first voyage to New Zealand. *Kumara* was launched on 8 May 1899, completed three months later, and departed London on 31 August on its maiden voyage via Cape Town to Wellington.

These vessels had only just entered service when the Boer War started, and on its maiden voyage *Kumara* carried a full load of supplies from Britain to South Africa, then went on to New Zealand to load meat for the voyage back to Britain. The New Zealand Government offered to send troops to South Africa, and the first contingent was embarked on the *Waiwera* in Wellington, leaving on 1 October 1899, these being the first New Zealand troops to be sent overseas. Later *Kumara* also carried troops from New Zealand to South Africa.

With the introduction of new passengers ships to the Shaw Savill fleet over the next few years, these two vessels were no longer needed on the main line service. *Kumara* made its last departure from London on this service on 13 December 1906, while *Waiwera* departed London on 4 April 1907.

Both vessels then operated as cargo ships, but from 1910 there was an increase in demand for migrant passages to New Zealand, so *Waiwera* and *Kumara* once again began carrying passengers in temporary quarters on the outbound voyages.

This ended when war broke out in 1914, and both vessels reverted to cargo ships for the duration of hostilities. After the war ended there was again a demand for migrant passages to New Zealand, and *Kumara* and *Waiwera* were again called on to carry about 200 third class passengers on their outward voyages until the mid-1920s, when they became cargo ships again.

In 1926 *Waiwera* was sold and renamed *City of Pretoria*, but this was quite brief as on 5 April 1928 the vessel arrived at Barrow to be broken up. In 1927 *Kumara* was sold to a Swedish company, the Gaspe Steamship Company, but not re-named, and soon sold to shipbreakers in Italy, arriving at Venice on 1 July 1928 to be scrapped.

Kumara

KARAMEA

Built: 1899 by Hawthorn Leslie, Newcastle
Tonnage: 5,564 gross
Dimensions: 420 x 54 ft/128 x 16.5 m
Service speed: 12 knots
Propulsion: Triple expansion/single propeller

This vessel was ordered by the Federal Line, and was named *Sussex* when launched on 22 August 1899. However it was purchased by Shaw Savill Line while being fitted out, and renamed *Karamea*. Primarily intended to serve as a cargo ship, accommodation was installed for 24 first class passengers in cabins, and the vessel was completed in November 1899.

Karamea had barely entered service when it was requisitioned to carry troops and horses from Britain to South Africa in connection with the Boer War. When this duty ended, the vessel resumed trading to Australia and New Zealand, initially being employed in the main line service on occasion until new ships were built.

From 1908 *Karamea* was used for a while on a cargo service from Canada to New Zealand. From 1910 there was a huge increase in the number of migrants seeking passages to both Australia and New Zealand, and as a result *Karamea* was one of many Shaw Savill cargo ships to be fitted with temporary quarters for up to 500 migrants in the holds for the voyage out from Britain. Up to 1914 *Karamea* made a number of voyages with migrants, though they were not carried on a regular basis.

During the war years *Karamea* remained on its regular trade under Government control, and from 1916 made the voyage from Britain to New Zealand through the Panama Canal in each direction. This continued after the war ended, and *Karamea* remained in the Shaw Savill fleet until 1925, when it was sold to an Italian firm, Soc. Anon. Alta Italia, being renamed *Mongolia*. The vessel served four years under this name before being broken up at Genoa, where it arrived on 16 April 1929.

Karamea

MEDIC, AFRIC and PERSIC

Built: 1899 by Harland & Wolff, Belfast
Gross tonnage: 11,816/11985/11,973
Dimensions: 570 x 63 ft/173.7 x 19.3 m
Service speed: 13 knots
Propulsion: Quadruple expansion/twin propellers

The first passenger vessels to be placed on the Australian trade by the White Star Line, these three ships were designed as giant cargo carriers which could also provide accommodation for 350 migrants, and would be the first ships exceeding 10,000 tons to use the Cape route to Australia.

The first launched, on 16 November 1898, was *Afric*, which was completed as a cargo ship only, and sailed from Liverpool to New York on 8 February 1899. On its return the ship went back to the shipyard on 23 March for accommodation to be installed.

Medic was launched on 15 December 1898, and departed Liverpool on 3 August 1899, calling at Teneriffe and Cape Town before reaching Albany on 9 September, then Adelaide on 12 September, Melbourne three days later, and Sydney on 21 September, berthing at Woolloomooloo. *Medic* became the largest ship operating to Australia, and also the first steamer on the route to provide only one class of accommodation, 320 third class. The *Sydney Morning Herald* reported on 22 September:

> It has been said that she carried 320 passengers; but if an intending voyager calls at Messrs Dalgety's office to engage a cabin he will be told that he can have a two-berth stateroom, a four-berth one, or an open berth; there is

neither first, second, nor third on board the *Medic* — they are all passengers, alone, family, all use the same saloon, smoking room, social hall, library etc, including the same bill-of-fare.

After going forward along a deck upon which the passengers play cricket, quoits and football, the forecastle is reached. Here the crew, comprising between 90 and 100 persons, all British sailors, have their quarters. Then the attendant leads the way to the bridge deck, where the officers have their quarters, and particularly fine quarters they are. Then, after passing the bridge deck, is a long stretch of what may be called the 'well-deck' of the vessel. Here is more promenading space and you enter the poop, the deck of which is also the passengers' exclusive camping ground.

That the introduction of vessels provided with so unusually good accommodation for the steerage traveller will prove a boon is certain, and the proprietors of the line are entitled to deserve full credit.

Speaking of the class of passenger who travelled out by the steamer, the chief officer said that 'they were altogether of the better class. There was no comparison between them and the emigrants to the States so called'. And that remark was certainly pretty well corroborated by the class of portmanteau etc which were going over the side. It is certain that the White Star has come to stay.

Medic was taken over by the various Australian colonies to carry troops to South Africa on its return trip to Britain. Once the troops disembarked, *Medic* continued its voyage to Britain with cargo.

Afric was completed as a passenger carrier in August

Medic

Persic

1899, and on 9 September left Liverpool on its first voyage to Australia, reaching Sydney on 27 October. *Persic* was launched on 7 September 1899, and left Liverpool on its maiden voyage on 7 December. Unfortunately, the rudder head fractured while *Persic* was en route to Cape Town, and on arrival there the vessel was delayed while a replacement part was sent out from Britain. It was not until 1 February 1900 that repairs were completed and *Persic* could continue its voyage, reaching Sydney on 3 March.

Throughout the Boer War the ships were used at times to carry troops and supplies to and from South Africa. With peace in May 1902, White Star Line was able to introduce a regular four-weekly schedule, and gain a large share of the migrant market. The third class accommodation offered by these vessels was superior to that on the ships of any other company. The cabins and public rooms were all located in the after half of the ships, and the dining room could seat all the passengers at one time.

The three ships operated to Australia until the outbreak of war in August 1914, and soon afterward both *Medic* and *Afric* were requisitioned by the Australian Government for service as troop transports, being allocated numbers A7 and A19. *Medic* was fitted out to carry 31 officers, 1,076 other ranks and 283 horses, while *Afric* carried 49 officers and 1,300 other ranks. Both vessels were in the first convoy to depart Australia, in November 1914. *Persic* was taken over late in 1914, and as A34 was included in the second convoy to leave Australia, in November 1914, having been fitted out to transport 40 officers, 520 other ranks and 491 horses.

On 20 September 1916, a torpedo fired at *Persic* by a German submarine just missed, but *Afric* was not so fortunate. Having left Sydney on 3 November 1916 with a full cargo and passengers, *Afric* was approaching the English Channel on 12 February 1917 when it was hit by a torpedo fired by the German submarine *UC66*, and sank, with the loss of twenty two lives.

In September 1918 *Persic* was also hit by a torpedo off Sicily, but remained afloat and reached port safely. The vessel spent almost nine months in drydock undergoing repairs, then returned to service with a departure from Liverpool on 13 July 1919.

In 1920 *Medic* and *Persic* were handed back to White Star Line, and their accommodation was revamped to carry 260 passengers in the newly designated cabin class. They returned to the Australian trade, following the same route as before the war but with an additional call at Brisbane.

In January 1927 the White Star Line became part of the Kylsant Group, and they decided to pull out of the Australian trade altogether. First to go was *Persic*, which left Liverpool on 26 September 1926 on its final voyage to Australia, returning to London on 26 May 1927. *Persic* was then sold to Dutch shipbreakers, leaving Liverpool on 7 July 1927 under tow for Rotterdam.

Medic made its final departure from Liverpool on 23 December 1927, arriving back in Southampton on 11 May 1928. In June 1928 the vessel was purchased by N. Bugge of Tonsberg in Norway, and rebuilt as a whaling mother ship, being renamed *Hektoria*. Following the German invasion of Norway the ship was taken over by the British Government, and used as tanker, but on 12 September 1942 *Hektoria* was torpedoed and sunk in the North Atlantic by a German submarine

OMRAH

Built: 1899 by Fairfield, Glasgow.
Gross tonnage: 8,130
Dimensions: 491 x 57 ft/149.6 x 17.3 m
Service speed: 18 knots
Propulsion: Triple expansion/twin screws

Omrah was the first Orient Line vessel to have a single funnel and two masts, being launched on 3 September 1898. Accommodation was provided for 175 first class, 175 second class and 500 third class passengers. *Omrah* sailed from Tilbury on 3 February on its maiden voyage, arriving in Sydney on 18 March. At the time *she* was the largest British flag ship operating to Australia. A description in the *Sydney Morning Herald* stated:

> There are no labyrinths within this ship. In spite of long passages, numberless bulkheads and countless cabins, the whole is so simply planned for convenience of communication that a child might find its way from stem to stern or from hold to hurricane deck.

> When heat becomes oppressive in the saloon one touch of a button sets the fans in noiseless motion, and to all appearance they work so satisfactorily that old-fashioned punkahs will be completely superseded. Above all, however, the *Omrah* differs from other ships on the Australian line in height between decks that gives to every cabin an airy spaciousness distinctly pleasant for travellers to contemplate with the prospect before them of a long voyage through the tropics.

> The saloon and drawing room, with sumptuous decorations in marqueterie, the smoking room admirably arranged in a series of cosy alcoves, all panelled with oak, and writing rooms in which work may be done without chance of disturbance from noise, are all as perfect as the most fastidious could desire.

Omrah quickly established itself as an efficient and popular member of the Orient Line fleet, as well as very economical to operate, and as a result her design provided the basis for subsequent Orient liners for many years.

Omrah arrived in Sydney in August 1914 from Britain. Requisitioned by the Australian Government as a troopship, number A5, *Omrah* embarked 32 officers, 999 other ranks and 15 horses in Brisbane, and joined the first convoy to transport Australian and New Zealand troops overseas, in November 1914. *Omrah* then returned to the Orient Line and resumed commercial voyages.

Omrah made its final commercial departure from London for Australia on 3 November 1916, leaving Sydney on 13 January 1917 carrying 7 officers and 730 other ranks to Britain. In July 1917 she was back in Sydney, but as a troopship, embarking 323 Australian troops for England. In the early months of 1918 a convoy of seven fast liners, including *Omrah*, was formed to carry troops from Alexandria to Marseilles. They completed two voyages successfully, and were returning to Egypt for more troops, but on 12 May, 40 miles (65 km) off Cape Spartivento, Sardinia, a torpedo hit *Omrah* forward of the bridge, and the ship sank, with the loss of four lives.

Omrah

ORTONA

Built: 1899 by Vickers, Barrow
Gross tonnage: 7,945
Dimensions: 515 x 55 ft/157 x 16.7 m
Service speed: 18 knots
Propulsion: Triple expansion/twin propellers.

Designed for the Pacific Steam Navigation Company's Australian service as part of the joint fleet with Orient Line, *Ortona* was the largest PSNC ship until 1902, and the last vessel the company would build for the Australian trade.

Launched on 10 July 1899, *Ortona* was the only ship placed on the Australian service by PSNC to be given twin screws. Accommodation was fitted for 130 first, 162 second and 300 steerage passengers, the first class quarters being considered second to none on the route, with the dining room extending through three decks and featuring a glass dome. *Ortona* departed London on 24 November 1899 on its maiden voyage to Australia.

In June 1902 *Ortona* was requisitioned by the British Government as a Boer War troopship, and made several trips to South Africa, being returned to PSNC in April 1903.

In 1906 Royal Mail Line bought the PSNC Australian service, and *Ortona* was transferred to their ownership. The only change made to the ship was having the funnel repainted yellow.

In 1909 the Royal Mail Line withdrew from the Australian route, and *Ortona* left London on 30 April 1909 on its last voyage to Australia. After one voyage from Britain to the West Indies and New York, and

another trip to the River Plate ports, *Ortona* went to Belfast for conversion into a luxury cruise ship.

This work included upgraded accommodation for only 320 passengers in one class, all cabins having beds instead of bunks. Additions included a gymnasium, an electric laundry, and an outdoor 35 ft/10m long swimming pool, then the largest pool afloat.

The ship was renamed *Arcadian*, and entered service in January 1912, voyaging from Liverpool to the West Indies and back to New York, where it was based for part of each year. On 17 August 1914 *Arcadian* was sent from Liverpool to New York with a large number of Americans who had been stranded in Europe when the war started. *Arcadian* returned to Liverpool, leaving there on 25 September for Quebec. On the return trip the vessel carried Canadian troops to Britain.

Arcadian was then laid up until February 1915, when she was requisitioned for duty as a troopship for Dardanelles campaign. *Arcadian* carried Headquarters staff from Avonmouth to Alexandria and then became an Army Headquarters Ship, spending some time at Mudros, and in April 1915 being involved in the Gallipoli landings, being based at Cape Helles and then Imbros until the Headquarters staff were able to go ashore. *Arcadian* then became an ordinary troopship.

On 15 April 1917 *Arcadian* was torpedoed while on passage from Salonica to Alexandria, and sank in ten minutes. Of the 1,335 persons on board, 279 lost their lives.

Ortona

HOULDER BROS SHIPS

LANGTON GRANGE   DENTON GRANGE   RIPPINGHAM
GRANGE/LIMERICK
Built: 1896/96/98 by Workman, Clark, Belfast
Gross tonnage: 5,807/5,851/5,790
Dimensions: 420 x 54 ft/128 x 9 m
Service speed: 12 knots
Propulsion: Triple expansion/single propeller

DRAYTON GRANGE
OSWESTRY GRANGE/ROSCOMMON
Built: 1901/02 by Workman, Clark, Belfast
Gross tonnage: 6,684/6,591
Dimensions: 450 x 55 ft/137.2 x 16.7 m
Service speed: 13 knots
Propulsion: Triple expansion/single propeller

EVERTON GRANGE/WESTMEATH
Built: 1903 by Furness, Withy & Co., West Hartlepool
Gross tonnage: 8,096
Dimensions: 475 x 56 ft/144.7 x 17 m
Service speed: 12 knots
Propulsion: Triple expansion/single propeller

Houlder Bros & Co. Ltd became involved in the Australian trade as early as 1863, when they were operating sailing ships, expanding into steamships in the 1880s, but by then their main interest was in the frozen meat trade from South America to Britain. In 1895 the company became involved in the Australian frozen meat trade, and subsequently decided to enter the migrant trade as well, for which they initially built three ships.

The first was launched as *Langton Grange* on 29 February 1896, being completed in May, closely followed by *Denton Grange*, launched on 27 May 1896 and handed over to Houlder Bros in August. There was then a gap of two years before the third was built, being named *Rippingham Grange* when launched on 18 April 1898, and delivered on 8 October.

All three ships were fitted out with quite comfortable cabin accommodation for about 26 first class passengers, but while the first two were given basic accommodation for only 50 third class passengers, *Rippingham Grange* could carry some 230 third class passengers.

The vessels would depart from either London Manchester or Liverpool and voyage via the Cape of Good Hope to Australia, usually calling at Adelaide, Melbourne, Sydney and Brisbane, with occasional visits to Fremantle. Meat would be loaded for the return trip at various ports in northern Queensland, then the vessels would come south to Sydney, Melbourne and Adelaide for the voyage back to Britain, again around South Africa.

In June 1900, *Rippingham Grange* departed London on a new round-the-world service, which followed the usual route out as far as Brisbane, then went to Noumea, and around Cape Horn to the River Plate ports, where frozen meat was loaded, then across the Atlantic to Britain. Apart from carrying migrants to Australia, first class passengers could stay on board for the entire voyage.

When the Boer War broke out, *Denton Grange* was one of many ships requisitioned by the British Government to carry supplies to South Africa, but on one voyage the vessel ran aground at Las Palmas, subsequently being refloated and returned to service. In 1901 *Denton Grange* was sold to the Clan Line and renamed *Glenlogan*. She was torpedoed and sunk 10 nautical miles South East of Stromboli Island on 31 October 1916.

The first of a larger pair of cargo/passenger ships, *Drayton Grange* was launched on 3 October 1901, and completed on 12 December, entering service by the end of the year. This vessel was fitted out to carry 46 first-class passengers and only 48 third-class passengers.

The second ship, *Oswestry Grange*, was launched on 23 January 1902, and joined *Drayton Grange* in the Australian trade in March that year. *Oswestry Grange* was also given first class accommodation for 46 passengers, but the third class was greatly enlarged to cater for a maximum of 320 passengers.

The last ship to be built for the Houlder Bros service from Britain to Australia was *Everton Grange*, which was launched on 15 February 1903. In 1902 Houlder Bros had formed a new subsidiary, Empire Transport Co., which was listed as the nominal owners of *Everton Grange* when it was completed on 15 August 1903. Unlike earlier ships, *Everton Grange* was not given any first class accommodation, instead being fitted to carry 204 third class passengers only in rather basic quarters. Early in her career, *Everton Grange* was also used to transport horses from Australia to Japan.

In 1904 Houlder Bros entered into an agreement with the Federal Steam Navigation Co. and Turnbull, Martin & Co., who operated as the Shire Line, to operate a joint service to Australia and New Zealand, to be known as the Federal-Houlder-Shire Line. Houlder Bros contributed four ships to the service, these being *Rippingham Grange*, *Everton Grange*, *Drayton Grange* and *Oswestry Grange*.

Langton Grange was reduced to operating as a cargo ship, and on 5 August 1909 was wrecked on the Welsh coast at North Bishops.

Oswestry Grange took the first sailing on the new service, departing Liverpool on 20 August 1904 and voyaging by way of Teneriffe and Cape Town to Adelaide, Melbourne, Sydney, Auckland, Wellington, Lyttelton and Port Chalmers.

In 1907 the Federal-Houlder-Shire Line established

an alliance with the British India Line, which operated a service from Britain through the Torres Strait to ports in Queensland. During 1909 both *Oswestry Grange* and *Rippingham Grange* made voyages on this joint service, going from London via the Suez Canal to Thursday Island, Cairns, Townsville, Rockhampton and Brisbane.

On one voyage *Drayton Grange* departed Liverpool in early March 1910 and voyaged direct to Durban, departing on 4 April for another long direct voyage to Sydney, arriving on 27 April. It was reported that on board there were 12 passengers for Sydney and 48 going on to New Zealand.

The four Houlder Bros ships provided a regular if unspectacular service on the Australian trade, being involved in only one major incident. Bound from Britain to Sydney with 190 migrants on board, *Everton Grange* arrived at Adelaide on the morning of Thursday, 5 January 1911, departing at 8pm the same evening for Melbourne. The course to be followed was through what is known as the 'backstairs passage', between Kangaroo Island and the mainland, and shortly after 1am the next morning the officer on watch sighted a light straight ahead, and called the captain. He thought it was a lighthouse they were expecting to see, but in fact it was a light in a building. At 1.45 am *Everton Grange*, proceeding at full speed, came to a sudden halt, having run aground on Kingscote Spit, which meant the vessel was about ten miles off course. The engines were put full astern for several hours, but the ship did not move.

Fortunately *Everton Grange* was sitting on a sandy bottom, so the hull was not holed, but it was firmly stuck. At high tide on the evening of Monday, 9 January, with a tug pulling and the engines full astern, the vessel was moved about 40 feet, but still remained aground.

On the Tuesday a lighter arrived to take off about 600 tons of cargo from the forward holds, but it was not until the afternoon of Friday, 13 January, that another attempt was made to refloat the vessel, which was successful. An inspection by divers confirmed that no damage had been suffered, so the voyage continued to Melbourne, with *Everton Grange* arriving there on 15 January, and in Sydney on Sunday, 21 January.

Everton Grange continued to operate a regular service from Britain to Australia and New Zealand, and occasionally a report on the vessel would appear in the local press, one such item on 19 July 1910 noting the vessel's arrival in Sydney with 217 migrants on board.

The master of *Everton Grange* for two voyages to Australia in 1911/12 was Captain Wilson, about whom the following information was found on the internet:

Though the company's principal focus was on the growing trade with Argentina, they had since 1902 carried migrants to Australia and in 1911, after seven years of trans-Atlantic crossings, Captain Wilson was given command of the *Everton Grange* an 8,000 ton twin screw steamship. Capable of a speed of 12 knots and carrying up to 204 third class passengers, she had been engaged since 1905 in migration from the United Kingdom to Australia and New Zealand as part of the Federal-Houlder-Shire Line partnership. During 1911 and 1912 [Wilson] was commander on two voyages to Australia via the Cape of Good Hope, taking English, Scottish and Irish migrants to Melbourne, Sydney and Brisbane. After visiting the northern Queensland ports of Bowen and Townsville gathering cargo such as frozen beef, hardwood and hides, the *Everton* turned south again picking up passengers for the return trip via Egypt's Port Said and Malta. The voyage to Liverpool, according to the Melbourne *Argus* of 7th October 1911, featured 'excellent accommodation for third class passengers....electric light throughout' for a fare of between thirteen and seventeen pounds. The journeys to Australia had taken over five months, a long time away

Everton Grange

Oswestry Grange

from his wife and three young daughters in Merseyside Liscard.

In 1912, Furness, Withy & Co. purchased a major holding in Houlder Bros, and in December that year they sold the Houlder Bros Australian interests to the New Zealand Shipping Company. The deal included the four ships the company was then operating on the Federal-Houlder-Shire Line service, *Drayton Grange*, *Everton Grange*, *Rippingham Grange* and *Oswestry Grange*, which were renamed *Tyrone*, *Westmeath*, *Limerick* and *Roscommon* respectively.

Following a voyage by *Roscommon* from London to Brisbane early in 1912, a spate of complaints resulted in an inquiry being held in Brisbane. The *Sydney Morning Herald* reported on 7 October 1912:

Arthur Clark, a passenger by the *Roscommon*, said that one thing he complained about was the food. On the voyage out witness stated that he found a ticket in the soup, which led him to believe it was not Australian meat. A Townsville witness said he was without bread for a day.

William Wylie, another passenger, complained about everything, the beef especially. A ticket was found in his wife's soup marked 'No. 4 Uruguay, September 11, 1910'. The purser said that they had guaranteed that all the meat was Australian. The potatoes had growths and were worm eaten. For two or three days they got no water downstairs for drinking purposes. There was a great deal of sickness during the voyage from Melbourne.

A..J. Douglas, surgeon and medical officer of the *Roscommon*, said he inspected the food on board ship, but received no complaint. There was some sickness on board,

but he did not think any of it was caused through lack of food or bad food.

Mary Bae, a passenger, said there was a plentiful supply of food, and, taking it all through, she thought they did very well.

George Bush, master of the vessel, said he received no complaints from any of the passengers on the voyage. He produced certificates from providers stating that both the beef and mutton were entirely Australian.

In 1913 it was arranged that all four ships would be transferred again, to the ownership of the Union Steam Ship Company of New Zealand, though they would retain their new names. However, on 27 September 1913 *Tyrone*, the former *Drayton Grange*, was wrecked near Otago Heads before the actual transfer took place.

The other three vessels operated on a cargo service between Britain and New Zealand, no longer carrying passengers, remaining in this trade after war broke out in 1914. Two of the vessel were torpedoed and sunk during the war, *Limerick* being lost on 28 May 1917, followed three months later by *Roscommon*, on 21 August 1917.

On 15 July 1917, *Westmeath* was torpedoed by the German submarine, *UC48*, in the English Channel, but the vessel remained afloat and was able to reach port. Following repairs, *Westmeath* returned to service, remaining under the New Zealand flag until 1925, when it was sold to an Italian firm, Soc. Ligure di Nav. a Vapeur, registered at Genoa, and renamed *Nordico*. In 1927 the vessel sold to D. & E. Fratelli Bozzo, Genoa, but not renamed, and remained in service until being sold to shipbreakers at Genoa during May 1932.

RHEIN and NECKAR

RHEIN
Built: 1899 by Blohm & Voss, Hamburg
Gross tonnage: 10,058
Dimensions: 520 x 58 ft/158.5 x 17.7 m
Service speed: 14 knots
Propulsion: Quadruple expansion/twin propellers

NECKAR
Built: 1901 by Tecklenborg, Geestemunde
Gross tonnage: 9,835
Dimensions: 518 x 58 ft/158 x 17.7 m
Service speed: 14 knots
Propulsion: Quadruple expansion/twin propellers

Members of the River class, these vessels were designed to operate both on the North Atlantic and to Australia for North German Lloyd, and for quick conversion into transports in case of war.

Rhein was launched on 20 September 1899, and completed two months later, on 9 December leaving Bremerhaven on its maiden voyage, to New York. In September 1901 *Rhein* left Bremen for Australia, going through the Suez Canal to visit Albany, Adelaide, Melbourne and Sydney.

The second ship of the class, *Main*, was completed in 1900, but never appeared on the Australian service. *Neckar* was launched on 8 December 1900, and completed in May 1901, being placed on the North Atlantic trade.

These ships could carry 369 second class and 217 third class passengers in cabins, with steerage space for a further 2,865 persons, though the crew numbered only 174. Thus if they sailed full they could carry 3,625 persons, more than some of the largest liners then afloat could accommodate.

Mostly the River class ships operated from Bremen to Baltimore, but for three years *Rhein* operated to Australia for part of each year. In October 1901 *Neckar* departed Bremen on its only voyage to Australia. In November 1904 *Rhein* made its final departure on the Australian route, and from that time was continuously employed on the North Atlantic trade.

Rhein was berthed in Baltimore when war broke out in August 1914, and was interned by the American authorities, together with *Neckar*, which sought refuge in American waters. The two ships lay idle until America came into the war in 1917, when both were seized by the United States Government, and converted into transports. *Rhein* was renamed *Susquehanna*, while *Neckar* became *Antigone*. They made many trips across the Atlantic taking troops to France, and after the Armistices made further voyages to bring troops home.

In 1920 *Antigone* was renamed *Potomac*, and with *Susquehanna* was chartered to the US Mail Steamship Co. for a service from New York to Bremerhaven and Danzig. In 1921 the company was renamed United States Line, and in August 1922 both vessels were withdrawn and laid up. In September 1927 the former *Neckar* was sold to shipbreakers in Holland, while the former *Rhein* went to Japan to be scrapped in February 1929.

Rhein

FEDERAL LINE VESSELS

CORNWALL DEVON KENT SURREY
Built: 1896/97/99/99 by Hawthorn Leslie, Newcastle
Gross tonnage: 5,490/5,489/5,464/5,455
Dimensions: 420 x 54 ft/128 x 16.5 m
Service speed: 11 knots
Propulsion: Triple expansion/single propeller

SUFFOLK (1) NORFOLK
Built: 1899/1900 by Sunderland S B Co., Sunderland
Gross tonnage: 5,464/5,310
Dimensions: 421 x 54 ft/128.2 x 16.5 m
Service speed: 13 knots
Propulsion: Triple expansion/single propeller

SUSSEX DURHAM
Built: 1900/1904 by Hawthorn Leslie, Newcastle
Gross tonnage: 5,474/5,760
Dimensions: 420 x 54 ft/128 x 16.5 m
Service speed: 11 knots
Propulsion: Triple expansion/single propeller

SUFFOLK (2) ESSEX DORSET SOMERSET
Built: 1902/1902/1903/1903 by John Brown, Clydebank
Gross tonnage: 7,530/7,573/7,630/7,010
Dimensions: 460 x 58 ft/140.2 x 17.7 m
Service speed: 13 knots
Propulsion: Triple expansion/twin propellers

The Federal Steam Navigation Company was established in 1895 to trade from Great Britain to Australia and New Zealand. It commenced with three second-hand vessels, and ordered two new vessels. The first was launched on 23 September 1896, and named *Cornwall*, commencing a policy of naming the ships after counties in England. The second ship, *Devon*, was launched on 20 November 1896. Both had accommodation for 12 first class and 156 third class passengers.

Cornwall departed London on 25 December 1896 on its maiden voyage, calling at Las Palmas and Cape Town en route to Fremantle, Albany, Adelaide, Melbourne and Sydney, then across the Tasman Sea to Auckland, Wellington, Lyttelton and Port Chalmers. *Devon* was delivered to the Federal Line on 6 February 1897, and left a few weeks later on its maiden voyage to Australia.

The Federal Line fleet expanded rapidly, with the addition of four vessels in two years. *Kent* was launched on 11 March 1899, and completed on 23 May, while the *Surrey*, was launched on 8 July 1899, and entered service in September. Both were fitted with cabins for 12 first class passengers as well as quarters for about 150 migrants.

On its second voyage, *Kent* was requisitioned by the New South Wales Colonial Government on arrival in Sydney to carry troops and horses to South Africa for the Boer War. Departing Sydney on 27 October 1899, *Kent* went to Albany, joining up with *Cornwall* with troops from Queensland, and two other ships, altogether carrying 1,200 men from five colonies. The convoy arrived in South Africa on 13 December 1899.

On 25 July 1899 another new vessel, *Suffolk*, was launched at Sunderland for the Federal Line, being delivered on 1 November that year. A sister was launched as *Norfolk* on 18 December 1899, and joined the Australian trade in April 1900. As with the previous vessels, this pair could accommodate 12 passengers in first class and about 150 migrants.

Suffolk had a very short career, as in August 1900 it was requisitioned to transport horses from Fiume to Cape Town, but on 24 September was wrecked near Port Elizabeth.

Surrey was one of three ships to leave Sydney on 17 January 1900 with troops and horses, picking up more at Adelaide and Fremantle, arriving in Cape Town on 20 February. At various times, *Cornwall*, *Devon*, *Kent* and *Norfolk* were also used to carry troops and horses to South Africa from Great Britain, Australia and New Zealand.

By the time *Suffolk* was wrecked, another new ship had joined the fleet, having been launched on 16 January 1900 as *Sussex*, entering service on 29 April 1900 with a departure from North Shields for Australia. In addition to 12 first class and 150 third class berths, it was also fitted with accommodation for 52 second class passengers.

Thus at the start of the new century the Federal Line had six recently built vessels to maintain their service, but soon placed orders for four more new ships. The first twin-screw vessels to be built for the company, these ships were primarily designed as large cargo ships, with permanent cabins for twelve passengers. However basic quarters for about 200 migrants could be installed in the holds on some voyages from Britain to Australia and New Zealand, but this was not done on a regular basis.

The first of the quartet to be launched, on 23 May 1902, revived the name *Suffolk*, being completed on 14 July that year. It was followed by *Essex*, launched on 1 November 1902 and completed only six weeks later, on 16 December. *Dorset* was launched on 14 February 1903, being handed over to the owners on 8 April, while the final ship, *Somerset*, was launched on 25 April 1903, and completed on 10 June.

These four ships operated primarily from Britain to Australia and New Zealand, but sometimes the outward voyage took them to North America. On 20 December 1902 the *Sydney Morning Herald* noted: 'Advices have been received in Sydney that the new steamship *Essex* will sail from New York on Jan 31 for Australian and New Zealand ports.'

Surrey

The final ship built for the company during its initial period of expansion was named *Durham*, when launched on 18 February 1904, but work on completing the vessel was held up, and it was not delivered to the company until 9 December. With the *Durham* in service, the Federal Line had a modern fleet of eleven vessels maintaining a regular service to Australia and New Zealand.

In 1904 the Federal Line joined with Houlder Bros, initially under a contract with the New Zealand Government, to operate a joint service, known as the New Zealand & South African Line, from New Zealand and Australia to South African ports, and later this was extended to include a call at River Plate ports in South America.

Another joint service was also started in 1904, when the Federal Line, Houlder Bros and Turnbull, Martin & Co. established the Federal-Houlder-Shire Line, which provided a regular service from Britain via South Africa to Australia and New Zealand. The first Federal Line steamer to depart under the new arrangement was *Suffolk*, which left Liverpool on 15 October 1904. All the other Federal steamers operated on this service, with departures being from London, Liverpool, Manchester, Glasgow, and occasionally Bristol, on a monthly basis.

Disaster almost struck when, in June 1906, the *Norfolk*, en route from Durban to Fremantle, lost its propeller in the Indian Ocean some 580 miles (930 km) west of Fremantle, and was left adrift. With no wireless on board it was not possible to summon help, and the ship was in danger of drifting far south, off the regular trade routes. Fortunately there were no passengers on board for the trip, but there was still quite a large crew on the vessel.

The master, Captain F. Corner, ordered that the fifteen canvas covers on the hatches be refashioned into sails, and a wooden bowsprit was also fitted, to carry a jib sail. With sails attached to the four masts, the vessel was able to proceed slowly towards Fremantle. Eleven days after the accident land was sighted, and a tug towed the crippled vessel into Fremantle on 21 June. A new propeller was sent from Sydney, and when it arrived the *Norfolk* was ballasted forward until the stern was lifted clear of the water, enabling the propeller to be fitted.

The operation of the Federal-Houlder-Shire line was revamped in 1910, when it was agreed with the New Zealand Shipping Company that the joint service would in future only operate to Australian ports. It was also in 1910 that a major surge began in the number of migrants seeking berths to go to Australia, which resulted in all the ships carrying migrants on every voyage over the next few years. Two more ships were also ordered, much larger than the existing vessels. They entered service in 1911 and 1912 as *Shropshire* and *Wiltshire*, but are dealt with separately along with a third sister, *Argyllshire*, which was owned by the Shire Line (see page 120).

On 3 January 1912 an agreement was reached whereby the New Zealand Shipping Company would acquire a major shareholding in the Federal Line, effective on 19 April. At the same time, the Houlder Line interest in the Australian trade was sold by its parent company, Furness, Withy & Co., to the New Zealand Shipping Co., and that effectively ended the Federal-Houlder-Shire Line joint service, which from May 1912 operated as the Federal & Shire Line. Despite these changes the names, funnel colours and operation of the Federal ships remained basically unchanged.

In late 1912 the first ship built for the company, *Cornwall*, was sold to Soc. Italia de Nav., being renamed *Atlantide*. This vessel was torpedoed and sunk off Madeira on 9 February 1918.

In July 1913, the *Devon* departed Montreal on a voyage to New Zealand, but at Cape Town the master had to be put ashore with typhoid fever, and the Chief Officer took over command. The vessel left Auckland on 23 August, bound for Wellington, but at 8.15pm on 25 August, in very bad weather with heavy rain and high seas, the *Devon* ran aground on Pencarrow Head, at the entrance to Wellington Harbour. The crew was rescued the next day by breeches buoy, but the *Devon* became a total loss. The Chief Officer was later exonerated of blame when it was found there were irregularities with the navigation lights ashore that he was relying on to bring the ship into the harbour.

After war broke out in Europe the Federal Line ships continued to operate on their regular trade, though no longer carrying passengers. On 8 November 1914 *Norfolk* was on its way from Melbourne to Sydney when a fire broke out that could not be contained. The vessel had to be abandoned, and eventually ran ashore at Ninety Mile Beach, and was wrecked.

Surrey struck a mine in the English Channel on 25 February 1915, but remained afloat and was towed into Dover.

Later in 1915 *Kent* and *Surrey* were sold to Blue Star Line, being renamed *Brodlea* and *Brodfield* respectively. *Surrey* was handed over after repairs to the mine damage, but on 13 November 1916 was wrecked near Church Point, St Mary's, in the Scilly Isles. *Kent* was renamed *Saxonstar* in 1919, altered to *Saxon Star* in 1929, and it survived until arriving at Savona in Italy on 17 September 1934 to be broken up.

Suffolk was proceeding up the English Channel to London when it hit a mine on 28 December 1916, but was able to reach Portsmouth safely.

On 29 April 1916 *Sussex* was chased by a surfaced submarine, which opened fire, but was able to outpace its adversary and escaped damage. However, on 1 January 1917, when in the English Channel off Calais, *Sussex* struck a mine, the explosion blowing a large hole in the hull at the bow. The vessel was beached near Calais, and after temporary repairs were completed was able to be refloated and return to England for full repairs.

Somerset was torpedoed and sunk in the North Atlantic on 26 July 1917, 230 miles west of Ushant, fortunately without loss of life. *Essex* managed to avoid a torpedo fired at it on 9 June 1918 when it was in the St George's Channel in the Irish Sea.

After the war the five survivors operated only as cargo ships until being sold. First to go was *Durham*, sold in July 1924 to an Italian, Andrea Zanchi, of Genoa, and renamed *Augusta*. When Italy entered the war in June 1940 the vessel took refuge in Brazilian waters, but was seized by the Brazilian Government in 1942 and allocated to Lloyd Brasiliero, based in Rio de Janeiro, and renamed *Minasloide*. In 1949 it was returned to its former owners. They again named the ship *Augusta*, and it survived under that name until May 1950, when it was broken up at Spezia.

Essex was bought in 1926 by a Belgian company, Compagnie International de Commerce et d'Armement, based in Antwerp. Renamed *Van*, the vessel served a further five years before being being broken up at Bo'ness, where it arrived on 18 January 1933. *Suffolk* and *Dorset* were both sold to shipbreakers at Bo'ness, *Suffolk* arriving there on 17 January 1927, and *Dorset* on 25 January. *Sussex* was sold in April 1929 to shipbreakers in Japan.

Essex

GROSSER KURFÜRST

Built: 1900 by Schichau, Danzig
Gross tonnage: 13,182
Dimensions: 581 x 62 ft/177.1 x 19 m
Service speed: 15 knots
Propulsion: Triple expansion/twin propellers

Grosser Kurfürst was the largest member of the Barbarossa class built for North German Lloyd. Launched on 2 December 1899, it departed Bremerhaven on 5 May 1900 and then Southampton before continuing on to New York.

On 11 November 1900 *Grosser Kurfürst* left Bremerhaven on its first voyage to Australia, going to Southampton then via the Suez Canal to Albany, Adelaide, Melbourne and Sydney, becoming the largest ship trading to Australia. The liner could accommodate 350 first class, 150 second class and 2,500 third class passengers.

Each year *Grosser Kurfürst* would make at least one trip to Australia, and in 1902 Fremantle was substituted for Albany. On 21 January 1912 *Grosser Kurfürst* left Bremerhaven on her final voyage to Australia.

Grosser Kurfürst sailed from Bremerhaven on 11 July 1914 to New York, and remained there when war was declared. When America entered the conflict in 1917 *Grosser Kurfürst* was seized by the United States Government and became an armed troop transport. Renamed *Aeolus*, the vessel spent the next two years operating across the Atlantic from New York to Brest, and bringing troops home again after the German surrender.

In September 1919 the vessel was allocated to the United States Shipping Board. Refitted at Baltimore, accommodation was installed for 300 passengers in first class only, and the boilers converted to oil firing. *Aeolus* was chartered to the Munson Line, who ran a service from New York to the River Plate, and on 1 December 1920 left New York on her first voyage for them.

On its final voyage for Munson Line in March 1922, *Aeolus* had the misfortune to collide with the British cargo ship *Zero* in the South Atlantic, causing that ship to sink.

Aeolus was then chartered to the Los Angeles Steamship Co., and in June 1922 left New York for the west coast. Renamed *City of Los Angeles*, and painted white with black funnels, the vessel was placed in service from Los Angeles to Hawaii.

City of Los Angeles made its first departure from Los Angeles on 11 September 1922, but by the end of 1923 the vessel was suffering serious engine problems. The Los Angeles Steamship Co. offered to buy the ship from the Shipping Board if they would first cover the cost of installing new engines. This was agreed, and geared turbines were installed. At the same time new accommodation was constructed for 446 passengers in first class only, and new funnels fitted. In June 1924 the vessel returned to service, now capable of maintaining 17 knots.

The Hawaiian trade began to wane as the Great Depression set in, and in 1932 *City of Los Angeles* was laid up and offered for sale. In 1933 Matson Line bought out the Los Angeles Steamship Co. *City of Los Angeles* was reactivated for a few more trips to Hawaii, then laid up again, and sold to Japanese shipbreakers in 1937.

Grosser Kurfürst (WSS Victoria)

EARLY NZSC VESSELS

WHAKATANE
Built: 1900 by Hawthorn Leslie & Co., Newcastle
Gross tonnage: 5,715
Dimensions: 420 x 54 ft/128 x 16.5 m
Service speed: 13 knots
Propulsion: Triple expansion/single propeller

RIMUTAKA   RUAPEHU
Built: 1900/01 by Wm Denny & Bros, Dumbarton
Gross tonnage: 7,765/7,705
Dimensions: 457 x 58 ft/139.3 x 17.8 m
Service speed: 13 knots
Propulsion: Triple expansion/twin propellers

TONGARIRO
Built: 1901 by Hawthorn Leslie & Co., Newcastle
Gross tonnage: 7,661
Dimensions: 457 x 58 ft/139.3 x 17.8 m
Service speed: 13 knots
Propulsion: Triple expansion/twin propellers

TURAKINA
Built: 1902 by Hawthorn Leslie & Co., Newcastle
Gross tonnage: 8,073
Dimensions: 473 x 59 ft/144.1 x 18 m
Service speed: 13 knots
Propulsion: Triple expansion/twin propellers

These five vessels were built for the New Zealand Shipping Company over a two-year period, with the last ship, *Turakina*, being lengthened while building. First to be launched was *Whakatane*, on 3 November 1899, being handed over to her owners on 23 January 1900. *Whakatane* had cabins for 26 first class passengers, while temporary quarters were provided in the 'tween decks for about 250 migrants on the outward voyage from Britain.

On 1 March 1900, *Whakatane* departed London on her maiden voyage to New Zealand, voyaging out by way of Cape Town, the return voyage taking the ship around the tip of South America.

Rimutaka was launched on 11 October 1900, delivered on 15 December, and left London on her maiden voyage to New Zealand on 3 January 1901.

On 24 November 1900 *Tongariro* was launched, being completed on 23 February, and departing London in March on its first voyage to New Zealand. The main obvious difference from *Rimutaka* was the extra tall upright funnel fitted to *Tongariro*, which also lacked the rake of funnel on the Denny-built ships.

Ruapehu was launched on 21 February 1901 and completed two months later. The ship was then chartered to the Allan Line for six months, and renamed *Australasian*, Leaving Liverpool on 23 May 1901 on her maiden voyage to Quebec and Montreal. In November the vessel was returned to the New Zealand Shipping Co., and reverted to its original name. *Ruapehu* departed London on 5 December on its first voyage to New Zealand.

Rimutaka, *Tongariro* and *Ruapehu* each had accom-

Tongariro

Ruapehu

modation for 40 first class, 50 second class and 80 third class passengers in permanent cabins, while a further 170 emigrants could be carried in temporary accommodation erected in the holds.

The last vessel in the group, *Turakina*, was launched on 23 April 1902 and completed in August, leaving London on 2 September 1902 on its maiden voyage to New Zealand. *Turakina* had accommodation for 60 first class, 50 second class and 80 third class passengers in cabins, with the same temporary arrangements in the holds for migrants.

Rimutaka and *Tongariro* were relegated to a secondary service in 1911, carrying third class passengers and migrants only.

When war broke out in August 1914, *Ruapehu* was requisitioned by the New Zealand Government and converted into a troopship, being in the convoy that took the first contingent of New Zealand troops to Egypt. The ship was then returned to her owners, and resumed her regular trade.

At first the ships continued to circumnavigate the world on each voyage, but from 1915 both journeys were made around South Africa, and in the middle of 1916 it was decided to use the Panama Canal passage instead.

This change did not affect *Tongariro* for very long, as on 30 August 1916 the vessel was voyaging down the east coast of North Island to Wellington in poor visibility, and about 7 pm ran aground on Bull Rock off Portland Island in Hawkes Bay. Attempts to refloat the vessel failed, and the ship broke in two across No. 3 hold, and became a total loss.

Turakina, on a voyage from New Zealand to Britain with her holds filled to capacity with New Zealand produce, was torpedoed 120 miles (190 km) west of the Scilly Isles on 13 August 1917, and sank soon afterward, fortunately without loss of life.

Whakatane remained on the New Zealand trade throughout World War I and in 1920 was relegated to being a cargo carrier only. *Rimutaka* and *Ruapehu* also survived the conflict, but needed refits before resuming their commercial careers.

Rimutaka departed London on 23 December on her first post-war voyage to New Zealand as a passenger ship. *Ruapehu* finished her refit shortly afterwards, and returned to the passenger service with a sailing from London on 14 January 1921.

Both ships were put back on the mail service to replace war losses. When *Rotorua* joined the service in 1923, *Rimutaka* and *Ruapehu* were taken off the mail route, and with their accommodation reclassified as saloon class, were placed on a secondary service catering to the migrant trade.

In 1924 *Whakatane* was sold to an Italian company, Soc. Anon. de Nav. Alta Italia, and renamed *Moncensio*. On 24 April 1929 the vessel was sold to shipbreakers at Savona in Italy.

Rimutaka left London on her final voyage to New Zealand on 15 November 1929, and not long after returning to Britain early in 1930 was sold to shipbreakers at Pembroke in Wales.

Ruapehu left London for the last time on 20 December 1930, returning to Britain in April 1931 and being laid up in Falmouth awaiting a buyer. In August 1931 she was sold to Italian shipbreakers, and steamed to Savona where she was scrapped.

RUNIC and SUEVIC

Built: 1900/1901 by Harland & Wolff, Belfast
Gross tonnage: 12,482/12,531
Dimensions: 565 x 63 ft/172.2 x 63.3 m
Service speed: 13 knots
Propulsion: Quadruple expansion/twin propellers

These two ships were enlarged versions of *Medic*, *Afric* and *Persic,* the first three ships White Star Line built for their Australian service (page 52). *Runic* was launched on 25 October 1900, handed over to White Star on 22 December, and left Liverpool on its maiden voyage on 3 January 1901, going via Cape Town to Albany, Adelaide, Melbourne and Sydney, where it arrived on 24 February.

Suevic was launched on 8 December 1900, and delivered on 9 March 1901. However, the vessel was taken over by the British Government to transport troops to South Africa for the Boer War, so its maiden sailing from Liverpool on 23 March 1901 was with 229 troops aboard as well as supplies. The troops disembarked at Cape Town, and passengers were embarked for the voyage to Australia, with the vessel arriving in Sydney on 18 May.

In 1901 *Runic* also began carrying troops to South Africa on some voyages, so it was impossible for White Star to operate a regular monthly service until after the war ended in 1902.

Runic and *Suevic* were just over 500 tons larger than the earlier trio, and could carry 400 passengers in one class. The accommodation was superior to the third class offered on ships of other companies, although not by any means up to first class standard. This meant that the pair quickly became popular with migrants who had a bit more money to spend on their passage to Australia, and also with travellers who preferred having the run of the ship rather than being confined by classes.

The ships called only at Cape Town when bound for Australia, but on the return trip additional stops were made at Durban and Teneriffe. From there they went to Plymouth and London, where passengers and cargo were offloaded. The ships then went around the coast empty to Liverpool to prepare for their next voyage.

Having left Sydney on 26 January 1907, on 17 March *Suevic* was approaching the English Channel, with 382 passengers aboard, when the vessel ran into thick fog, and went hard aground on Stag Rock, near the Lizard. A heavy swell was running, and attempts to refloat the ship by putting the engines full astern proved futile, so lifeboats were lowered and the passengers safely removed.

The Liverpool Salvage Association was hired to refloat the vessel, but their initial attempts met with failure, the ship being firmly held forward of the bridge. The area was prone to bad storms, and locals predicted the ship would eventually become a total loss and be broken up by the seas, but the salvors decided on a daring, and at that time untried scheme to save at least part of the ship.

As the engines, bridge and superstructure of the ship were in no way damaged, it was decided to cut the ship in two just forward of the bridge, leaving the after portion intact. A series of small dynamite charges were needed to cut the ship in two, and the stern section floated free. A coffer-dam was built across the forward section of the salvaged part, and it was towed to Southampton during April 1907, and drydocked.

Runic

Suevic

Harland & Wolff built a new bow section to the original plans, and this was towed to Southampton, arriving on 25 October, and the two sections were joined. On 14 January 1908 *Suevic* left Liverpool on her first voyage to Australia since the accident, looking exactly the same as before.

Soon after the outbreak of war in 1914, *Suevic* was taken over by the Australian Government, becoming transport A29, and fitted out to carry 40 officers, 510 other ranks, and 527 horses. *Suevic* was included in the second convoy to carry Anzacs and supplies to Egypt. *Runic* was taken over early in 1915, becoming A59, with quarters for 90 officers and 1,534 other ranks. *Runic* carried her troops to Britain, but off Beachy Head in the English Channel on 1 May 1915 collided with and sank another vessel, *Horst Martini*. *Runic* was not seriously damaged, and soon back in service.

Both vessels continued to operate to Australia throughout the war, and in September 1917 *Suevic* was transferred to the Shipping Controller, as was *Runic* in November 1917, this continuing for some time after the Armistices, when *Suevic* made several voyages to New Zealand as well.

Suevic was returned to White Star in January 1920, and was still in its wartime configuration when, on 2 February, the vessel left Liverpool for Australia. After two voyages *Suevic* went to Portsmouth for an extensive refit, during which the accommodation was improved to carry 266 passengers in cabin class only. *Runic* was similarly altered at about the same time, and they then resumed their places on the Australian trade.

Runic missed one voyage in October 1925, being replaced by *Vedic* (see page 170), but otherwise the two ships remained in service until the continuing world slump rendered them uneconomic. On 14 April 1928, *Suevic* left Liverpool on its last voyage to Australia, and in October was sold to the whaling firm Yngvar Hvistandahl Finnhavl A/S, of Tonsberg, Norway, who sent the ship to the Krupp Germaniawerft shipyard at Kiel to be converted into a whaling mother-ship and factory ship, with storage space for 80,000 barrels of whale oil.

When the work was completed the vessel, renamed *Skytteren*, had an opening in the stern through which whales could be hauled up a ramp to the main deck, while the superstructure was extended forward. The foremast was retained, but the other three masts were removed and four stump masts fitted.

On 14 December 1929 *Runic* left Liverpool on its final voyage for White Star, and in May 1930 was sold to the Scottish whaling firm of Chr. Salvesen & Co., of Leith, though the registered owners were shown as Seville Whaling Co. Also converted into a whaling mother and factory ship by the Krupp yard at Kiel, the vessel was renamed *New Sevilla*. Its career came to an end on 20 September 1940, when it was torpedoed and sunk off Galway by a German submarine, with the loss of two lives.

When the Germans invaded Norway, *Skytteren* escaped to Gothenburg in Sweden. In March 1942 the crew decided to try and get the ship to England, but on 1 April 1942 they were stopped by units of the German Navy while off Maseskjaer on the Swedish coast. To prevent their ship falling into German hands it was scuttled by the crew.

ATHENIC, CORINTHIC and IONIC

Built: 1902 by Harland & Wolff, Belfast
Gross tonnage: 12,234/12,231/12,232
Dimensions: 516 x 63 ft/157.1 x 19.3 m
Service speed: 14 knots
Propulsion: Quadruple expansion/twin propellers

These three ships, built by White Star Line for the New Zealand joint service with Shaw Savill Line, were designed along similar lines to the liners operated by White Star on the North Atlantic, though on a smaller scale. They would be the only White Star vessels to operate to New Zealand to offer second class accommodation, and the only ones to be given quadruple-expansion machinery, chosen for reliability rather than speed.

The first to be completed was *Athenic*, launched on 17 August 1901 and handed over to White Star on 23 January 1902. On 14 February *Athenic* left London on her maiden voyage, going by way of Cape Town to New Zealand. At that time the joint service had only one passenger vessel, *Gothic*, backed up by cargo ships, so the new ship was a welcome addition to the service.

These two ships maintained the service through most of 1902, as *Corinthic* was not launched until 10 April 1902. Handed over to White Star on 14 July, *Corinthic* was first used on the Atlantic service briefly before making her first departure from London on 20 November 1902 for New Zealand, by which time the third member of the group was almost completed.

This ship was christened *Ionic* when launched on 22 May 1902, reviving the name of one of the first White Star ships to operate to New Zealand, which had been sold in 1900. *Ionic* was delivered on 15 December,

and left London on 16 January 1903 on her maiden voyage.

The accommodation provided by the three ships was very roomy, well ventilated and also well lit, and revolutionised travel to New Zealand as it was vastly superior to anything offered previously. The actual breakdown of the passenger complement varied over the years, but when the ships entered service they could cater for 121 first class, 117 second class and 450 third class passengers, the latter being mainly used by migrants on the southbound journey. The ships also had a huge cargo capacity with seven holds and considerable refrigerated spaces. They became extremely popular with travellers within a short time, and were very profitable ships for the White Star Line.

Over the next few years the demand for migrant berths grew, while the number of first and second class passengers' being carried declined, so by 1910 the accommodation of the three ships had been altered to cater for 93 first class, 81 second class and 500 third class.

In 1904 Shaw Savill had added two new cargo ships to their fleet, *Matatua* and *Mamari*, which could carry several hundred emigrants in temporary berths in their holds when required (page 82), but the next major additions to the service were the Shaw Savill passenger ships *Arawa* and *Tainui*, which were smaller than the Athenic class, and joined them in 1907 and 1908 (pages 94, 95). *Gothic* was taken off the route in 1907, so that it was then operated by the three large White Star liners and the new Shaw Savill pair, offering four-weekly departures from London.

These five ships would comprise the Shaw Savill-White

Ionic

Star fleet until 1914, when some would be required for service as troop transports. *Athenic* was in New Zealand when war was declared, and immediately taken over by the New Zealand Government for service as troop transport number NZ11. The vessel carried elements of the New Zealand Expeditionary Force to the Middle East in the first convoy to leave the country in October 1914.

However, with their huge refrigerated cargo spaces these ships were needed to carry essential foodstuffs to Britain, so early in 1915 *Athenic* was returned to her owners' service, though her accommodation was controlled by the Government, as was those of her sisters.

Throughout the war the three ships remained on the New Zealand trade, but were diverted to other ports of call at times, including several visits to Australia. *Athenic* called at several ports in 1915 on a voyage from Liverpool to New Zealand. *Ionic* made at least four visits to Australia in the course of similar trips, the first in 1915, with two more in 1916 and one in 1918.

In 1916, following the example of the New Zealand Shipping Co., the White Star ships were frequently routed though the Panama Canal, which reduced travelling time and was safer. All three ships survived the war without incident, but were retained by the Government for some time after the Armistices.

Ionic was the first to be returned, and made the first commercial sailing for the Shaw Savill-White Star joint service when she left London on 31 January 1919. It would be another year before *Athenic* and *Corinthic* returned to the service, as they were not released from Government duty until late in 1919. *Athenic* made her first post-war departure from London on 10 January 1920, followed by *Corinthic* on 20 January.

There was a major change in the route followed in the post-war years, as the Panama Canal was transitted in both directions, and from July 1921 the ships called at Southampton to embark their passengers, though cargo was still loaded in London. During the immediate post-war years there was a boom in migration to New Zealand, and in 1926 the first class accommodation on *Athenic* was regraded second class, and she joined *Arawa* in a secondary service to New Zealand, making some departures from Liverpool.

This phase was to be of short duration for *Athenic*, which on 23 April 1927 departed Liverpool on a voyage to Australia on behalf of the Aberdeen Line. The vessel arrived in Melbourne on 23 June, and Sydney two days later, disembarking passengers at each port. *Athenic* continued to New Zealand and returned to Britain through the Panama Canal.

On 18 October 1927 *Athenic* made its final departure from Liverpool for New Zealand, and was then withdrawn. In May 1928 she was sold to Hvalfangerselskapet Pelagos A/S, a Norwegian whaling company from Tonsberg, Norway.

At Smith's Dock Co., North Shields, the vessel was rebuilt as a mother-ship for the whaling fleet, during which most of the superstructure was removed, the hull built up one deck, the tall masts removed and replaced by two pairs of goal-post masts and two pairs of short masts, and her boilers converted to oil firing. Renamed *Pelagos*, the ship was unrecognisable as her former self, and was sent to the Antarctic each year for the whaling season.

In 1929 the first class accommodation on *Ionic* was regraded second class, but on 14 August 1931 *Corinthic* left Southampton on its final voyage to New Zealand, and on returning to Britain was laid up. In December 1931 *Corinthic* was sold for breaking up to Hughes, Bolckow & Co., being scrapped at their Blyth yard in 1932.

Ionic remained the sole survivor on the New Zealand service, and in February 1932 her accommodation was again altered, to cater for 280 passengers in a single class. *Ionic* and *Tainui* were the only coal-burning vessels left in the combined fleet by this time, and both were nearing the end of their careers.

On 4 September 1936 *Ionic* left Southampton on its seventy-ninth and last voyage to New Zealand, and on returning to Britain was offered for sale. It was not surprising that the only interest should come from shipbreakers, and in January 1937 *Ionic* was purchased by a Japanese firm, making the voyage from Liverpool under its own steam to Osaka, where the vessel was broken up.

Meanwhile, former sister ship *Athenic* was continuing her career as the whaling ship, and even after war broke out in 1939 *Pelagos* was sent off as usual in September 1940 to the Antarctic. On 15 January 1941 the German auxiliary cruiser *Pinguin* captured *Pelagos* and her fleet of whalers in the Antarctic, and she was sent to Bordeaux with a prize crew aboard.

Placed under the German flag and managed by Erste Deutsche Waifang-Gesellschaft, she was sent to Norwegian waters for experimental operations with the 24th U-boat flotilla. When the Germans were withdrawing from Norway, they scuttled *Pelagos* on 24 October 1944 at Kirkenes, but in 1945 the Norwegians managed to raise her.

The ship was still in good enough condition in spite of her age to be refitted for further service as a whaling mother-ship, and her superstructure was enlarged at this time as well. *Pelagos* returned to her duties in the Antarctic summer, and served for another eighteen years. Finally, at the ripe old age of sixty, the former liner was sold to Eckfeardt & Co., arriving at their Hamburg shipbreaking yard on 28 June 1962.

COMMONWEALTH and GEELONG

COMMONWEALTH
Built: 1902 by Barclay, Curle & Co., Glasgow
Gross tonnage: 6,616
Dimensions: 450 x 52 ft/137.2 x 15.8 m
Service speed: 14 knots
Propulsion: Triple expansion/twin propellers

GEELONG
Built: 1904 by Barclay, Curle & Co., Glasgow
Gross tonnage: 7,951
Dimensions: 450 x 54 ft/137.2 x 16.4 m
Service speed: 14 knots
Propulsion: Triple expansion/twin propellers

This pair, built for the Blue Anchor Line, were considerably larger than previous ships owned by the company, and the first to be fitted with twin propellers. Launched on 23 August 1901 by the Countess of Hopetoun, the first was named *Commonwealth*, as Australia had become a commonwealth on 1 January 1901.

Permanent cabin accommodation was provided for 75 first class and 70 third class passengers, but in addition about 250 migrants could be carried on the outward voyage in temporary quarters erected in the 'tween decks.

On 28 October 1902 *Commonwealth* left London on its maiden voyage to Australia via Cape Town, arriving in Sydney on 19 December. The next day this description of the vessel appeared in the *Sydney Morning Herald*:

Accommodation is provided for about 75 first-class passengers amidships in specially large and well-lit and ventilated staterooms. The saloon, which is situated at the fore end of the bridge, extending the full breadth of the vessel, is tastefully fitted up in polished oak and teak wood. A large music room, panelled in oak, and a smoke room in mahogany are fitted on the bridge deck. A boat deck is fitted over the full length of the bridge, forming an exceedingly fine sheltered promenade for passengers.

Third class passengers to the number of 70 are accommodated in a long poop. The staterooms are arranged for two, three, four and six passengers; and a large dining saloon is provided under the poop deck. A smoking room, ladies room, and saloon entrance are fitted up in good style in houses upon the poop deck. Separate galleys, fitted up with steam ovens, grills, and all other cooking apparatus, are provided for first and third class passengers, and the pantries, sculleries, bakeries etc are carefully arranged to

Commonwealth in Blue Anchor Line colours.

Geelong (David Finch collection)

facilitate the preparation and dispensing of passengers' meals. Large porcelain baths with hot and cold water and showers, and all other sanitary fittings are provided for the passengers, officers and crew. The upper 'tween decks fore and aft are arranged to accommodate about 1,200 troops when required.

It had been the original intention of the Blue Anchor Line to name the second vessel *Australia*, but the P&O Line already had a ship of that name on the Australian trade. Instead the vessel was named *Geelong* when launched on 19 March 1904. It provided accommodation for 90 first class passengers and a maximum of 450 in third class. *Geelong* left London on 27 May 1904 on its maiden voyage, going via Cape Town to Albany, Adelaide, Melbourne and Sydney, arriving there on 11 July. On that day the *Sydney Morning Herald* reported:

The *Geelong* is a really magnificent vessel, and cost about £140,000 to build and equip. The passenger accommodation is excellent, that in the first-class being situated amidships. The dining hall is an especially handsome and well-lighted apartment, done in light oak and teak, and capable of seating 90 persons at one time. The social hall, smoking room and state rooms leave nothing to be desired, and are quite up to those to be found in the most modern mail liners, plenty of space and ventilation being the striking features throughout. The bridge deck, amidships, is 167ft long, and affords a splendid promenade. A remarkable thing about the passenger accommodation is that passengers can get from any of the cabins to the dining saloon, smoking rooms, bathrooms etc, without having to go onto the outer deck, all these being under one cover.

The steerage accommodation is under the poop, and is probably unsurpassed in any vessel of similar size afloat. It comprises state rooms, fitted with lavatories,

and wire mattresses, and containing all the conveniences to be found in the first class, whilst a smoking room, social hall etc, with piano, are also provided. The poop deck supplies an ample promenade. The ship is lit with electricity throughout, and a large section of the cargo space is insulated for the carriage of perishable products.

In 1908 a larger ship, *Waratah*, joined the Blue Anchor fleet, but on its second voyage it sank off the coast of South Africa in July 1909 (page 98). The loss destroyed the Blue Anchor Line, and six months later the assets of the company were purchased by the P&O Line.

Commonwealth had been scheduled to depart London on 1 March 1910 for Australia, but this sailing was taken by a P&O ship, and *Commonwealth* was refitted, the first class accommodation being removed, increasing capacity to 450 in third class only. *Geelong* was also refitted, to carry a maximum of 700 third class passengers only.

Commonwealth made its first sailing as a P&O ship from London on 15 September 1910, still on the same route. The service continued under the Blue Anchor name for six months, but in June 1910 it was renamed the P&O Branch Line, though the Blue Anchor funnel was kept until late 1913, when the two ships were given the P&O black funnel.

Geelong was taken over by the Australian Government for trooping service soon after war broke out in August 1914, being allocated number A2. Converted in Melbourne to carry 62 officers and 1,539 other ranks, it went to Hobart to board troops. *Geelong* then went to Albany, where the first convoy to be sent overseas in the war was assembled, departing on 1 November, and disembarking the troops in Egypt.

Several months later *Commonwealth* was also requisitioned by the Australian Government, being allocated number A73, and fitted out to carry 23 officers and 982 other ranks.

On 1 January 1916 *Geelong* was in a convoy in the Mediterranean when it collided with the British steamer *Bonvilston* some 100 miles (160 km) north of Alexandria, as a result of which *Geelong* sank.

After a quick refit it was *Commonwealth* that reopened the P&O Branch Line service with a sailing from London to Australia in October 1919, but with new ships being built for the trade, the vessel was withdrawn in 1922 and offered for sale. Although only twenty years old, in 1923 *Commonwealth* was sold to Italian shipbreakers.

ORONTES

Built: 1902 by Fairfield SB & E Co., Glasgow.
Gross tonnage: 9,028
Dimensions: 530 x 58 ft/161.5 x 17.6 m
Service speed: 18 knots
Propulsion: Quadruple expansion/twin screws

Orontes was ordered by the Orient Line in February 1901, launched on 10 May 1902 and ran trials four months later off Skelmorlie, averaging 18.18 knots over a 24 hour period.

As *Orontes* was intended for conversion into an armed merchant cruiser in the event of war, the Admiralty was involved in the design of the ship, and the hull was very heavily subdivided, there being ten main watertight bulkheads, and the vessel could float with any two flooded. *Orontes* was the first Orient liner to be given quadruple-expansion machinery, and had 32 furnaces.

The accommodation for first and second class passengers was based on the Bibby system to provide more cabins with portholes. There was accommodation for 323 first class, 323 second class and 320 third class passengers.

Orontes left London on 24 October 1902 on its maiden voyage to Australia, and proved to be an excellent seaboat. On the day the vessel arrived in Sydney, 6 December, the *Sydney Morning Herald*, under the headline 'A New Mammoth Mail Steamer', carried this report:

The magnificent new mail steamship *Orontes*, the latest addition to the fleet of the Orient-Pacific Company, will complete her maiden voyage by arriving at Sydney early this morning. The new vessel is described as a strikingly handsome ship with a straight stem, elliptical stern, forecastle, long promenade deck, and poop.

The *Orontes*, which has been specially designed and built for the mail and passenger trade between London and Australia, of the Orient-Pacific Line, is the largest vessel which has yet taken her place in the service of British mail steamers to the Southern Colonies. The Orient-Pacific Line have endeavoured to embody in the *Orontes* all modern improvements for the comfort and safety of passengers, of whom she has accommodation for 323 first and second saloon passengers, and 320 third class. The cabins are arranged for one, two or three passengers, and are all particularly large and airy, and furnished with every requirement for passengers' comfort.

The first class dining saloon, upon the upper deck, is 43ft long by 42½ ft wide. The centre of it rises to twice the height of the sides, and is surmounted by a dome having wood ribs and intermediate panels of stained glass. This dome, with its 'clerestory' of low arched windows (a device partly for light and partly for ventilation), is carried on mahogany columns, with carved capitals. The general scheme of decoration in this saloon is mahogany, with ebony moulded panels and pilasters of Coromandel wood, inlaid with devices in mother-of-pearl and green shell. The dome is of white mahogany, with a carved coat of arms at each end — at one end that of Great Britain, and at the other the arms of the Australian Commonwealth — finished in heraldic colours. The electric light fittings, very simple in character, harmonise well with the general scheme. They are simple, and unobtrusive in character, and are so placed as to give an even distribution of light through the saloon.

The smoking room is on the promenade deck, aft of the dining saloon, and has a floor area of 700ft. It can be

Orontes

entered from the saloon by a stairway, without going out on deck. The fitting is carried out in grey fumigated oak. The seats — some settees and some armchairs — are grouped for the most part around small tables, where reading, card playing, and other games can be carried out in good light.

The drawing room is upon the promenade deck, forward of the dining saloon. The sides are panelled in two heights; below of bleached Italian walnut, and above of satinwood, with inlays of various stained and painted woods. The ceiling has white rafters and interspaces of white painted wood, forming panels on which are stencilled a design of stems and leaves in tones of purple and green. The sofas and chairs are covered with Morris cretonnes; the curtains are of silk brocade in blues and greens; the floor is laid with bright Eastern carpets. There is a grand piano in a specially designed case of bleached Spanish mahogany, and a well-fitted bookcase. Opposite each of the entrances to the drawing room is a small and convenient writing room. The staircase from the main deck to the dining saloon and drawing room, constructed of dark mahogany, is spacious and handsome. The sides are lined with dark teak panels.

The second dining saloon, placed on the main deck aft, occupying the whole width of the ship for about 35ft in length, is a very commodious apartment, with seats for 126 persons. The panelling round the saloon is of pitch-pine, in teak stiles. The columns supporting the roof beams are cased in teak. At the head of the staircase leading from the second saloon to the promenade deck is a commodious vestibule fitted with upholstered lounge seats, with doors leading on to the promenade deck at each side.

The provision of deck space for exercise and amusement is very liberal. First saloon passengers have a length of 272ft of the promenade deck, with a maximum width at each side of the vessel of 14ft, besides the forward part of the boat deck above. The latter being 30ft above the water level affords a commanding view all round the vessel. Part of the boat deck is appropriated to second saloon passengers, who have also the entire use of the after promenade deck, 120ft long by over 21ft wide. The promenade deck, besides being well provided with comfortable fixed deck seats in sheltered positions, is well arranged for accommodating passenger deck chairs. The greatest part of this deck is sheltered from sun and rain by the boat deck above.

In 1905 the third class accommodation was improved and enlarged. When first placed in service Orontes had a black funnel, as did all Orient Line vessels, but when the Royal Mail Line took over the PSNC interest in the joint service to Australia in 1906 the funnel was painted yellow, to match those of the new partner.

On 19 June 1914, Orontes departed London on its 53rd voyage to Australia, being there when war broke out, but completing the voyage back to Britain as scheduled. Orontes remained on the Australian service, eventually being the lone Orient liner on the route. During October 1916 the vessel was finally taken over, and used as a troopship, spending considerable time plying between South and East Africa and also making some trips from South Africa to France, with a couple of trooping to trips to Australia late in 1916. In August 1917 Orontes was handed over to the Shipping Controller and put back on the Australian route, voyaging by way of South Africa in both directions, but in June 1918 made a voyage from Sydney across the Pacific and through the Panama Canal to New York and then to Liverpool, followed by a trip from there to Boston and return.

After the Armistices, Orontes was used to repatriate Australian troops, the first sailing being from Liverpool on 20 December 1918, returning to London. It was not until June 1919 that Orontes was handed back to the Orient Line, and following a very basic refit returned to the Australian trade with a departure from London on 25 October.

By the beginning of 1921 Orontes was in need of a major refit, but it was considered not worth the expense. In February 1921 Orontes left Tilbury on its final voyage to Australia, only the fifth since returning to the route, after which the vessel was laid up off Southend as a reserve ship.

In February 1922 a British syndicate, British World Trade Exhibitions Ltd, took out an option to buy the ship for use an exhibition ship for British goods, and renamed British Trade. Work on the conversion began at Tilbury, but then the syndicate ran into various problems, including lack of government support, and in August 1922 Orontes was taken back by the Orient Line and laid up at anchor off Southend.

In 1923 the idea was revived, and Orontes voyaged to Hull in February for conversion. In May a fire caused some damage to the ship, and in July work was suspended due to the owners' financial problems. In January 1924 they went bankrupt, and Orontes reverted to Orient Line yet again, as it had not been paid for.

Orontes remained at Hull until August 1924, then was towed back to Southend, and soon after went to the River Blackwater to lay up. In 1925 the vessel was sold to shipbreakers.

THE GERMAN GENERALS

GNEISENAU/CITTA DI GENOVA
Built: 1903 by A. G. Vulcan, Stettin
Gross tonnage: 8,081
Dimensions: 454 x 56 ft/138.3 x 17 m
Service speed: 14 knots
Propulsion: Triple expansion/twin propellers

ZIETEN SEYDLITZ
Built: 1903 by F Schichau, Danzig
Gross tonnage: 8,066/7,942
Dimensions: 450 x 55 ft/137.2 x 16.7 m
Service speed: 14 knots
Propulsion: Triple expansion/twin propellers

ROON SCHARNHORST
Built: 1903/1904 by Tecklenborg, Geestemunde
Gross tonnage: 8,022/8,131
Dimensions: 453 x 56 ft/ 138.1 x 17 m
Service speed: 14 knots
Propulsion: Triple expansion/twin propellers

In 1903 North German Lloyd began taking delivery of a group of five steamers, known as the General class, from three shipyards. They were of basically the same design but slightly different dimensions, and designed to be interchangeable between the Far East and Australian services. The first, Zieten, was launched on 12 July 1902, and entered service in January 1903 with a voyage to the Far East, as did the second ship,

Seydlitz, which was launched on 25 October 1902 and entered service in March 1903. They were followed by Roon, which was launched on 1 November 1902, and on completion in April 1903 also went onto the Far East service.

The first of the series to make a voyage to Australia was Gneisenau, which was launched on 1 April 1903, completed in August, and departed Bremen on 2 September, with a call at Southampton en route to Fremantle, Adelaide, Melbourne and Sydney. Gneisenau provided accommodation for 124 first class, 116 second class and 1,862 third class passengers.

In November 1903 Zieten departed Bremen to become the second vessel of the class to make a voyage to Australia. The next member of the group to enter the Australian trade was the last to be delivered, Scharnhorst, which was launched on 14 May 1904, completed in August that year, and the following month departed Bremen for Australia. Seydlitz was placed on the Australian trade with a departure from Bremen in February 1905.

In 1906 North German Lloyd began introducing a series of new ships of the Bulow class (page 92) on the Australian route as well, and from September 1906 operated an accelerated schedule to Australia using only twin-propeller vessels, going from Bremerhaven and Southampton to Genoa and Naples, Port Said, Colombo and on to Fremantle, Adelaide, Melbourne and Sydney. Under this new arrangement the sailings for most of the year were taken by ships of the General or Bulow classes, but in the northern winter the larger vessels of the Barbarossa class (page 42) continued

Gneisenau

Zieten

to make appearances in Australian waters, but for only one trip at a time.

The last member of the General class to appear in Australia was *Roon*, which had been the third completed, but did not make its first voyage to Australia until February 1908. Thus all five of these vessels were in use on the Australian trade, but only on an irregular basis, when the war brought the service to a swift end.

Scharnhorst made its final departure for Australia in April 1914, followed by *Zieten* in May, *Seydlitz* in June and then *Roon*, which left Bremerhaven in early July.

Seydlitz was in Sydney when it become obvious that war was about to break out between Germany and Britain. On 3 August the vessel hurriedly left Sydney and managed to make its way right across the Pacific, around Cape Horn and reach Bahia Blanca in Argentina, where it was interned, and later seized by Argentina.

Zieten was homeward bound from Australia, and took refuge in Portugal, being seized by the Portuguese authorities in 1916 and renamed *Tungue*. On 27 November 1917 the vessel was torpedoed and sunk by a German submarine in the eastern Mediterranean north of Port Said.

Roon terminated its outward voyage to Australia and returned to Germany, while *Scharnhorst* was in Bremerhaven when war broke out.

Gneisenau had left Germany on 29 July for Australia, and sought sanctuary at Antwerp on 31 July, but was seized by the Belgians on 4 August, though the crew was sent back to Germany. In October 1914 the vessel was scuttled by the Belgians in the River Scheldt to obstruct and delay the Germans, but the current turned the vessel lengthwise and it settled on its starboard side. The Germans captured Antwerp in October 1914, and in August 1916 began salvage operations on the vessel. After being refloated, on 23 May 1917 it was towed back to Antwerp.

When the war ended, *Scharnhorst* went to the French Government in 1919, and was sold to Cie Generale Transatlantique in 1921. Renamed *La Bourdonnais*, and refitted to carry 122 cabin class and 212 third class passengers, it left Le Havre on 2 April 1921 on a service to New York, though from 1923 the terminal port became Bordeaux. On 11 October 1934 the vessel arrived in Genoa to be broken up.

Roon was taken over by the British in 1919, and then sold to the Greek Government. Renamed *Constantinoupolis*, it served until being sold in 1925 to shipbreakers in Italy.

Seydlitz was operating under the Argentine flag, but in 1922 North German Lloyd bought the ship back again, and used it to recommence their North Atlantic service with a sailing from Bremerhaven in February 1922 to New York. The Australian service was not restored.

In November 1918 *Gneisenau* was again seized by Belgium as a war prize, and on 20 June 1919 was sold at auction to the Soc. Ind. Transporti Maritimi, of Genoa. Repaired by the Antwerp Engineering Co., in 1920 the vessel was chartered by the British Government, being managed for them by C. T. Bowring, and left Antwerp on 23 January 1921, still named *Gneisenau*.

Later in 1921 *Gneisenau* was handed back to Soc. Ind. Transporti Maritimi, and renamed *Citta di Genova*. Refitted to carry 28 first class and 596 third class passengers, *Citta di Genova* was employed on a service to South America for the next two years, but at the end of 1922 it was purchased by another Italian shipping firm, Navigazione Generale Italiana, who at that time were operating on the emigrant trade to Australia in a joint service with Lloyd Sabaudo.

On 14 January 1923 *Citta di Genova* left Genoa on its first voyage to Australia, going through the Suez Canal to

Fremantle, then Melbourne on 2 March, arriving in Sydney on 6 March, continuing north to Brisbane. It had been intended that the vessel would carry about 500 migrants on the voyage, but this did not happen, as was explained in a report in the *Sydney Morning Herald* on 7 March (see page 158):

Owing to difficulties which arose in regard to the Italians who came to Australia by the *Re d'Italia* early in January and most of whom returned to their native country by the same vessel, between 400 and 500 prospective emigrants were forbidden by the Italian Government to board the steamer *Citta di Genova* when she was about to leave Genoa for Australia. This statement was made by officers of the steamer after she had berthed at Woolloomooloo yesterday morning.

The emigrants, it was stated, had booked their passages, and some even had luggage aboard when the news was received in Italy of the experiences of the *Re d'Italia* emigrants in Australia. The Government immediately issued an edict forbidding those who proposed to leave by the *Citta di Genova* to embark. The only new arrivals at

Sydney yesterday were a saloon passenger and six Greek immigrants.

The present is the *Citta di Genova*'s first visit to Sydney. She had an uneventful voyage, meeting with bad weather only in the Red Sea and between Melbourne and Sydney. On Monday night, when a short distance from the Heads, a dense fog enveloped the steamer. This was described by one of the officers as the worst he had ever experienced. He said that his pair of night-glasses, with which he ordinarily could see 25 miles, were only effective for three miles.

Citta di Genova continued to voyage to Australia until 1930, when she it laid up in Genoa, and sold on 16 October 1930 to shipbreakers at Naples.

By this time only two members of the original quintet were still active. *La Bourdonnais* continued to operate for Cie Generale Transatlantique until being withdrawn in 1933, and sold to shipbreakers at Genoa, arriving there on 11 October 1934. *Seydlitz* continued to serve North German Lloyd on the North Atlantic until 1933, and then it too was sold to shipbreakers.

Gneisenau as *Citta di Genova*.

DUMBEA and NERA

DUMBEA
Built: 1888 by Forges et Chantiers de la Mediterranee, La Seyne

NERA
Built: 1888 by Soc. Provencale de Cons Nav., La Ciotat

DUMBEA   NERA
Gross tonnage: 5,809/5,876
Dimensions: 463 x 46 ft/141.3 x 11.1 m
Service speed: 16 knots
Propulsion: Triple expansion/single propeller

These ships were built for the Messageries Maritimes service from France to South America. *Nera* was christened *La Plata* when launched on 18 June 1888, and on 5 April 1889 departed Bordeaux on its maiden voyage to Brazil and Argentina. *Dumbea* was named *Bresil* when launched on 7 November 1888, and joined the South American trade in the middle of 1889. They were fitted with accommodation for 132 first class, 90 second class and 745 third class passengers.

In 1903 both vessels were extensively refitted and renamed prior to commencing a service from Marseilles to Colombo, Australia and Noumea. The first departure was by *Dumbea* from Marseilles on 15 March, arriving at Fremantle on 17 April, then Melbourne on 22 April and Sydney two days later. On 25 April *Dumbea* left for Noumea, where the voyage terminated.

Nera left Marseilles on 11 May, reaching Fremantle on 11 June and Melbourne six days later, arriving in Sydney on 20 June. After an overnight stay, *Nera* also continued on to Noumea.

On its second voyage *Dumbea* departed Sydney for Noumea on 20 August, but two days later the high pressure cylinder cover blew off, and the vessel limped back to Sydney for repairs.

Nera did not depart Marseilles on its second voyage to Australia until 17 February 1904, arriving in Sydney on 28 March and continuing to Noumea. Both ships subsequently operated on a regular basis between France, Australia and Noumea.

In July 1909, *Nera* was caught in a cyclone off the east coast of Australia, and limped into Melbourne suffering considerable damage, including the loss of the foremast.

On 2 October 1911, *Nera* was backing out of its wharf in Darling Harbour when *Taviuni*, owned by the Union Steam Ship Company of New Zealand, tried to pass on its way in to another wharf. The two ships collided, the propeller of *Nera* tearing a large hole in the hull of *Taviuni*, which managed to reach its berth, but then sank.

Nera departed Marseilles on 29 April 1914 for what was to be its final voyage to Australia, while *Dumbea* left Marseilles on 22 July on its final voyage on the route. In August 1914 both vessels were requisitioned for service as troopships.

Both survived the war and underwent extensive refits prior to returning to service. On 19 September 1919, while being removed from a drydock at Marseilles, *Dumbea* capsized and sank, being refloated on 23 October. It did not return to service until a departure from Marseilles on 30 August 1920 for Madagascar, on which route both vessels were permanently placed.

Nera was sold to Italian shipbreakers in April 1923, but *Dumbea* survived another five years, no doubt due to the extensive work done after the sinking in 1919. It was not until September 1928 that *Dumbea* was sold to shipbreakers and scrapped.

Dumbea

ORITA

Built: 1902 by Harland & Wolff, Belfast.
Gross tonnage: 9,239
Dimensions: 485 x 58 ft/147.9 x 17.7 m
Service speed: 16 knots
Propulsion: Quadruple expansion/twin screws

This vessel, which was built to operate on the South American service of the Pacific Steam Navigation Company, made only one voyage to Australia, but at that time was the largest British flag vessel to have visited Australia. Launched on 15 November 1902, *Orita* was completed in March of 1903, and on 8 April departed London on an 18-day cruise to the Mediterranean. This was followed by the voyage to Australia in place of *Orizaba* which was undergoing a major refit (page 14).

On 8 May 1903, *Orita* departed London, calling at Naples on 17 May, then passing through the Suez Canal, and stopping at Colombo on 1 June. Fremantle was reached on 11 June, followed by a call at Adelaide on 15 June, and Melbourne two days later, the voyage terminating in Sydney on 19 June. The *Sydney Morning Herald* reported:

The passenger accommodation is all that can be desired. The *Orita* is not a large passenger carrier, but the cabins are more spacious than those of the other ships. She has accommodation for 114 first class passengers situated on the main and spar decks, and special attention has been devoted to the subject of ventilation and light. All the cabins are fitted with wardrobes, and have been elegantly furnished. The dining saloon is on the spar deck, running the whole width of the ship, and is elaborately furnished. Seating accommodation has been provided for 122 persons, and a separate dining room has been provided for nurses

and children. The whole of the first class accommodation, it should be stated, is amidships.

The second saloon accommodation for 118 passengers is situated on the main deck running from amidships aft, and the dining saloon, with seating accommodation for 100 persons, runs the full width of the ship. There is also accommodation for about 200 third-class passengers forward. No expense has been spared in fitting up the new vessel in the most modern style and all the latest improvements in ship construction have been introduced. Needless to say the electric light is installed throughout the vessel.

Orita departed Sydney on 4 July for the voyage back to London, calling at Melbourne, Adelaide and Fremantle. The liner then joined the service from Liverpool to Valparaiso in Chile via Rio de Janeiro, Montevideo and the Straits of Magellan, on which it remained the largest vessel until 1908.

In 1910 PSNC was taken over by the Royal Mail Steam Packet Company, but the two companies retained their separate identities and *Orita* continued on the same route as before.

During the World War I *Orita* saw service as a troop transport, and was handed back to PSNC at the end of 1918. On 10 February 1919, *Orita* departed Liverpool on its first post-war voyage to Valparaiso, but the route now went through the Panama Canal.

On 22 September 1927, *Orita* departed Liverpool on its final voyage to South America, which followed the original route via the Straits of Magellan, and on returning to Britain the vessel was laid up in the River Dart. It remained there for five years, then in 1932 was sold to shipbreakers.

Orita

KAIKOURA and KAIPARA

Built: 1903 by John Brown, Clydebank
Gross tonnage: 6,998/7,392
Dimensions: 460 x 58 ft/140.2 x 17.7 m
Service speed: 13 knots
Propulsion: Triple expansion/single propeller

Basically designed as cargo ships, the first of this pair to be launched was *Kaikoura*, on 27 June 1903, being delivered to the New Zealand Shipping Company on 11 September. Two days later *Kaipara* was launched, being completed on 11 November.

Both vessels were fitted with permanent accommodation for 22 first class passengers, but could also carry about 200 migrants in temporary quarters erected in the holds for the outward voyage.

These vessels were placed on a secondary service from Britain to New Zealand via South Africa, returning around Cape Horn. Migrants were not carried on all voyages, and on occasion it was necessary to use these ships on the main line service to New Zealand when the regular passenger liners were out of service.

When war broke out in August 1914, *Kaipara* was on a voyage from New Zealand to Britain, carrying a large cargo of produce and dairy products. On 16 August 1914, only two weeks after the war started, *Kaipara* was approaching Las Palmas, where it was due to take on coal for the final leg of the voyage to Britain, when the vessel was captured by the German armed merchant raider *Kaiser Wilhelm der Grosse*.

Once all the crew had been removed, *Kaipara* was sunk by gunfire, though it took 53 shells to send the ship to the bottom. Ten days later the German raider met a similar fate at the hands of a British cruiser.

Kaikoura survived the war, and continued to operate for the New Zealand Shipping Company into the 1920s, though only as a cargo ship. In August 1926 the vessel was sold to an Italian, Ditta L. Pittaluga of Genoa, and renamed *Giano*. The following year the name of the ship was changed to *Ferrania*. In March 1929 the vessel was sold to shipbreakers at Savona in Italy.

Kaipara

AUSTRALIND, ARMADALE and *AJANA*

AUSTRALIND
Built: 1904 by Charles Connell & Co., Glasgow
Tonnage: 5,568 gross
Dimensions: 384 x 50 ft/ 117.1 x 15.3 m
Service speed: 11 knots
Propulsion: Triple expansion/single propeller

ARMADALE
Built: 1909 by Charles Connell & Co., Glasgow
Tonnage: 6,153 gross
Dimensions: 395 x 52 ft/ 120.5 x 15.8 m
Service speed: 11 knots
Propulsion: Triple expansion/single propeller

AJANA
Built: 1912 by Russell & Co., Port Glasgow
Tonnage: 7,753 gross
Dimensions: 454 x 56 ft/ x 138.4 x 17.1 m
Service speed: 13 knots
Propulsion: Quadruple expansion/single propeller

The first vessel to be built for the Australind Steam Navigation Co. was appropriately named *Australind* when launched on 24 June 1904, entering service two months later. Primarily a cargo ship, *Australind* could carry up to 450 migrants in temporary quarters located in the holds on the outward passage from Britain to Fremantle.

The next two vessels built for the company, *Ashburton*, launched on 8 June 1905, and *Arrino*, which was launched on 27 June 1906, were exclusively used to carry cargo.

The fourth ship to be built for the company, *Armadale*, was launched on 14 September 1909. It originally operated only as a cargo ship, but a report in the *Sydney Morning Herald* on 10 November 1910 stated: 'The Orient Company, at the request of the Acting Agent-General, has chartered the steamer *Armadale* to bring 600 migrants to Western Australia next month. The *Armadale* will carry no other passengers.'

The vessel was fitted out with temporary accommodation in London prior to this trip, which in fact carried 336 migrants to Fremantle, where it arrived on 26 December 1910. According to records held in Perth, *Armadale* arrived in Fremantle on 10 July 1911 again with migrants on board, and another migrant voyage reached Fremantle on 1 July 1912.

On Monday, 8 May 1911, the *Sydney Morning Herald* carried a story regarding the arrival of the *Australind* in Fremantle:

The steamer *Australind*, which arrives on Sunday, brings 434 immigrants, of whom 73 have been nominated by immigrants who have come to the State within the last year. Fifty are domestic servants, for whom there is a strong

demand. The Government Labour Bureau is absorbing all new arrivals without overtaking the demand for country workers. Last month the bureau was only able to supply 256 men to applicants.

A report appeared in the *West Australian* on Monday, 20 May 1912, regarding a voyage made by the *Australind* departing Tilbury on 30 March 1912, and arriving in Fremantle on 18 May:

The *Australind* of 7,500 tons, commanded by Captain A. Hunter, arrived at Fremantle on Saturday from London. She left Plymouth on April 1, coaled at St Helena on the 19th, and again at Cape Town on the 28th. She brought with her 492 immigrants, all of whom are for this State. The majority of the passengers were women, coming to Australia to join their husbands and bringing with them many children from the age of three months upwards. One hundred and seventy six of the small passengers were under 12 months, and of the complete register of immigrant passengers 377 were nominated. The *Australind*'s trip was uneventful and good weather was met with all the way out. She will remain in Fremantle for a fortnight, and then go east via Albany. This is the *Australind*'s third journey with immigrants, and the *Ajana* which is building to the order of the company will shortly be in commission for the trade.

Ajana was launched on 22 February 1912, and ran sea trials on 25 May, achieving a maximum speed of 14.373 knots. Permanent accommodation was fitted for about a dozen first class passengers, while temporary quarters were provided for about 700 migrants on the outward voyage from Britain. On her maiden voyage *Ajana* left Liverpool and went to Avonmouth to embark more migrants, leaving there on 19 June 1912, this being the first time a ship for Australia had boarded migrants at that port. Only two stops for coal were made on the outward voyage, at Las Palmas and Cape Town, and the voyage took 38 days.

On 16 July a description of the vessel appeared in the *Sydney Morning Herald*:

The new steamer *Ajana*, which has been specially built for the trade between London and Western Australia, is described to be a fine type of vessel. The first-class accommodation is fitted amidships, with a spacious saloon, smoke-room, and six large spare staterooms. A special feature of this steamer is the accommodation for immigrants, which is most perfect and up-to-date. The whole of the shelter 'tween decks is fitted with two, four and eight berth cabins, and on the shelter deck there are large houses for music-room, smoking-room, dining-room, pantry, bar, and lavatories etc. She has 14 lifeboats and one 'D' boat sufficient to carry more than all the passengers and crew.

Ajana (Western Australia Maritime Museum)

Ajana docked in Fremantle at noon on 28 July, with a crowd of 2,000 waiting on Victoria Quay to welcome the new arrivals. Of the 645 migrants on board, 228 travelled on an assisted passage scheme, comprising 24 married couples, 82 single men, 48 single women, 48 children under 12, and two wives coming out to join their husbands. The other 417 migrants had been nominated for work in Western Australia, and comprised 23 married couples, 35 single men, 72 single women, 191 children under 12, and 73 wives joining their husbands.

Ajana continued to carry migrants to Western Australia, though not all survived long in their new country. On her second voyage, 61 of the 513 migrants were on an assisted scheme, the rest being nominated, and there were about 250 children.

At the time *Ajana* departed Britain, several areas in the Midlands were being affected by a measles epidemic, and within a few days departure there was an outbreak of measles among the children on board. When the ship arrived at Gage Roads off Fremantle on 1 February 1913, medical authorities found 25 children were seriously ill, including a number of infants, and they with their parents were transferred to the Woodman Point Quarantine Station, where sadly four died within days of arriving, including two young brothers aged two and four.

Ajana made another voyage to Australia with migrants later in 1913, arriving in Fremantle on 13 October,

and its final migrant voyage ended in Fremantle on 23 March 1914.

During 1913 *Armadale* is recorded as arriving in Fremantle on 4 January, 10 June and 7 December, with migrants on each voyage, with a final arrival on 12 June 1914.

When the war came all these vessels were taken over for military duty. *Ajana* was requisitioned by the Australian Government on arrival in Sydney in December 1914, and allocated pennant number A31. It was in the second convoy to be sent overseas since the war began, the troops being landed at Alexandria. Over the next three years *Ajana* was used from time to time to transport Australian troops overseas.

Australind was used to transport New Zealand and Australian troops from Alexandria to Gallipoli for the landing there on 25 April 1915. *Armadale* was sunk by a German submarine on 27 June 1917, but *Australind* and *Ajana* survived the war.

In 1920 *Ajana* joined the New Zealand Shipping Company fleet, being renamed *Otarama*, and operated only as a cargo ship between Britain and New Zealand. In 1928 *Otarama* was sold to D. & E. Fratelli Bozzo, of Genoa, and renamed *Amaranto*. In November 1932 the vessel arrived at Genoa to be broken up.

Australind was sold in 1928 to a French company, being renamed *Colbert*. In 1933 she was again sold, and renamed *Scandinavie*, but on 8 October 1934 the vessel arrived at Savona in Italy to be broken up.

MATATUA and MAMARI

MATATUA
Built: 1904 by Workman, Clark, Belfast
Gross tonnage: 6,488
Dimensions: 448 x 56 ft/ 136.6 x 17 m
Service speed: 12 knots
Propulsion: Triple expansion/twin propellers

MAMARI
Built: 1904 by Harland & Wolff, Belfast
Gross tonnage: 7,062
Dimensions: 454 x 56 ft/ 138.4 x 17 m
Service speed: 13 knots
Propulsion: Quadruple expansion/twin propellers

Designed primarily as cargo ships for the Shaw Savill Line trade from Britain to Australia and New Zealand via South Africa, this pair had permanent accommodation for six first class passengers, but temporary quarters could be installed in the holds for about 200 steerage passengers.

Matatua was the first to be launched, on 15 January 1904, being delivered the following month. *Matatua* was the first vessel built for a service from Glasgow and Liverpool to Australia and New Zealand via South Africa.

Shortly before *Matatua* was due to depart on its maiden voyage another ship rammed it in the stern. The damage was not thought to be serious, and only minor repairs were completed before *Matatua* left for its scheduled voyage. However, during the voyage the propeller shaft snapped and the rudder jammed, which resulted in the ship being laid up for some time undergoing repairs. A later court case ruled the earlier ramming had caused damage to both the shaft and rudder that was not identified when the inspection of damage was made.

Mamari was launched on 24 September 1904, and handed over to Shaw Savill on 3 December. The vessel departed Britain at the end of 1904 on its maiden voyage to Australia and New Zealand.

For the first four years of their careers *Mamari* and *Matatua* were occasionally included in the main line service, operating to a strict schedule, but when *Tainui* joined the fleet in 1908 (page 95) both ships were relegated to being primarily cargo carriers. However, from 1910 to 1914 demand for emigrant passages was extremely high, and each vessel would carry up to 500 migrants on the outward voyage from Britain.

On 16 January 1911 the *Sydney Morning Herald* carried the following report on a voyage to Sydney by *Mamari*:

Matatua

Mamari

When the steamer *Mamari*, which has just arrived in Sydney with 490 immigrants, reached Capetown, a number of those on board, not content with having 'a jolly time' there, laid in a secret stock of liquor on board for celebrating New Year's Eve.

When New Year's Eve came they gathered together in the dining saloon, forward, where the men's quarters were, and began the celebration. It eventually became so pronounced that the steward informed Captain Holmes that he couldn't keep the men quiet, and thereupon the captain visited the scene, and remonstrated with them. He told them that he would have all lights put out if they did not keep quiet.

The captain went away, only to be called again by the steward some time later. The men had become worse, and were creating a good deal of disturbance. This time the captain ordered the lights to be turned off, and at the same time be ordered the men to go to their beds. 'If you don't get into your berths and shut your doors,' he said, 'I'll have the hose turned on you.'

The men openly defied him. 'I'd like to 'see you turn the hose on me,' said one. They refused to leave the dining saloon, and as the room was in darkness, and they kept striking matches, thereby exposing the ship to the risk of fire, the captain's next order to the steward was: 'Send for the boatswain and tell him to get the seamen to connect the hose.'

Captain Holmes stood on the stairway, and the second officer stood by him in case of trouble. The hose was brought and the captain said to the second officer, 'Tell them to turn the water on full as soon as my whistle goes.' He took out his watch and addressing the men said, 'I give you two minutes. If you are not all in your berths in two minutes, I'll have the hose turned on you.'

The men took the hint and went, and as they were going the captain called out to the second officer, 'Stand by for half an hour, and if one of them shows his head, let him have it. '

Fortunately the trouble ended there. The men did not come out again. Discussing the matter with a *Herald* reporter, Captain Holmes said the disturbance was confined to a few men, and he did not wish to reflect upon the immigrants as a body. 'They are as fine a lot as you have had,' he said. 'but there are always a few rough ones in every lot.'

On 8 May 1911 the *Sydney Morning Herald* carried a report from London dated 5 May: 'The *Mamari* has sailed with 640 emigrants for New South Wales.' Both vessels continued to carry migrants to Australia and New Zealand over the next few years, and in the early period of World War I. *Mamari* departed London on 16 October 1914 with a full complement of migrants bound for New Zealand. Later in the war both *Mamari* and *Matatua* were taken over for military duty.

After World War I there was a huge demand for migrant passages to New Zealand, and *Mamari* was refitted to carry 450 steerage passengers, while *Matatua* was provided with quarters for 200.

In 1928 both vessels were sold to well-known European shipowner Arnold Bernstein, being placed under the German flag. *Mamari* was renamed *Gerolstein*, and *Matatua* became *Ilsenstein*. Initially they operated from Europe to North America as cargo ships, but in 1931 both were fitted with economical one class passenger accommodation.

Ilsenstein was sold to British shipbreakers in 1939, but was still afloat when war broke out. The vessel was taken to Scapa Flow, the major British naval base in the north, and scuttled on 18 February 1940 as a blockship in the entrance to Skerry Sound, to prevent German submarines attacking the warships at anchor.

Gerolstein, the former *Mamari*, was sold early in 1939 to German owners, the Horn Line, and renamed *Consul Horn*, changed soon after to *Horn*, then back to *Consul Horn* in 1940. On 20 July 1942 the vessel struck a mine off the Dutch coast in the North Sea and sank.

MILTIADES and MARATHON

Built: 1903/1904 by A. Stephen, Glasgow
Gross tonnage: 6,793/6,795
Dimensions: 454 x 55 ft/138.4 x 16.7 m
Service speed: 13 knots
Propulsion: Triple expansion/twin propeller

When Geo Thomson & Co., who traded as the Aberden Line, ordered two new steamships in 1902 it was not surprising, for a company so steeped in the lore of the sailing ship, that the new ships were designed with clipper bows, including bowsprit and figurehead. They were destined to be the last large steam vessels to be built in the world to this design.

The first of the new ships to be completed was named *Miltiades* when launched on 11 August 1903, leaving London on 3 November 1903 on its maiden voyage, going around South Africa to Albany, Adelaide and Melbourne before arriving in Sydney on 14 December. Next day the *Daily Telegraph* carried an extensive article extolling the merits of the new steamer, which read:

Named after a famous clipper ship which for years figured prominently in the Australian trade, the *Miltiades*, Messrs Geo. Thompson & Co.'s latest steamer, had many admirers at Smith's Wharf yesterday. The *Miltiades* is the largest steamer carrying the Aberdeen Line flag, and she is also the fastest. Proof of her excellent steaming capabilities were given on this, her maiden voyage from London, the steamer having made a record trip. Her actual steaming time for the voyage to Melbourne was 34 days 16 hours, representing an hourly average speed of 14.2 knots, or 340.8 miles per day.

The passenger accommodation has been fitted up in a luxurious and most comfortable manner. Most of the staterooms have been designed with two berths; others for the use of families, while several single-berth rooms have been provided for the convenience of those who prefer travelling alone. All the staterooms are on the upper and bridge decks, and are fitted with every provision for comfort. Besides the main saloon there is a ladies' room, writing-room and library — the latter room being fitted in satinwood with marquetry inlaid panels. A large handsome cupola is fitted over the saloon with ornamental stained glass sky-light overhead. The smoking-room is exceptionally large and airy, with a height of over 10ft between the decks, and is handsomely decorated. The third class accommodation is placed aft in the poop and on the main deck, and fitted up in a superior manner with smoking and music rooms in deck houses on the poop deck. The sanitary accommodation for both classes is very complete.

Miltiades as built. (David Finch collection)

Miltiades' maiden voyage terminated in Brisbane, from where the vessel began the return trip to Britain, with Fremantle being substituted for Albany, and an extra call made at Durban.

Marathon was launched 18 November 1903 and completed two months later, leaving London on 26 January 1904, arriving in Sydney on 10 March. Each ship had accommodation for about 100 first class passengers and 300 in third class, though extra migrants could be carried in temporary quarters.

In June 1907, *Miltiades* was chartered by the Orient Line, whose vessel *Oroya* had suffered a major breakdown, to make a voyage on their behalf from London to Australia and back through the Suez Canal, the scheduled voyage via South Africa for Aberdeen Line being cancelled. This was the only time *Miltiades* passed through the Suez Canal. In October 1910, *Miltiades* became the first vessel in the Aberdeen Line fleet to have a wireless fitted.

An account of a voyage by *Miltiades* appeared in the *Sydney Morning Herald* on 5 February 1912:

The Aberdeen liner *Miltiades* includes in her passenger list a number of new settlers. On her prior trip to Australia she brought an exceptionally desirable lot of immigrants, whose appearance and conduct aroused favourable comment. In the opinion of Captain Schleman, those by the liner on her present visit are in every respect equal to their forerunners, and he has no doubt they will prove their worth in the Commonwealth. Unfortunately the voyage was marred by two deaths. A third-class passenger, named Mrs Taylor, died shortly after leaving Capetown from meningitis, whilst a steward, named Ferrars, who sustained a fractured skull through a fall, also succumbed to his injuries. After leaving Capetown the vessel for five days encountered strong head winds and heavy seas, which greatly retarded her progress, but she subsequently made up a good deal of leeway, a speed of 15 knots at times being recorded. The night before arrival in Melbourne a highly successful dance was given on deck, whilst musical selections in the saloon contributed to one of the most harmonious functions ever held on the vessel.

In 1911 two new liners, *Themistocles* and *Demosthenes*, had entered service for the Aberdeen Line and to make *Miltiades* and *Marathon* better running mates for the new vessels, they were withdrawn for extensive reconstruction in 1912. They returned to the yard where they were built to be cut in two, and a new section 50ft/15m long constructed forward of the boiler room, increasing their length to 504 feet/151.2 m, and gross tonnage to 7,814 for *Miltiades* and 7,848 for *Marathon*. A dummy forward funnel was added, the first time a dummy funnel had been fitted on a British ship, and was used as a ventilator for third class accommodation.

Marathon was the first to be extended, after its arrival in London on 17 June 1912, the work taking just four months, so the ship was able to depart London again on 19 October. *Marathon* arrived back in Sydney again on 1 December 1912, and the *Sydney Morning Herald* reported:

Since the last occasion on which the steamer *Marathon* visited Australia, she has undergone considerable alteration. Her tonnage has been increased by about 1250 tons, making her 8,000 gross register, to effect which a modern operation in ship surgery has been carried out. The steamer had to be cut in half, just aft of the bridge, and a further 50 feet has been added to her length. Those who have travelled out in her speak in high terms of her seagoing qualities, while a second funnel somewhat enhances the appearance of the vessel, giving her yacht-like lines of striking beauty. Certain improvements have also been carried out on the internal arrangements, several notable features being added to the saloon accommodation. A very fine lounge has been furnished on the bridge deck, while on the same deck ladies and gentlemen's bathrooms have been fitted, in addition to some single-berth rooms. Additional single-berth rooms have also been erected on the awning deck, while on this deck several bibby-rooms - now so popular with travellers — have been arranged. A barber's shop is another improvement, and there have been minor additions to the third-class accommodation. The *Marathon*'s outward voyage has been most successful, the run from London to Sydney, including time spent at ports of call, occupied 43 days.

The rebuilding of *Miltiades* took longer than her sister. Having arrived at Plymouth on 27 August 1912, *Miltiades* did not depart London until 24 April 1913, arriving in Sydney on 9 June, and next day the *Daily Telegraph* gave an interesting account of the voyage:

The steamer *Miltiades*, of the Aberdeen Line, which arrived yesterday from London, was recently lengthened 50 feet, and the alterations have added considerably to her appearance. On arrival, the steamer berthed at Dalgety's wharf. The *Miltiades* left London at 2 pm, on April 24 and Plymouth at 4 pm the following day, with a total of 589 passengers. Moderate weather was experienced on the run to Teneriffe, which reached at 11 am on 30 April. A stay of 6 hours, for coal, enabled passengers to take a run ashore. The steamer left again at 5 pm, and fine weather was enjoyed for the rest of the run to within a few miles of Capetown, where a slight delay occurred owing to fog, the ship anchoring in Table Bay at 8 pm on May 14. Leaving again on the morning of the 16th, the weather encountered was very favourable for the time of year, the run across to Melbourne being made on the 40th parallel. The *Miltiades* was in constant touch by wireless with the *Corinthic*, to the southward, and *Saldanha* to the northward. Communication was also effected with Durban, for a distance of one thousand miles, and Fremantle at 1600 miles.

Marathon and *Miltiades* joined *Themistocles* and *Demosthenes*, with occasional sailings by the old *Moravian*, in providing one of the best migrant services

Marathon as rebuilt with two funnels.

from Britain to Australia. The route followed was from London and Plymouth to Teneriffe, then Cape Town, Albany, Adelaide, Melbourne and Sydney, with calls at Fremantle and Durban instead of Albany westbound.

In September 1914, *Miltiades* was taken over by the Australian Government when it arrived in local waters, and as troop transport A28 took part in the first convoy to take Australian and New Zealand troops overseas in the World War I.

In 1915 *Marathon* was taken over by the British Government and began service as a troopship. Both ships survived the war, and *Marathon* departed London on 15 November 1919 with Australian troops returning home. The vessel arrived at Albany on Christmas Day, then went on to Melbourne, berthing on 30 December, reaching Sydney on 6 January 1919.

Miltiades departed London on 21 December, also with returning troops, voyaging by way of South Africa to Fremantle, Adelaide and Melbourne before arriving in Sydney on 13 February 1919.

Both ships carried a number of first class passengers on their voyages back to Britain. *Marathon* was back in Sydney again on 10 June, when 200 troops disembarked, while *Miltiades* arrived on 8 August with 600 returning troops.

Marathon departed Sydney on 9 July to return to Britain, and as the voyage neared its end ran into a thick fog in the English Channel. A few minutes before midnight on 9 September the Japanese freighter *Heijin Maru* slammed into *Marathon*, and as water poured into the forward holds *Marathon* had to be beached near Dungeness to prevent it sinking. *Marathon* was refloated on 14 September, and limped to London for repairs.

Marathon made one more repatriation voyage to Australia, arriving in Sydney on 1 January 1920 with about 150 men on board, and a similar number of dependents. *Miltiades* also made a similar voyage to Australia, and on the return trip, which departed Sydney on 21 February 1920, carried third class passengers for the first time since the war.

Miltiades was the first to be handed back to its owners, and was given only a very basic refit before taking the first post-war Aberdeen Line sailing from London, on 4 June 1920, following the same route as had been operated in 1914, with the omission of the call at Adelaide. *Marathon* was the last Aberdeen liner to return to service, departing London on 21 October 1920.

This was also destined to be last voyage to Australia by *Marathon*, which was laid up on its return to Britain. *Miltiades* made a final departure from London with its second post-war sailing to Australia on 26 November 1920, then joined *Marathon* at the laying-up berth. The reason for this was the reluctance of the company to spend the large amounts of money that would be needed to upgrade the ships to a standard where they could compete with the large number of new ships that had been ordered for the Australian service after the war ended. They were also extremely expensive to operate, with their outmoded machinery, and their appearance made them look older than they were.

Marathon and *Miltiades* were offered for sale, and bought in 1922 by the Royal Mail Line, who intended to use them as reserve ships for the entire Kylsant Group, which included the Pacific Steam Navigation Company, and it was to this company that the pair were allocated. *Miltiades* was renamed *Orcana*, while *Marathon* became *Oruba*.

Orcana made a few voyages on the PSNC service from Liverpool to South America, but *Oruba* broke down at Rio de Janeiro while on its first voyage, and on returning to Britain was handed back to the parent company and laid up. *Orcana* was also laid up after only a short period of service. In 1924 *Oruba* was sold to German breakers, while *Orcana* was sold to a Dutch shipbreaking firm in the same year.

THE P&O M CLASS

MOLDAVIA   MONGOLIA
Built: 1903 by Caird & Co., Glasgow
Gross tonnage: 9,505
Dimensions: 545 x 58 ft/166.1 x 17.8 m
Service speed: 16 knots
Propulsion: Triple expansion/twin propellers

MARMORA   MACEDONIA
Built: 1903/1904 by Harland & Wolff, Belfast
Gross tonnage: 10,509/10,512
Dimensions: 564 x 60 ft/171.9 x 18.4 m
Service speed: 17 knots
Propulsion: Quadruple expansion/twin propellers

MOOLTAN
Built: 1905 by Caird & Co., Glasgow
Gross tonnage: 9,621
Dimensions: 545 x 58 ft/166.1 x 17.8 m
Service speed: 16 knots
Propulsion: Quadruple expansion/twin propellers

MOREA
Built: 1908 by Barclay, Curle & Co., Glasgow
Gross tonnage: 10,890
Dimensions: 562 x 61 ft/171.3 x 18.5 m
Service speed: 18 knots
Propulsion: Quadruple expansion/twin propellers

MALWA   MANTUA
Built: 1908/1909 by Caird & Co., Glasgow
Gross tonnage: 10,883/10,946
Dimensions: 560 x 61 ft/170.7 x 18.5 m
Service speed: 18 knots
Propulsion: Quadruple expansion/twin propellers

MALOJA
Built: 1911 by Harland & Wolff, Belfast
Gross tonnage: 12,431
Dimensions: 625 x 63 ft/173.7 x 19.1 m
Service speed: 18 knots
Propulsion: Quadruple expansion/twin propellers

MEDINA
Built: 1911 by Caird & Co., Greenock
Gross tonnage: 12,350
Dimensions: 625 x 63 ft/173.7 x 19.1 m
Service speed: 18 knots
Propulsion: Quadruple expansion/twin propellers

Between 1903 and 1912 P&O took delivery of five new ships for the Australian trade, all with names beginning with M. They were the first ships P&O built for this trade with two propellers, though an unusual feature of the first two was that the propellers overlapped, a setup not repeated in future vessels.

Four of the new ships were launched during 1903, the first being named *Moldavia* when launched on 28 March, and completed in August. *Moldavia* was sent to India on its maiden voyage, departing London on its first voyage to Australia on 11 December 1903, arriving in Melbourne on 19 January 1904 and Sydney on 22 January. The *Sydney Morning Herald* reported:

She has been fitted for the conveyance of 348 first class and 166 second class passengers. The arrangements in connection with the passengers' accommodation are in advance of anything hitherto attained in respect to comfort, roominess, light and ventilation. All the cabins are on the main, spar, hurricane and boat decks, and most of the

Mongolia

Macedonia

inside ones are lighted from the outside by a passageway to the scuttle.

The second ship, *Mongolia*, was launched on 13 August 1903, and completed in October. After a maiden voyage to India, *Mongolia* left Tilbury on 5 February 1904 on its first voyage to Australia.

Work on the two ships being built in Belfast had commenced simultaneously, and they were launched only two days apart, *Marmora* on 9 April 1903, followed by *Macedonia* on 11 April. *Marmora* was completed in seven months, and was sent on a voyage to Bombay during December 1903. *Marmora* then entered its designed route to Australia, departing Tilbury on 18 March 1904.

Macedonia was not handed over to P&O until January 1904, and also went to Bombay on a shakedown voyage before making its first departure for Australia from London on 29 April. They were the first P&O liners to exceed 10,000 tons, and had berths for 377 first class and 187 second class passengers,

Mooltan was launched on 3 August 1905, and unique in not having an exact sister, though very similar to *Moldavia* and *Mongolia*. The Caird-built ships could be distinguished from the Harland & Wolff ships by their thinner funnels. *Mooltan* was given quadruple-expansion machinery, but the accommodation was identical, 348 first class and 166 second class passengers, all in cabins located on or above main deck. Delivered to P&O in October 1905, *Mooltan* was sent to Bombay on its maiden voyage, and left Tilbury on 19 January 1906 on its first voyage to Australia.

The success of these ships resulted in the P&O

ordering three more of the same basic design, but slightly larger than its predecessors. *Morea* was the first to be launched, on 15 August 1908, being handed over to P&O in November and departing Tilbury on 4 December on its maiden voyage to Australia. *Malwa* was launched on 10 October 1908 and completed two months later. On 29 January *Malwa* left London on its maiden voyage to Australia.

The last was *Mantua*, launched on 20 February 1909 and making its maiden departure on the Australian trade on 4 June from Tilbury. These ships provided accommodation for 407 in first class and 200 in second class, while the crew numbered 307.

Morea could be distinguished from the other two by having thicker funnels, and was also the largest liner in the P&O fleet until 1911. *Malwa* had been in service for little more than a year when it was involved in a collision with the British steamer *Nairn* off Colombo, but fortunately did not suffer serious damage.

There were now eight M class liners maintaining the Australian service for P&O and soon afterward the class was completed with the delivery of the final two. This meant P&O could operate a two-weekly schedule using ships of similar design, and none more than nine years old, a situation they were to enjoy but briefly, and would never know again.

In October 1910 P&O began extending some voyages on their Australian service to Auckland. Between then and 1913, when the extension was abandoned, *Moldavia* made four visits to the New Zealand port, while *Mongolia*, *Morea*, *Mooltan* and *Mantua* each made two round trips to New Zealand.

Malwa

The final two M class ships were considerably larger than their predecessors, though of the same basic design. *Maloja* was launched in Belfast on 17 December 1910, and a description of the vessel appeared in the *Sydney Morning Herald* on 24 January 1911, as follows:

The vessel is a passenger and mail steamer of the highest class, and the largest vessel built for her owners...and in her construction and design will represent the latest and most approved practice. She has two steel pole-masts and two funnels, and ten watertight bulkheads carried up to the spar deck, and seven steel decks. The double bottom extends right fore and aft, the depth and strength being increased under the engine room, thus giving great rigidity to the structure.

The *Maloja* will have accommodation for over 450 first class and about 220 second class passengers, and the various public rooms and staterooms will be furnished and decorated in a style well in keeping with the traditions of the line. The first class dining saloon on the spar deck extends the full breadth of the ship, and will seat 318 people. The second class accommodation includes smoking room and music room. The dining saloon extends the whole breadth of the vessel, and will seat about 200.

Handed over to P&O on 9 September, *Maloja* made a short cruise to the Hebrides, and was then sent on a voyage to Bombay, carrying advance people preparing for the royal tour to India later that year, in which sister ship *Medina* would play a major role. *Maloja* entered the Australian service with a sailing from Tilbury on 9 February 1912, arriving in Sydney on 21 March. Next day the *Sydney Morning Herald* reported:

Though vessels as large as the Maloja have visited the port, none of them has been so completely fitted up. Accommodation is provided in the steamer for 458 first saloon and 212 second saloon. A feature of the Maloja is that the first saloon smoking room is placed on the promenade deck. The seating accommodation in the first saloon dining room is for 300 people. Second saloon passengers are accommodated aft. Their quarters are very comfortable and the smoking room and library are situated on the poop deck, which is used as a promenade.

Medina was launched on 14 March 1911 and completed as the Royal Yacht for the visit to India by King George V and Queen Mary. *Medina* was painted white with a blue riband around the hull, and yellow funnels, while an additional chartroom was constructed above the bridge and a third mast fitted behind the bridge. Private suites for the King and Queen were built into the area designed as the first class dining saloon. During the tour the ship was to be manned by officers and men from the Royal Navy. They were berthed in the second class cabins, while the second class dining room was converted into a wardroom for officers. For formal occasions, the ship also carried a party of one hundred Royal Marines.

One of the more unusual features was the provision of a huge tank filled with live fish from which the royal table would be supplied, and three cows from the King's own herd at Windsor were taken on board to supply fresh milk.

Medina was completed in October 1911. The royal party embarked at Portsmouth on 11 November, arriving in Bombay on 2 December, departing on 10

January 1912 for the return trip to Portsmouth, and docking there on 5 February 1912. The ship was then decommissioned, and handed back to P&O, being sent back to the Caird yard for completion to the original design, though a few of the royal tour cabins were retained and offered as special suites.

The conversion was completed late in May 1912, and on 28 June the vessel left Tilbury on its first voyage to Australia, arriving in Sydney on 8 August. An interesting sidelight to *Medina*'s maiden voyage to Australia of *Medina* was the fact that the senior radio operator for that trip was Harold Bride, who had been serving in a similar capacity on *Titanic* only four months previously. He had sent out distress calls until it was impossible to continue, and survived the sinking of the giant liner.

With the *Titanic* tragedy so fresh in the mind, an article on the arrival of *Medina* in Sydney that appeared in the *Sydney Morning Herald* on 9 August included the following:

An interesting feature about the Medina's life-saving equipment is that there are 24 lifeboats — eight more than were carried on the Titanic. These boats can accommodate 50 persons each, so that were the *Medina* fully taken up, and including 414 of a crew, there would still be room for 200 more people in the boats should the occasion arise.

The arrival of *Medina* in Australia marked the completion of the M class, and for the next two years they provided a balanced and profitable fleet for P&O.

However, only nine ships were needed to provide a schedule of two-weekly departures, so in 1913 *Mantua* became a full-time cruise ship from British ports, making summer trips to the Baltic and Norwegian fjords and in winter going south to the Atlantic islands and the Mediterranean.

When war came in 1914, P&O was forced to unite their Indian and Australian services, sending their ships by way of Bombay to Australia, with *Mooltan* making the first sailing from Tilbury on 7 August.

On 2 August 1914 *Mantua* was on a cruise to the Baltic, but was ordered to return to Britain immediately. *Mantua* made the voyage at high speed and without stopping, burning furniture and other fittings when the coal bunkers ran low. *Mantua* arrived back in Tilbury on August 5, and was immediately requisitioned for service as an armed merchant cruiser. The conversion work took only nine days, in which time eight 4.7 inch guns were fitted. Attached to the 10th Cruiser Squadron, *Mantua* was sent to patrol the waters north of Britain, and in 1915 was altered for service as a troopship, in which capacity it served for the rest of the war.

Marmora was taken over in August 1914 and *Macedonia* a month later. They were both converted into armed merchant cruisers, and *Marmora* also joined the 10th Cruiser Squadron, which consisted entirely of converted merchantmen which had the thankless task of patrolling the waters north of Britain searching for German blockade runners. *Macedonia* saw only brief service as an auxiliary cruiser, as in 1915 it became

Medina

a troopship, and in 1916 was bought outright by the Admiralty.

In October 1915 *Morea* was taken over and converted into a hospital ship, but only served six months in this role. In April 1916 she became a troopship, and in April 1917 was altered into an armed merchant cruiser, fitted with seven 6-inch guns and commissioned as HMS *Morea*.

In 1917 *Malwa* was requisitioned and converted into a troopship, and in 1918 was one of seven liners formed into a fast convoy to carry troops from Egypt to France.

It is ironic that the four liners retained by P&O all became victims of the war. *Maloja* left Tilbury on 26 February 1916 with 121 passengers on board, and the next day struck a mine off Dover in the English Channel. As the ship was listing heavily the engines could not be stopped, and it was still under way when it sank, with the loss of 122 passengers and crew.

During the first three years of the war vessels on commercial service usually travelled alone and maintained a regular schedule, but in 1917 the British Government established the Liner Requisition Scheme, whereby they controlled the movements of all British ships, concentrating them into convoys whenever possible.

1917 was a bad year for the M ships, three being lost while engaged on the Australian trade. On 28 April *Medina* was torpedoed and sunk off Start Point, shortly after leaving Plymouth, with six crew members being lost.

On 28 June 1917 *Mongolia* struck a mine off Bombay, and sank in just 13 minutes, with the loss of 23 lives.

Mooltan was proceeding from Egypt to Marseilles in company with the French vessel *Lotus,* escorted by two Japanese destroyers, when it was hit by a torpedo shortly after dawn on 26 July 1917. All 554 persons on board were saved, as was the mail, but it was not possible to tow the stricken vessel to safety because of the danger of another submarine attack, so it was abandoned to sink. This left P&O with no ships on their Australian service.

On 23 May 1918 *Moldavia* was torpedoed and sunk in the English Channel. At the time the vessel was employed ferrying American troops to Europe, and had a full complement of soldiers on board, fifty of whom lost their lives when the ship sank.

Marmora was the last M class ship to be lost in the war, being sunk off the Irish coast on 23 July 1918 by a torpedo fired from the German submarine *UB64*, with the loss of ten lives.

When the war ended, there were only four 'M' class ships still afloat, *Macedonia*, *Morea*, *Malwa* and *Mantua*.

Morea was returned to P&O early in 1919, and following a refit made the first post-war commercial sailing for P&O with a departure from Tilbury for Australia on 7 October 1919.

Mantua was also returned to the company in 1919 and, after being refitted by Vickers Armstrong at Barrow, resumed its place on the Australian trade on 3 January 1920.

Malwa was not released from military service until the end of 1919, and it was 24 September 1920 before the vessel left Tilbury on its first post-war voyage.

Morea made only six voyages to Australia after the war. *Malwa* and *Mantua* made several more, but by 1923 all three had been transferred to the service from London to Bombay and the Far East, their place on the Australian route being taken by new liners. They served the rest of their careers on this route. In June 1930 *Morea* was sold to shipbreakers in Japan. *Malwa* lasted a couple of years longer, but in December 1932 was also disposed of to Japanese shipbreakers.

Macedonia had been bought outright by the Admiralty in 1916, but was sold back to P&O in 1920. Following an extensive refit, the vessel returned to service on the route from London to Bombay, Singapore, Hong Kong and Japan, and was to give the company a further ten years service. *Macedonia* made only one more voyage to Australia, which departed from Tilbury on 24 November 1922. *Macedonia* then reverted to the Far East trade until being sold in 1931 to shipbreakers in Japan.

This left *Mantua* as the last survivor of the M liners, and it remained on the Far East service until May 1935, when it was sold to shipbreakers in Shanghai.

THE NDL BULOW CLASS

BULOW
Built: 1906 by Tecklenborg, Geestemunde

YORCK   KLEIST
Built: 1906/1907 by F. Schichau, Danzig

GOEBEN
Built: 1907 by AG Weser, Bremen

Gross tonnage: 9,028/8,901/8,950/8,792
Dimensions: 462 x 58ft/140.9 x 17.6 m
Service speed: 14 knots
Propulsion: Quadruple expansion/Twin propellers

Of the five ships of the Bulow class built for North German Lloyd, only the last of the series, *Lutzow*, did not appear in Australian waters. They had accommodation for about 100 first class, 110 second class and 1,400 third class passengers.

Bulow was launched on 21 April 1906, and after one voyage to the Far East left Bremerhaven in January 1907 on its first voyage to Australia. *Yorck*, which was launched on 10 April 1906, left Bremerhaven in February 1907 on the same route, and *Kleist* took the April sailing. In 1908 *Yorck* was transferred to the Far East trade.

Bulow and *Kleist* made more trips to Australia, but were also used on the Far East and Atlantic services. In June 1911 *Goeben* made her first voyage to Australia, but after only two round trips reverted to the Far East trade.

On 11 May 1913 *Kleist* made its final departure from Bremerhaven for Australia. *Bulow* left Bremerhaven on 13 July 1914 bound for Australia. When war became inevitable, *Bulow* turned back, and was interned in Portuguese waters.

At the end of July 1914, *Lutzow* left Bremerhaven for Australia, and when the war started tried to make its way back to Germany. Captured by British naval forces and renamed *Huntsend*, it served the British through the war.

In 1916 *Bulow* was seized by the Portuguese Government, and renamed *Tras-Os-Montes*. In 1927 the vessel was sold to a Portuguese shipping company, Cia Nacional. Renamed *Nyassa*, it survived until November 1951, when it was sold to British shipbreakers.

Yorck was at Tsingtao in China when war broke out, and escaped to Valparaiso, where it was interned, and later seized by the Chilean Government. *Kleist* and *Goeben* were in Germany and remained there throughout hostilities. At the end of the war *Kleist* was allocated to Japan in 1919 and renamed *Yoshina Maru*. This vessel was torpedoed and sunk by an American submarine in the North Pacific on 31 July 1944. *Goeben* went to the French, and in 1920 was purchased by Cie Générale Transatlantique. Renamed *Roussillon*, in 1920 it began operating between Havre and New York, transferring to the Bordeaux service in 1923. The vessel remained under the French flag until being sold to shipbreakers in February 1932.

In 1922 North German Lloyd bought *Yorck* back from the Chilean Government, and in 1924 *Lutzow* was bought back from the British Government, both being placed on the New York trade. At the end of 1932 they were both sold to shipbreakers at Danzig.

Kleist (WSS Victoria)

ASTURIAS

Built: 1908 by Harland & Wolff, Belfast
Gross tonnage: 12,002
Dimensions: 535 x 62 ft/163.1 x 19 m
Service speed: 16 knots
Propulsion: Quadruple expansion/Twin propellers

Built for the Royal Mail Line to operate to South America, *Asturias* was launched on 26 September 1907, and completed in January 1908. There was accommodation for 300 first, 140 second and 1,200 third class passengers, and at the time *Asturias* was the largest vessel in the Royal Mail Line fleet.

However, In 1906 Royal Mail Line had bought out the PSNC interest in Orient-Pacific Line, a joint service with the Orient Line to Australia, and to make a grand impression on this route it was decided to send *Asturias* to Australia on its maiden voyage.

Asturias left London for Australia on 24 January 1908, reaching Fremantle on 27 February, Adelaide on 2 March and Melbourne two days later. Unfortunately, *Asturias* proved to be slower than the contemporary vessels of the Orient and P&O lines, possibly due to poor quality coal taken on during the voyage, and was running four days behind schedule when it arrived in Sydney on 7 March, terminating the trip at Brisbane on 13 March. *Asturias* was the largest liner to have visited Australia up to that time, creating enormous interest at every port visited.

Asturias returned to Britain and joined the South American trade, but did make one more voyage to Australia. Departing London on 5 February 1909, this voyage went much more smoothly than the earlier trip. Passing through Fremantle on 11 March, *Asturias* stopped at Adelaide before berthing in Melbourne on 17 March, arriving in Sydney on 20 March, and Brisbane on 26 March. As before, *Asturias* was returned to the South American trade when it returned to Britain.

Asturias remained on the South American trade until being requisitioned for military service on 1 August 1914, and converted into a naval hospital ship. On 20 March 1917 *Asturias* was proceeding up the English Channel when a torpedo hit the stern, killing 35 men. The liner was beached near Bolt Head, where it was decided the ship was a total loss.

The British Government bought the wreck, and had it towed to Plymouth, where it remained for the next two years as an ammunition hulk. After the war Royal Mail repurchased their former liner, which was towed to Harland & Wolff at Belfast, rebuilt as a cruise ship, and renamed *Arcadian*.

Leaving Belfast on 3 June 1923, the first cruise was to Norway, followed by trips to the Mediterranean and West Indies, a pattern followed for the next eight years. In October 1930 *Arcadian* was laid up at Southampton, staying there until sold in February 1933 to shipbreakers in Japan.

Asturias

ARAWA

Built: 1907 by Swan, Hunter & Wigham Richardson, Newcastle
Gross tonnage: 9,372 gross
Dimensions: 460 x 60 ft/140.2 x 18.3 m
Service speed: 14 knots
Propulsion: Triple expansion/twin propellers

The second ship of the name to be built for Shaw Savill, *Arawa* was launched on 29 November 1906. *Arawa* had accommodation for 44 first class, 70 second class and 200 third class passengers, but a large number of migrants could also be carried in temporary accommodation in the 'tween decks. First class was situated in the superstructure midships, with second class also midships on the shelter deck, and third class aft on lower decks. On 22 August 1907 *Arawa* departed London, going via Cape Town to New Zealand, returning around Cape Horn with calls at Rio de Janeiro and Montevideo.

In 1909 *Arawa* dropped her starboard propeller shortly after leaving Cape Town outward bound, but continued on to New Zealand on the port one only.

In August 1914 *Arawa* was in Lyttelton when war broke out, and was requisitioned by the New Zealand Government, designated HMNZT10. After boarding troops, *Arawa* went to Albany where the first convoy of Australian and New Zealand troops was being assembled. The troops were carried to Egypt, and after they had disembarked *Arawa* continued on to Britain. The vessel was then put back on its regular service for the next two years, but in 1916 the route was changed to transit the Panama Canal in both directions, and this marked the end of the round-the-world service.

In 1917 *Arawa* came under the Shipping Controller, but still remained on its usual service. *Arawa* remained under the Shipping Controller until 1921, when it was handed back to Shaw Savill.

The New Zealand and British Governments started a migrant scheme in 1926 that resulted in a passenger boom on the route, and *Arawa* was converted into a cabin class ship to operate a secondary service from Liverpool to New Zealand.

In 1928 *Arawa* was sold to the Arnold Bernstein company and used as a cargo ship across the Atlantic between Antwerp and New York, being renamed *Konigstein*.

In 1931 *Konigstein* was refitted for passenger service once again, its external appearance being altered by the construction of a deck house forward from the superstructure over No. 3 hold, to contain a lounge, with an observation deck on top. The ship continued to operate from Antwerp to New York, carrying amongst the passengers large numbers of German Jews escaping from Nazi tyranny.

In 1937 *Konigstein* was sold to the Belgian shipping company, Cia Maritime Belge, renamed *Gandia*, and placed on a service from Antwerp to West Africa. On 22 January 1942 *Gandia* was torpedoed and sunk by a German submarine in the North Atlantic.

Arawa

TAINUI

Built: 1908 by Workman & Clark, Belfast
Gross tonnage: 9,957
Dimensions: 478 x 61 ft/145.7 x 18.6 m
Service speed: 14 knots
Propulsion: Triple expansion/twin propellers

Built for Shaw Savill & Albion *Tainui* was launched on 1 September 1908, and left London on 12 November 1908 on its maiden voyage to Cape Town, then Hobart and on to Wellington, the return voyage being around Cape Horn. Accommodation was provided for 40 first class, 74 second class and 300 third class passengers, while a large number of migrants could be carried in temporary accommodation in the 'tween decks.

On 22 April 1911, the *Sydney Morning Herald*, reported on the arrival of the first group of 'Dreadnought Boys' in Australia:

> The scheme devised by the executive committee of the Dreadnought Fund for obtaining boys from England, and training them to Agricultural pursuits, has received practical application in so far that 12 fine strapping young fellows have reached Sydney, and have received a very cordial welcome.
>
> The boys were passengers by the steamship *Tainui* from London to Hobart, which port they reached on 12th inst. From Hobart they came along in the *Paloona*, which arrived in Sydney at half-past 10 o'clock on Thursday night, and were met and welcomed by officers of the Immigration Bureau.

In May 1913 *Tainui* was damaged in a collision with the steamship *Inca* in the English Channel, and had to miss its next voyage for repairs.

In the war *Tainui* remained on the New Zealand trade, though under Government control, and in 1916 began using the Panama Canal on both outward and homeward voyages. On 8 April 1918 *Tainui* was torpedoed by a German submarine in the approaches to the English Channel. At first it was thought the ship was sinking, being abandoned by passengers and crew, but when it remained afloat, Captain R. A. Kelly and the crew returned aboard, and nursed the ship stern first the 130 miles (200 km) to Falmouth where it was beached.

After repairs *Tainui* returned to service, still under Government control, and was not released until 1921. Following a refit the vessel returned to the New Zealand trade. Passengers were now embarked at Southampton, though cargo continued to be worked at London. For some time in the twenties the migrant boom returned to the New Zealand trade, but as the thirties began demand for migrant passages declined, and *Tainui* was altered to carry 200 passengers in one class. On 25 November 1938 the vessel left Southampton on its final voyage to New Zealand, and during the following year was sold to British shipbreakers.

They had not started dismantling the ship when World War II broke out, so *Tainui* was purchased by the Ministry of Transport, renamed *Empire Trader*, and put back on the New Zealand trade as a cargo ship, being managed by Shaw Savill Line. On 21 February 1943 the old ship was torpedoed by a German submarine in the North Atlantic, and sank.

Tainui

PERICLES

Built: 1908 by Harland & Wolff, Belfast
Gross tonnage: 10,925
Dimensions: 518 x 62 ft/157.9 x 19 m
Service speed: 14 knots
Propulsion: Quadruple expansion/twin propellers

Launched on 21 December 1907, *Pericles* ran trials on 6 June 1908, and left London on 8 July, going first to Plymouth, then Teneriffe and Cape Town, Fremantle, Melbourne, Sydney and Brisbane.

The 100 first class passengers were carried in excellent conditions, *Pericles* being the most luxurious ship on the service to Australia via South Africa, while facilities for 250 third class passengers were also of a very high standard. Extra temporary berths could be installed in the holds on the outbound voyage for carrying several hundred migrants.

Pericles arrived in Sydney for the first time on 24 August 1908, and that morning the *Sydney Morning Herald* carried a report on the new liner under the headline 'A Floating Palace', which included a special mention of the safety features of the hull:

The arrival at Sydney at daybreak this morning of the new Aberdeen twin-screw liner *Pericles*, of 11,000 tons, on her maiden voyage from London will mark an important epoch in the rapid development of our overseas shipping trade. She is the largest vessel engaged in carrying saloon passengers between England and Australia by the Cape route, and is the first vessel specially built for this trade to be equipped with receivers for submarine signalling. The *Pericles* was launched from the yard of Harland & Wolff on December 21 last year, and has been constructed under Lloyd's survey for the 100 A1 class. She also conforms to the Admiralty Transportation Department and Board of Trade passenger regulations, and, generally speaking, her scantlings and fittings are considerably beyond the utmost requirements of these bodies.

The one feature of the *Pericles* which will probably cause disappointment amongst those who have watched the progress of the line is her straight stem, which takes the place of the graceful clipper bows for which the Aberdeen liners, both sail and steam, have for so many years been famous. The new steamer is 500 ft long and 62 ft in beam, and although her great size ensures her being very comfortable even in heavy seas, additional precautions have been taken against rolling by fitting bilge keels. Her motive power is provided by two sets of quadruple expansion engines, balanced so as to prevent any vibration, and of ample power to ensure regular adherence to timetable dates. The *Pericles* is constructed on the cellular double-bottom principle, the double-bottom extending the whole length of the ship, and is divided by eight watertight compartments, thus providing ample safety even in the event of a serious collision.

No less than four decks are utilised for the accommodation of saloon passengers, although only 100 are carried. The dining saloon, which is on the main deck, is a broad spacious apartment extending the full width of the ship. Large portholes are fitted for light and ventilation, while an auxiliary arrangement of fans is also provided in order to ensure comfort and fresh air in all weathers. Following the company's invariable custom, there is sufficient seating accommodation for all passengers to dine at one sitting, even when the steamer is full, but a new feature has been introduced in entirely eliminating large tables, replacing them with small ones on the restaurant principle, which is now becoming popular.

The predominating colour of the carpet and upholstery is crimson, and the floor polished oak parquetry. The walls are of carved white panelling, relieved with gold, and with a dado of oak, and the ceiling is white. The saloon, library and lounge are situated at the forward end of the bridge deck, and are divided by a handsome glass screen, each room having a separate entrance. The library is fitted up as a reading and writing room, and is reserved for non-smokers. The lounge is also sumptuously furnished, and in it smoking is permitted.

The first class smoking room, which, like all other public rooms on this steamer, is of very large size, is placed at the after end of the bridge deckhouse. The smoking room, library and lounge, and deck cabins are all fitted with Messrs Harland & Wolff's type of open square windows, which afford a great amount of light and ventilation. The first class staterooms are situated on the awning and bridge decks. Those on the awning deck are mostly arranged on the popular tandem principle; so that there are no inside rooms, each stateroom having direct light and ventilation from the outside. The staterooms in the deckhouse on the bridge deck are also all outside rooms, and are particularly light and airy, being nearly 10 ft in height, beam to beam. All the rooms are fitted with wardrobes, and contain one, two and three berths, and a feature which will appeal to travellers is the roominess of the cabins.

An account of the *Pericles,* however, would be far from complete unless mention were made of the exceptionally comfortable third class accommodation, which surpasses anything of the description in the trade. In this class there is accommodation for 250 passengers. The general room, smoking room and dining room are comfortably fitted up. All the cabins are enclosed, and are provided with wash basin, electric light etc, and the large number of rooms arranged for two or four passengers will prove an acceptable feature of the ship. The third class cabins are all on the main deck, immediately aft of the dining room, which extends the whole width of the steamer. The smoking room and general room are on the awning deck. Whilst preserving all the best characteristics of their earlier vessels, and retaining the single berth cabin ——which they were the first to use in the Australian-South African trade

— the Aberdeen Line owners have, in the shelter deck, tandem cabins, lounge, and small dining tables, again led the van.

The size and appearance of the *Pericles* created much interest, and next day the *Sydney Morning Herald* noted:

Interest along the waterfront yesterday was centred in the mammoth 11,000 ton twin-screw Aberdeen liner *Pericles*, which arrived early in the morning on her maiden voyage from London, via Capetown. The great beam of the *Pericles* seemed to take everybody's fancy, and the noble commanding appearance of the great liner called forth many expressions of admiration.

Glancing at the Pericles from the wharf, she appeared to tower right over the 12,000 ton White Star liner *Persic*, berthed alongside. She is probably the most lofty vessel that has visited this port, for the distance from the waterline to the chart room is no less than 66 ft ——the height of a four storey house. The exact gross tonnage of the Pericles is 10,925, and her net tonnage is 6,898, and her deadweight carrying capacity 11,200 tons. If called upon at any time to act as a transport the *Pericles* can accommodate between 3,000 and 4,000 troops in the fore 'tween decks. The officers and crew of the *Pericles* number 167 all told.

Captain Alex Scott, who commands the new liner, is the commodore of the fleet, and has for 43½ years been in the service of the company. With the arrival of the Pericles yesterday he completed his 77th voyage between England and Australia.

Pericles quickly gained acceptance with passengers and seemed set for a long and successful career. This was not to happen, unfortunately, as within two years of entering service this fine ship would be lost. *Pericles* departed London on 15 January 1910 on its fifth voyage to Australia, and on 14 March 1910 sailed from Brisbane at the start of the voyage back to Britain, leaving Sydney on 18 March, Hobart on the 22nd and Melbourne on 24 March.

When *Pericles* left Melbourne there were over 200 passengers on board, and a mixed cargo that included 30,000 boxes of butter, 6,000 bales of wool, 900 tons of tallow, 300 tons of copra, 600 tons of lead, 40,000 carcases of meat, 36,000 cases of apples, 500 tons of wheat and 1,250 crates of rabbits. There were also 91 bags of mail, all destined for South Africa.

Crossing the Great Australian Bight the vessel encountered heavy weather for several days, but as it approached the west coast the weather moderated, and on 31 March it was fine and sunny as *Pericles* neared Cape Leeuwin on the way to Fremantle.

At 3.30 in the afternoon *Pericles* gave a sudden lurch to starboard when about six miles off Cape Leeuwin. Almost immediately the ship came upright, but then began to list to port quickly, and the bow began to sink. Apparently the vessel had hit an uncharted rock, and the damage caused to the bottom must have been enormous.

At first the master tried to beach his stricken vessel, but water was now pouring into the ship, and it was abandoned by passengers and crew within half an hour, without casualties. Two and a half hours after the first jolt, *Pericles* went to the bottom, bow first.

Fortunately the keeper of the Cape Leeuwin Lighthouse witnessed the whole incident, and was able to raise the alarm. The coastal steamer *Monaro*, owned by the Melbourne Steam Ship Co., was berthed at Bunbury, and left that port to go to the scene of the sinking, rescuing all the survivors from lifeboats, taking them back to Bunbury. The next day, *Monaro* left Bunbury with the survivors still on board and carried them to Fremantle, where they arrived on the afternoon of 2 April.

Pericles

WARATAH

Built: 1908 by Barclay, Curie & Co., Glasgow
Gross tonnage: 9,359.
Dimensions: 480 x 59 ft/146.3 x 18 m
Speed: 13.5 knots.
Propulsion: Quadruple expansion/Twin propellers

In this day and age it seems inconceivable that a brand new passenger liner could vanish completely, leaving no trace, but such was the fate of *Waratah*. Built for the Blue Anchor Line, *Waratah* was launched on 12 September 1908 and on trials reached 15 knots, being delivered to the owners on 23 October

Permanent accommodation was provided for 128 first class and 300 third class passengers, with first class being located on the upper decks of the superstructure, having very comfortable and roomy facilities. On southbound voyages 400 migrants could be carried in temporary berths erected in the holds.

Waratah departed London on 5 November on its maiden voyage, carrying 67 first class and 689 third class and migrants. The vessel was under the command of Captain Josiah Ilbery, now aged 68 and the commodore of the Blue Anchor Line fleet. Going by way of Cape Town to Adelaide and Melbourne, *Waratah* arrived in Sydney on 24 December. That day the *Sydney Morning Herald* reported:

At daylight today the new steamer *Waratah* of 9,300 tons — the latest addition to Lund's Blue Anchor fleet — will arrive at Sydney on her maiden voyage from London, via Capetown, with a record number of passengers in both classes. On arrival she will berth at the Central Wharf at Miller's Point.

The *Waratah* is classed 100A1 at Lloyds. She is divided into seven watertight compartments, and has a cellular double bottom extending practically the full length. In order to ensure the greatest amount of comfort in heavy seas the vessel is fitted with bilge keels, as are all the other ships of the fleet.

The new vessel caters for the conveyance of first and third class passengers. No first saloon cabins are situated lower than the bridge deck, so that passengers are able at practically all times to have their cabin ports or windows open.

On this deck there are 24 cabins, each containing two sleeping berths and a long sofa, fitted with a spring mattress, and there are also two exceptionally large four-berth cabins each with a sofa in addition, suitable for families. At the forward end of the bridge deck is placed the dining saloon, which is a fine apartment capable of seating 100 passengers, and a large number of the tables are arranged on the restaurant system.

Next to the family cabins on this deck is a good-sized nursery, so that for the first time on steamers trading to Australia, via South Africa, the children will have a place of their own. At the after end of the bridge deck, accessible to both first and third class passengers, is the doctor's surgery and the purser's office. Ascending to the promenade deck there is a large lobby, at the forward end of which is the drawing room, containing piano, four writing tables, and lounges. This room is lighted by means of large square windows and a dome from the boat deck above, which runs through to the dining saloon below.

Right at the after end of this deck is a recessed deck lounge, fitted with tables, and here passengers obtain perfect shelter whilst at the same time being able to sit out in the open.

On the after end of the boat deck is a spacious smoking room, panelled in oak, with skylight overhead, and containing writing and card tables, and a bar. Outside this room is another open air lounge with tables.

The forward end of the boat deck is reserved for passengers, in addition to the promenade deck. On this deck are also arranged the captain's and navigating officer's cabins, and above is the navigating bridge, at a height of about 50ft above sea level.

Every saloon cabin for more than one passenger contains a chest of drawers, a large wardrobe for ladies' dresses, in addition to patent wash-basin, boot locker, and drawers underneath the sofas.

Waratah

In the after part, situated on the upper and main decks, is accommodation for 300 third-class passengers, in cabins arranged with two, four, six and eight berths. On a the upper deck is a comfortable dining saloon extending the full breadth of the vessel, fitted with revolving chairs, and at the after end of the deck and completely shut off from the cabins are five bathrooms and lavatory accommodation.

Above the upper deck is a promenade reserved exclusively for third-class passengers, and a further promenade is provided on the boat deck overhead. Also on the promenade deck are found the smoking room and ladies lounge. A piano is fitted in the dining room for use of third-class passengers.

The *Waratah* is fitted with ample hospital accommodation. Two or more stewardesses are carried to attend to the requirements of ladies. The ship is lighted by electricity throughout, and all saloon cabins and public apartments are fitted with electric bells.

The steamer is fitted with two sets of quadruple expansion engines, balanced to ensure little or no vibration. They are of great power, capable of driving the ship at a high speed. The most up-to-date refrigerating plant is fitted, so that all on board are provided with fresh provisions, vegetables, fruit etc throughout the voyage.

On the return leg of its maiden voyage *Waratah* left Sydney on 9 January, spending several days loading cargo in Melbourne before departing on 15 January for Adelaide, from where the vessel sailed on 20 January. *Waratah* steamed directly to Durban, made a call at Cape Town, then went non-stop to London, arriving on 8 March.

When *Waratah* returned to London a few in the crew said that the ship seemed to be top heavy, while others spoke about it having a tendency to maintain a permanent list. However the captain pronounced himself satisfied with the ship, except that it should not be moved in dock without ballast aboard.

Waratah departed London on 27 April 1909 on its second voyage to Australia, arriving in Sydney on 17 June. Again Captain Ilbery was in command, and it was reported he had said this would be his last voyage before retiring. The vessel left Sydney on 26 June and Melbourne on 1 July on the return leg. On 25 July *Waratah* berthed at Durban were some passengers disembarked and cargo was off-loaded. Passenger, Mr C. G. Sawyer, booked to London, left the ship in Durban, claiming it hung badly when rolling. *Waratah* took on coal and more passengers before sailing on the evening of 26 July, having on board 119 crew, 92 passengers and 6,500 tons of cargo.

On the first day out from Durban *Waratah* ran into a full gale, and was sighted in the morning by the British cargo ship *Clan Macintyre*. *Waratah* forged ahead and disappeared into the murky weather.

When *Waratah* did not arrive in Cape Town on 29 July, there was no immediate concern, it being thought the vessel had slowed up, but the next day anxiety began to mount. The arrival of *Clan Macintyre* with its sighting report created major concern, and on 31 July a tug was sent from Cape Town to search for the missing ship, which was presumed to have broken down. A tug and two British cruisers were also sent from Durban to search.

The Australian Government and the underwriters jointly chartered the Union-Castle ship *Sabine*, which left Cape Town on 11 September, but sighted nothing and returned on 7 December. On 15 December *Waratah* was officially posted missing at Lloyds, but in Australia funds were raised for another search. On 10 February 1910 the steamer *Wakefield* left Melbourne for Durban, and spent three months searching, but found nothing.

An inquiry into the loss of the *Waratah* opened in London late in 1910, and on 13 January 1911 the *Sydney Morning Herald* carried a report from London dated 11 January:

At the Board of Trade inquiry into the loss of the steamer *Waratah* today Captain Bidwell, Marine Superintendent for Wilhelm Lund and Son, gave evidence that after the first voyage of the *Waratah* the captain and officers eulogised the *Waratah* and made no complaint. The witness said he did not remember telling Messrs Lund that the Waratah was less stable than the *Geelong*. Witness added that Captain Ilbery treated the rumours on the subject among the clerks in the employ of Wilhelm Lund and Sons as idle talk.

Admiral Davis quoted a letter of the chief engineer, Mr Hodder, informing Mr Shanks, engineer superintendent for Wilhelm Lund and Sons, of the difficulty about coaling the *Waratah* in Sydney, and of his compelling the captain to stop coaling twice because he was afraid of the possible list. The witness replied: 'Captain Ilbery told me nothing of this.'

Captain Bidwell was unable to explain why the ballast tanks were full on the first voyage, and left empty on the second voyage homeward to Durban. The deposition of Latimer, tally clerk at Sydney, giving the opinion of the second officer, that the *Waratah* had a deck too many, and of the Sydney pilots informing Captain Ilbery that the vessel was tender, together with the depositions of Lusakin, a steward, that the boatswain told him that the lifeboats were the most awful he had ever seen, were read.

Saunders, a stowaway, said that the behaviour of the *Waratah* scared him. He believed she was bound to topple over in a squall.

In the end the inquiry could determine no reason for the tragedy, which remains one of the great mysteries of the sea.

THE ORSOVA CLASS

ORSOVA
Built: 1909 by John Brown, Clydebank

OTWAY
Built: 1909 by Fairfield, Glasgow

OSTERLEY
Built: 1909 by London & Glasgow SB Co., Glasgow

Gross tonnage: 12,036/12,077/12,129
Dimensions: 553 x 63 ft/168.5 x 19.3 m
Service speed: 18 knots
Propulsion: Quadruple expansion/twin propellers

OTRANTO   ORVIETO
Built: 1909 by Workman, Clark & Co., Belfast
Gross tonnage: 12,124/12,133
Dimensions: 554 x 64 ft/168.8 x 19.5 m
Service speed: 18 knots
Propulsion: Quadruple expansion/twin propellers

The Royal Mail Line purchased the Australian service of the PSNC in 1906, and the following year the mail contract with the British Government from 1910 came up for tender. The current contract was shared between P&O Line and the Orient Line, with the PSNC not included despite their joint service with the Orient Line. However, the Royal Mail Line wanted to obtain a share of the contract, and subsequent subsidies, so they submitted a share tender. When the new mail contract was once again awarded jointly to P&O and the Orient Line, being signed on 15 November 1907 to become effective in February 1910, the Royal Mail Line gave notice they intended to withdraw from the Australian trade in May 1909.

Meanwhile the Orient Line was making preparations to meet the terms of the new mail contract, the most important clause requiring them to provide five new vessels on the service prior to commencement, with a sixth vessel to be added within eighteen months, and a seventh within six years.

The Orient Line drew up plans for the first five ships within months of signing the contract. They were to be built in two groups. The first group of three ships would all be built on the Clyde, though at different yards, while the other two, of a slightly different design would come from the Workman & Clark yard at Belfast.

The first to be launched was *Orsova*, which entered the water on 7 November 1908, being followed two weeks later by *Otway* on 21 November, the last of the trio, *Osterley,* being launched on 26 January 1909. *Orsova* completed trials on 20 May 1909 and made its maiden departure from Tilbury on 25 June, going by way of the Suez Canal to Fremantle, Adelaide, Melbourne and Sydney, where it arrived on 7 August, and on to Brisbane, returning to Britain by the same route.

Otway was delivered to the Orient Line on 29 May, and left Tilbury on its maiden voyage on 9 July, while *Osterley* was handed over on 22 June, and made its first departure on 6 August, arriving in Sydney on 19 September.

Next day the *Sydney Morning Herald*, in a report on the *Osterley*, noted:

On June 18 she ran a series of progressive trials over the

Otway

Otranto

measured mile, beginning at a speed of 13 knots, and working up to 14, 15½, 16¾ and 17½ knots. After these trials she ran a double run over the mile at full speed. On this run the maximum speed obtained was 19¼ knots, the mean of the two runs being 18¾ knots. The indicated horsepower was 13,790, and the mean of revolutions, 93.9. The stopping trials, which followed, showed that when running at 14 knots the vessel could be brought from full speed ahead to full speed astern within twice her own length within two minutes.

Orsova, *Otway* and *Osterley* each carried some 270 first class, 120 second class and 660 third class passengers, and introduced the Admiralty-type funnel tops that were to become a trademark of Orient Line ships built up to the late 1930s.

The final two ships were distinguishable from the initial trio in having a much squarer superstructure and the bridge was one deck higher. *Otranto* was the first to be launched, on 27 March 1909; *Orvieto* was launched on 6 July the same year. In late July 1909 *Otranto* ran trials, and a description of the vessel appeared in the *Sydney Morning Herald* on 10 August:

The *Otranto*, the first of two steamers built by Messrs Workman, Clark and Co. of Belfast for the Orient Company's mail service with Australia, was last month taken on her speed trials. The vessel, which has a gross register of 12,000 tons, has accommodation for 400 first class, 140 second class and 400 third class passengers, as well as for 450 emigrants.

The first class dining saloon, a noble apartment on the upper deck, has its tables arranged on the restaurant system. The walls are beautifully panelled in light French grey oak, whilst the ceiling is delicately moulded and decorated in white and gold. Conveniently placed is a nursery, which may be best described as a miniature saloon devoted to the use of the children.

The lounge and music room are two impressive and lofty apartments situated in the forward deck house. A distinguishing feature is the large bow windows, which command uninterrupted views over the sea. The decorations are in the Georgian style, the walls being panelled and relieved with carved columns, mirrors and tapestries. The furniture consists of reproductions of some of the finest models of the eighteenth century. In the lounge the decorations and furniture are of Italian walnut, whilst in the music room they are of satinwood. An electric hoist for conveying passengers to the dining saloon corridor is approached from the lounge.

The smoking room, a room of lofty proportions, is situated at the after end of the promenade deck. The arrangements are such that small parties of friends can enjoy privacy, whilst writing tables and chairs are placed conveniently near the windows. At the end of the room a bar has been fitted up. Doors at the after end lead to a sheltered alcove, furnished with tables and chairs, where a comfortable lounge can be enjoyed in the open air.

A feature of the vessel's arrangement is in respect of the galleys. The first and second class galleys are in one compartment on the upper deck, the first class pantry opening off the fore end and the second class pantry off the after end. The ship has a fully equipped laundry on board, and is heated throughout. The ventilation of all parts of the vessel has been carefully considered with a view of securing the comfort of passengers while the vessel is passing through tropical waters. The propelling machinery consists of two independent sets of quadruple-expansion engines. On the trial run the vessel behaved in an eminently satisfactory manner, attaining a mean speed of 18.95 knots.

On 1 October 1909 *Otranto* left London on its maiden voyage to Australia. The *Sydney Morning Herald* on 13 November 1909 reported:

The RMS *Otranto*, the fourth of the Orient Company's new 12,000-ton mail steamers, is due this morning, and will berth at 7am alongside the Orient Company's wharf at Circular Quay. She left London with a record number of passengers in all classes, and arrives in Sydney with 1,000 passengers, and a crew of 350, which is the record of any ship to Australia.

Orvieto made its maiden departure from Tilbury on 26 November 1909, arriving in Sydney on 9 January 1910. Accommodation on the second pair differed slightly from the Clyde-built ships, providing berths for 235 first class, 186 second class and 696 third class passengers.

The route followed by the ships went through the Mediterranean, with a call at Naples, and the Suez Canal, stopping at Aden and Colombo before arriving in Fremantle, then continuing to Adelaide, Melbourne, Sydney and Brisbane.

On 5 January 1912, *Otway* departed Tilbury on a voyage to Australia, and for the first time included a stop at the port of Toulon, in southern France, which would subsequently become a regular port of call for the Orient Line. The voyage was described in the *Sydney Morning Herald* on 13 February as:

having been of a most enjoyable nature, and since practically a full list of passengers had been carried in all classes, sports, games, and evening entertainments have been on an unusually large scale, and were gone through in a most hearty manner. Dances or concerts have taken place in all classes on almost every evening since the ship entered the Mediterranean, and two highly successful fancy dress balls were held.

However, on 12 February 1912, *Otway* dropped its starboard propeller when approaching Port Phillip Heads from Adelaide. On 13 February the *Sydney Morning Herald* reported:

How the accident happened can only be conjectured, but it is believed that the propeller, with its four big blades intact, snapped as the vessel was in the act of going astern when about to pick up the pilot four miles outside Port Phillip Heads, at half past 2 o'clock this morning. Her officers are positive that she did not strike any obstruction. In consequence of the accident, and having to proceed with only one propeller at slower speed than usual, the vessel will leave for Sydney at 10 am tomorrow, instead of 3 pm, as originally arranged.

The voyage was terminated at Sydney, and *Otway* was laid up while a new propeller could be cast. To avoid disruption to schedules, the ship following from Britain, *Orvieto*, terminated in Sydney, and departed for

London on 3 March, only three days later than *Otway* had been due to leave. *Otway* entered Woolwich Dock on 21 February to have the new propeller fitted, the tail shaft repaired and the hull cleaned and painted, being refloated on 10 March. *Otway* then took the departure originally scheduled for *Orvieto* back to Britain.

Orvieto was requisitioned by the Australian Government when it arrived in Brisbane on 17 August 1914 on a voyage from Britain, and became troopship A3. Accommodation was installed for 209 officers and 1,425 other ranks, and the vessel became the Commodore ship for the first convoy to leave Australia in World War I. After embarking troops in Melbourne, *Orvieto* proceeded to King George Sound, near Albany in Western Australia, from where the convoy departed on 1 November 1914. The troops disembarked in Egypt, then the vessel continued to Britain, and began carrying British troops.

Orvieto served as a troopship until March 1915, when it was converted into minelayer, and served in this capacity until January 1916, then became an armed merchant cruiser and was attached to the 10th Cruiser Squadron, which patrolled the waters to the north of Scotland.

Otranto becoming an armed merchant cruiser, while *Otranto* was attached to the South Atlantic Squadron, which was mainly composed of warships, and on 1 November 1914 the Squadron encountered the German Far Eastern Squadron, which consisted of five cruisers under the overall command of Admiral von Spee. The ensuing battle would go down in history as the Battle of Coronel, during which two British cruisers were sunk, but *Otranto* was able to avoid the major conflict, and at nightfall made good its escape from the vastly superior enemy ships. The British soon realised the folly of combining warships and converted merchantmen in the same formations, and *Otranto* was reassigned to convoy escort duty.

Otway had departed London on 31 July 1914 on the last pre-war sailing to Australia, leaving Sydney on 26 September to return to Britain. In December 1914 *Otway* was taken over for service as an armed merchant cruiser, joining *Orvieto* in the 10th Cruiser Squadron.

On 7 May 1915 *Orsova* left London carrying British troops for Malta, Mudros and Alexandria, then continued on to Australia, where it was taken over by the Australian Government in July 1915. Designated Australian troopship A67, and fitted out to carry 217 officers and 1,328 other ranks, *Orsova* left Sydney on 14 July with a full complement of Australian troops, bound for Britain.

Orsova made two more trips carrying Australian troops to Britain before voyaging to the Persian Gulf, then made another voyage to Australia to collect troops. As this voyage was nearing its end, *Orsova* was in the vicinity of the Eddystone Lighthouse when, on the afternoon of 14 March 1917 the vessel was struck by a torpedo fired by a U-boat. The missile struck on the port side at the engine room, killing six men instantly, and putting the port engine out of action, but fortunately the starboard engine continued to operate, and with brilliant seamanship the crippled vessel was beached at Cawsand Bay, near Plymouth, later to be towed to Devonport Naval Dockyard.

Once temporary repairs had been completed *Orsova* steamed to Liverpool for permanent repairs. At that time priority was being given to naval ships, so it was not until September 1918 that *Orsova* was ready to return to service, still as a troopship.

In June 1917 *Osterley* was requisitioned for trooping duties, leaving the Orient Line with no ships, and their Australian service was suspended.

On 22 July 1917 *Otway* was torpedoed by *UC49* while patrolling in the Minch, north-west of the island of St Kilda. The explosion killed ten ratings instantly, and the port propeller shaft was broken. The survivors abandoned the ship in lifeboats, and two hours after the torpedo hit, *Otway* sank.

Meanwhile *Otranto* was continuing its escort work in the North Atlantic, and also carrying troops from America to Europe. *Otranto* was in a convoy travelling from New York to Britain when, on 6 October 1918, in gale-force winds and huge seas, the P&O liner *Kashmir* collided with her amidships on the port side.

Otranto was almost cut in half by the force of the collision, and in the subsequent abandonment of the stricken vessel, 431 men lost their lives, among them 335 American soldiers. *Otranto* remained afloat, and drifted ashore on the island of Islay, in the Irish Sea, where it was soon smashed to pieces by the huge waves, and became a total loss.

Orsova, *Osterley* and *Orvieto* survived the war, and *Osterley* left Liverpool on 10 January 1919 carrying 977 Australian troops and their dependants to various ports as far as Brisbane. On returning to Britain in May the vessel was released from Government control.

Osterley departed London on 27 September 1919 on its first post-war commercial voyage to Australia, to reopen the Orient Line service.

Orsova made two voyages to Australia after the war, repatriating Australian troops, before being returned to the Orient Line on 12 May, and refitted. *Orvieto*, handed back to Orient Line earlier in 1919, made its first post-war departure from London on 1 November 1919, followed on 22 November by *Orsova*.

As soon as possible after the war the Orient Line placed orders for five new ships which would be improved versions of the Orsova class, but it was 1924 before the first of them entered service, and late in 1929 before the last member of the new quintet was completed.

Osterley left London on its final voyage to Australia on August 1929, being sold in March 1930 to the Glasgow shipbreaking firm of P. & W. MacLellan. On 30 August 1930 *Orvieto* left London on its final voyage, being sold to British shipbreakers in March 1931.

Surprisingly, the pioneer vessel of the series, *Orsova*, survived a further five years, and in 1933 the accommodation was altered to cater for 660 passengers in tourist class only. The vessel was also used for cruises from Britain in the off-season. On 30 June 1936 *Orsova* left London for the last time, this being its seventieth voyage for Orient Line to Australia, returning to Tilbury on 24 September. The next month the old vessel steamed to Bo'ness to be broken up by Douglas & Ramsey.

Orsova

RUAHINE

Built: 1909 by Wm Denny & Bros, Dumbarton
Gross tonnage: 10,832
Dimensions: 497 x 60 ft/146.4 x 18.4 m
Service speed: 14 knots
Propulsion: Triple expansion/twin propellers

The first New Zealand Shipping Company ship to exceed 10,000 tons, *Ruahine* was launched on 19 August 1909, completed on 6 November and left London on its maiden voyage to New Zealand on 25 November that year, going out via Cape Town and returning around South America.

Accommodation consisted of permanent cabins for 56 first class, 88 second class and 126 third class passengers, while up to 250 migrants could be carried in portable berths erected in the holds on voyages from Britain to New Zealand

After the outbreak of war in 1914 *Ruahine* remained on the New Zealand trade. Late in 1915 the route was changed so that voyages in both directions went around the Cape of Good Hope. When this route was considered too dangerous, in 1916 the vessel began using the Panama Canal in both directions.

In March 1917 *Ruahine* came under the Shipping Directors' control, but continued to maintain its regular service, and in the same year survived a submarine attack near Fastnet when a torpedo fired at her missed. In 1920 *Ruahine* was handed back to the NZSC, and sent for a refit, during which it was converted to oil firing.

On 2 December 1920 the vessel sailed from London on its first post-war voyage to New Zealand, but now her first port of call was Southampton, where passengers embarked, then across the Atlantic and through the Panama Canal to New Zealand, returning the same way.

During a refit in 1926 the accommodation was improved and reduced by about fifty passengers. In 1933 *Ruahine* was refitted to carry 220 passengers in tourist class only. In 1938 the vessel was relegated to a cargo service, and would have been disposed of in 1939 but for the outbreak of war. The passenger accommodation was reactivated and *Ruahine* operated a regular service to New Zealand, sometimes carrying troops instead of passengers.

In 1946 *Ruahine* was refitted to carry 180 passengers in one class, and mainly used to carry migrants to New Zealand. On 2 September 1948 the veteran liner left London on its 92nd and last voyage to New Zealand and in January 1949 was sold to an Italian firm, Fratelli Grimaldi.

Refitted and modernised in Italy, the vessel was renamed *Auriga* and placed on the migrant services from Europe to South America and Canada. The vessel was also chartered by Chargeurs Réunis for their service to the Far East during 1954, but mainly traded on the migrant routes until arriving on 18 January 1957 at Naples at the end of its final voyage and being laid up. Shortly afterwards the liner was sold to shipbreakers at Savona, where it arrived on 22 March 1957 to be scrapped.

Ruahine

ROTORUA and REMUERA

Built: 1910/1911 by Wm Denny & Bros, Dumbarton
Gross tonnage: 11,140/11,444
Dimensions: 497 x 62 ft/146.4 x 19 m
Service speed: 15 knots
Propulsion: Triple expansion/triple-twin propellers

These vessels were improved versions of *Ruahine*, but were fitted with different propulsion systems, *Rotorua* being given three propellers. *Rotorua* was launched on 9 July 1910, and handed over to the New Zealand Shipping Co. on 6 October, leaving London on 27 October that year on its maiden voyage to New Zealand, going out around the Cape of Good Hope and returning around Cape Horn. Accommodation was provided for 52 first class, 72 second class and 160 third class passengers, while on voyages to New Zealand temporary berths for 250 migrants could be installed in the holds.

Remuera was launched on 31 May 1911, being delivered on 8 September, and leaving London on its maiden voyage on 28 September. *Remuera* had berths for 60 first class, 90 second class and 130 third class passengers, with similar arrangements for migrants as *Rotorua*.

These ships continued on their regular service after war broke out in 1914, but at the end of that year *Remuera* came home through the Panama Canal, becoming the first British vessel to transit the waterway. During 1915 both outward and return passages were made around South Africa, but in July 1916 this was dropped and the vessels transitted the Panama Canal in both directions.

Rotorua was approaching Britain when it was torpedoed on 22 March 1917 east of Start Point in the English Channel by the German submarine *UC17*. The explosion caused so much damage that *Rotorua* was immediately abandoned by the crew, one of whom was killed, and the ship sank.

Also in March 1917, *Remuera* came under the Shipping Controller, but remained on its regular route until being released in 1919. During a refit an extra deck was built on top of the existing superstructure, and at the same time the boilers were also converted from coal to oil firing.

Returning to service in March 1921, *Remuera* went through the Panama Canal in both directions. By 1933 *Remuera* was no longer required on the main line service, and the accommodation was re-graded cabin class, with a capacity of 200 passengers. During 1938 *Remuera* was transferred to an independent schedule and visited numerous islands in the Pacific on its voyages.

Remuera remained on the New Zealand trade after the World War II started in 1939, and was approaching Britain at the end of its seventy-fourth round trip to New Zealand when it was attacked by German aircraft off Rattray Head on the north-east coast of Scotland on 26 August 1940. Several bombs struck the old vessel, which sank soon after, fortunately without loss of life.

Remuera

AENEAS, ASCANIUS and ANCHISES

Built: 1910/1910/1911 by Workman, Clark & Co., Belfast
Gross tonnage: 10,049/10,048/10,046
Dimensions: 509 x 60 ft/155.1 x 18.4 m
Service speed: 14 knots
Propulsion: Triple expansion/twin propellers

These three ships were built for the Blue Funnel Line, or to give the firm its official title, Alfred Holt & Co., the first, *Aeneas*, being launched on 23 August 1910. *Aeneas* achieved a maximum speed of 16 knots on trials, was handed over to the Blue Funnel Line on 1 November, and on 18 November sailed from Glasgow to open a new passenger service. After a call at Fishguard, *Aeneas* went on to Las Palmas and Cape Town, where more passengers joined, including the Prime Minister of Australia, Andrew Fisher, returning home. *Aeneas* went to Adelaide and Melbourne, where the Prime Minister disembarked, and arrived in Sydney on 6 January 1911. A description of the vessel in the *Sydney Morning Herald* on 7 January noted:

The passenger accommodation occupies the midships portion of three decks. Provision has been made for two, three and four-berth staterooms, some being arranged on the tandem system. The dining saloon on the main deck is lighted by side-lights arranged in pairs, and by a central lighting well rising through two decks.

A children's nursery is situated near the main saloon. A series of staircases leads from the dining saloon to the main entrance hall on the promenade deck. Opening off the after end of the entrance hall is the music room. The smoke-room is at the after end of the promenade deck. The bar, placed at the forward end of this room, is fitted with cold lockers. Doors at the after end lead out to the verandah, sheltered from the weather and suitably furnished.

The vessel has a wireless telegraph-room. Electric light is fitted throughout, and electrically driven fans have been fitted in all the public rooms. Steam heating pipes and radiators have also been provided. Other features are the steam laundry and the barber's shop.

On the return trip to Britain extra stops were made at Fremantle, Durban and Liverpool, where *Aeneas* arrived on 20 March, having completed the voyage in 41 days, which was only four days longer than the mail ships using the Suez Canal route.

The second ship was named *Ascanius* when launched on 29 October 1910, making its first sailing from Glasgow on 30 December 1910. Last of the trio to enter service was *Anchises*, launched on 12 January 1911, and departing Glasgow on 3 March on its maiden voyage.

Anchises

Ascanius

These three ships had accommodation in the superstructure for 288 passengers in first class only, and quickly became popular with travellers to both South Africa and Australia. Blue Funnel Line was able to offer a sailing from Glasgow every six weeks, but less than a year after the ships entered service World War I started.

In August 1914 *Ascanius* was requisitioned by the Australian Government as a troop transport, and allocated pennant number A11. After conversion the vessel went to Adelaide to board AIF troops being sent overseas in the first convoy. *Ascanius* departed Adelaide on 20 October, going to Fremantle to board more troops from Western Australia. On 3 November *Ascanius*, accompanied by *Medic*, left Fremantle and joined the convoy, which headed across the Indian Ocean to Colombo, and then to Aden and the Suez Canal.

Crossing the Arabian Sea, *Ascanius* rammed the ship ahead of it, *Shropshire*, in the stern, and the pair remained locked together for a short time. When the two ships separated, *Ascanius* managed to strike *Shropshire* a second time. The collisions left *Ascanius* with a hole in the bow, while *Shropshire* had a damaged stern, but both ships continued their voyage in the convoy, which arrived at Alexandria in the first days of December.

Aeneas and *Anchises* were left on their regular route a few months longer, but then were taken up by the British Government for service as troopships. The only major incident affecting them occurred in May 1918 when *Aeneas* ran aground on Rathlin Island and suffered some damage, but was refloated and returned to service.

Following a full refit, *Aeneas* reopened the Blue Funnel service when it left Glasgow on 29 May 1920 for Australia, and made a call at Liverpool that would remain a permanent feature of the itinerary from then on. On 21 August 1920 *Ascanius* began its first post-war voyage, but *Anchises* was not returned to Blue Funnel until 1921, and it was September 1922 before it resumed service to Australia.

On 10 January 1925 *Aeneas* made its last departure from Glasgow for Australia, and was then transferred to the service to the Far East. In 1926 the passenger accommodation on *Ascanius* and *Anchises* was reduced to 180 in first class only, while *Aeneas* was by then only carrying 135 passengers to the Far East.

None of these ships was requisitioned in World War II, but remained on their regular routes, though under Government control, and often voyaging in convoys especially in the Atlantic. On 2 July 1940 *Aeneas* was sailing in convoy when it was bombed by German aircraft off Start Point, and sank, with the loss of nineteen lives. On 27 February 1941 *Anchises* was damaged during another German bombing raid on a convoy, and the next day the bombers returned to finish the job, with *Anchises* being sunk off the northwest coast of Ireland, with twelve fatal casualties.

Ascanius was torpedoed in the English Channel on 30 July 1944, but reached port safely, and was repaired at Birkenhead. During 1945 the vessel was used to transport displaced persons between Marseilles and Haifa, then returned to the Australian trade in 1946, but only as a cargo ship.

In 1949 *Ascanius* was sold to Cia de Nav. Florencia, registered in Panama, and renamed *San Giovannino*. The only voyage made under this name was to La Spezia, where the vessel was laid up until being sold to local shipbreakers in March 1953.

NORSEMAN

Built: 1898 by Harland & Wolff, Belfast
Tonnage: 9,546 gross
Dimensions: 516 x 61 ft/157.1 x 18.9 m
Service speed: 12 knots
Propulsion: Quadruple expansion/twin propellers

On 12 May 1910 a brief item appeared in the *Sydney Morning Herald* advising that, as a temporary replacement for the lost *Pericles*, which had sunk two months earlier, the Aberdeen Line had secured the charter of the steamer *Norseman* from the Dominion Line. This vessel was built for Hamburg-America Line, being the first completed of a class of five ships that were intended for a new service to carry migrants and cargo across the Atlantic from Germany to Baltimore.

When launched on 27 November 1897, the vessel was named *Brasilia*. Accommodation was provided for 300 second class passengers in permanent cabins, while up to 2,400 persons could be carried in temporary steerage quarters erected in the holds. The crew numbered only 150.

On 21 March 1898, *Brasilia* departed Belfast on its maiden voyage to New York, but subsequently operated from Hamburg to Baltimore, its first departure being on 4 May, but after two more voyages the vessel also began making some trips between Hamburg and New York carrying cargo only.

Unfortunately the service was not a success, and on 12 February 1900 *Brasilia* was sold back to Harland & Wolff, who sold the vessel to the Dominion Line, which at that time was one of the major operators across the North Atlantic. Harland & Wolff undertook a major reconstruction of the vessel, the original pair of short masts being removed and replaced by four much higher masts; a new funnel, taller and raked, was fitted, and the interior was completely rebuilt.

The vessel was then renamed *Norseman*, but immediately taken over for duty was as Boer War transport No. 80, leaving Liverpool at the end of 1900 carrying 27 officers, 1,115 other ranks and 430 horses to South Africa. On her return to Britain, *Norseman* began running for the Dominion Line on a secondary service between Liverpool and Portland, Maine, though some voyages also went to Boston and even Galveston, Texas. This continued over the next nine years, though migrants were not carried on every westbound voyage. Apparently *Norseman* turned out to be something of a misfit in the Dominion Line fleet, so they were quite pleased when the opportunity suddenly arose to charter the vessel to the Aberdeen Line.

On 7 June 1910, *Norseman* departed London on its first voyage to Australia, making a brief call at Plymouth to embark more passengers, then steaming around South Africa directly to Melbourne, where it arrived on 26 July. Next day *The Argus* reported:

Some interest was created by the arrival in Melbourne of the steamer *Norseman* because she has been chartered

Norseman

by the Aberdeen Line to act as a substitute for the lost *Pericles* until the first of the new Aberdeen liners now being constructed is ready to enter the Australian service. In many respects the *Norseman* resembles the *Pericles*, being approximately of the same tonnage and speed of that vessel. Only one class of passengers are carried by *Norseman*. When she arrived in Hobson's Bay last evening there were 480 passengers on board, of whom 80 were booked for this port.

Included in the staff of the *Norseman* is Mr S. Atkinson, purser of the *Pericles*, who was on that liner when she foundered some months ago. He lost all his belongings in the disaster. The *Norseman* began her voyage at Gravesend on June 7, and, with the exception of a brief call at Plymouth, made no stoppage on the way to Melbourne. No unusual incidents happened, and generally fine weather prevailed, a pleasant sojourn was spent by all on board. The liner, which is under the care of Captain G. Berry, a stranger to Australia, was berthed in the Victoria Dock to land passengers and a cargo of general merchandise.

Norseman arrived in Sydney on 29 July, with the voyage terminating at Brisbane. Leaving Brisbane on 7 August, *Norseman* stopped again at Sydney and Melbourne, but then steamed directly to Durban, and then back to London.

On its second voyage to Australia, *Norseman* arrived in Melbourne on Friday, 10 December 1910, and the next day the following story appeared in the *Sydney Morning Herald* under the heading 'Record Passenger List':

The *Norseman*, chartered by the Aberdeen Line to replace the lost *Pericles*, brought to Australia today the largest number of passengers ever carried across the seas to these shores. The *Norseman*, to save time, came direct from London to Melbourne. She had aboard 895 passengers, or a total company, including the crew, of 1,071 people. Of the 895 passengers 322 are for Victoria. Two hundred represented more of the fruits of the M'Kenzies-Mead delegation.

Among the most interesting of the passengers on the *Norseman* were the three sons of the late Jennings Carmichael. They were taken to the home of Mrs Edwards, who has undertaken to care for and supervise them until arrangements are completed for permanent homes.

Norseman arrived in Sydney on 15 December, on which day it was reported that 340 of the passengers would be disembarking there, while about 200 were destined for Brisbane, where the voyage would terminate.

On its next voyage, *Norseman* arrived in Melbourne on 24 May 1911, and on Thursday, 25 May, the following item appeared in the *Sydney Morning Herald*:

The Aberdeen liner *Norseman*, from London, via South Africa, is due in Sydney on Saturday. Captain Berry stated in Melbourne that the voyage had been one of the finest and most harmonious he had ever known. Making no stoppage on her way, the *Norseman* covered the 12,000 miles in 42½ days. Passengers, of whom there were over 1,000 on board, indulged in an endless series of shipboard amusements, of which several successful concerts were a conspicuous feature, and in these diversions long days passed merrily by. Unfortunately, an epidemic of measles which broke out on board somewhat marred the voyage, 12 cases of the disease being reported when the liner arrived in Melbourne. This, however, proved no bar to her being awarded health clearance.

When the new *Themistocles* and *Demosthenes* joined the Aberdeen fleet in 1911 (see page 12), the charter of *Norseman* was continued, as in 1912 the older Aberdeen Line vessels *Miltiades* and *Marathon* were withdrawn for lengthy periods to be lengthened, and *Norseman* was used to fill the gap. When those two vessels returned to service, *Norseman* continued to operate on charter to the Aberdeen Line, as there was a strong demand for migrant passages to Australia.

Norseman arrived in Sydney on 24 September 1912 with 593 migrants on board, but unfortunately eleven of them had the measles. This meant that the ship had to be placed in quarantine, and nobody was allowed to disembark until medical authorities had checked every passenger and cleared them.

On Friday, 21 February 1913 it was reported in the *Sydney Morning Herald* that 'On Saturday the Aberdeen steamer *Norseman* is due at Melbourne. She has on board 551 passengers, including landseekers with capital of £6,370.'

On 30 January 1914, *Norseman* departed London on its last voyage for the Aberdeen Line. The vessel left Brisbane on 3 April and Sydney four days later, and on returning to Britain on 17 June was handed back to the Dominion Line. At no time when operating for the Aberdeen Line did the vessel carry their colours on its funnel.

Norseman returned to service across the Atlantic, but soon after war broke out in August 1914 was taken over for military duty. *Norseman* was passing through the Gulf of Salonica on 22 January 1916 when it was torpedoed by the German submarine *U39*. The vessel stayed afloat long enough to be towed to the nearby island of Mudros, where it was beached, and remained there for the rest of the war, with the after deck under water.

After inspection after the war it was decided *Norseman* was a constructive total loss. The wreck was sold to an Italian firm of shipbreakers, who refloated it and broke it up during 1920.

RANGATIRA, PAKEHA, ZEALANDIC and WAIMANA

RANGATIRA
Built: 1910 by Workman, Clark & Co., Belfast
Tonnage: 10,118 gross
Dimensions: 494 x 61 ft/150.6 x 18.6 m
Service speed: 13 knots
Propulsion: Triple expansion/twin propellers

PAKEHA ZEALANDIC
Built: 1910 by Harland & Wolff, Belfast
Tonnage: 10,481/10,898 gross
Dimensions: 494 x 63 ft/150.6 x 19.2 m
Service speed: 13 knots
Propulsion: Quadruple expansion/twin propellers

WAIMANA
Built: 1911 by Workman, Clark & Co., Belfast
Tonnage: 10,389 gross
Dimensions: 494 x 63 ft/150.6 x 19.2 m
Service speed: 13 knots
Propulsion: Triple expansion/twin propellers

These four vessels were designed as large cargo steamers with permanent accommodation for just six passengers, but the cargo holds could be fitted with temporary quarters for up to 1,100 migrants on voyages from Britain to Australia and New Zealand. Although all four were to be operated by Shaw Savill Line, *Zealandic* was owned by White Star Line. The route these vessels followed was from Liverpool or London to Teneriffe, Cape Town and Hobart on the way to New Zealand, but sometimes an additional call would be made at Melbourne, Sydney and Brisbane.

The first to be launched was *Rangatira*, on 16 December 1909, being handed over to Shaw Savill Line on 7 February 1910, and entering service shortly afterward on a voyage from Liverpool to Wellington. *Rangatira* had the misfortune to run aground on a mudbank when departing Brisbane on 27 October 1910, remaining stuck for several days before being pulled free.

Pakeha was launched on 26 May 1910, and entered service in August that year, also with a voyage from Britain to New Zealand. On 13 April 1911 *Pakeha* departed Liverpool on a voyage to Australia, passing through Fremantle on 20 May and arriving in Sydney on 25 May 1911 with a large number of migrants, some of whom disembarked while others went on to New Zealand when the vessel departed on 27 May.

Zealandic was launched on 29 June 1911, four weeks after *Titanic* was launched at the same yard for the same owners, but its launch did not receive any publicity. *Zealandic* was delivered to White Star on 12 October 1911, and differed from the Shaw Savill

Zealandic (WSS Victoria)

Waimana

ships in having a longer forecastle and bridge deck.

Zealandic departed Liverpool on its maiden voyage on 1 November 1911, being at Cape Town on 22 November, and arriving in Fremantle on 7 December, when 501 migrants disembarked. The vessel then went to Adelaide on 12 December, and proceeded directly to Sydney, arriving on 17 December, and more migrants were landed, before *Zealandic* left for New Zealand ports.

The last of the four to be completed was *Waimana*, which was launched on 12 September 1911, and handed over to Shaw Savill on 27 November. On 24 December 1911 *Waimana* departed Liverpool on its maiden voyage to Australia and New Zealand. *Rangatira* left Tilbury on 11 January 1912 with 1,154 migrants bound for Australia.

On its second voyage, *Zealandic* departed London on 22 April 1912, a week after *Titanic* sank. On this voyage *Zealandic*, under the command of Captain Breen, again carried migrants to Australia as well as New Zealand, and the vessel arrived in Sydney on the evening of 4 June, going to anchor overnight, and berthing at No. 3 Miller's Point the following morning. A report on the vessel and its voyage appeared in the *Sydney Morning Herald* on 5 June 1912:

The twin-screw steamer *Zealandic*, the latest addition to the fleet of vessels employed in the White Star line's service, arrived at Sydney last night. She has very large cargo capacity in six holds. Two are for general cargo, and the other four are insulated for carrying frozen cargo. There is accommodation for a number of first-class passengers, with

a comfortable saloon on the bridge deck. The smoke-room is also situated on the bridge deck, adjoining the saloon. A feature of the ship is the cabin accommodation, specially arranged for over 1,100 third-class passengers, with space on the shelter deck for a third-class smoke-room and dining-room. There is also a third-class ladies' room. The vessel is lighted throughout with electric light, and is fitted with wireless telegraphy. The steering gear is capable of being worked by telemotor from the flying bridge.

She sailed from London on April 22, and experienced exceptionally fine weather through the Bay of Biscay. Capetown was left on May 15, and during the run across the Indian Ocean excellent weather prevailed except for two days — May 27 and May 28 —when the vessel ran into a moderate gale. On May 17 the old barque *Carmonsey* was passed. Right along the Australian coast calm weather prevailed. The time occupied on the passage was 42 days, an average speed of 13½ knots an hour being maintained.

Zealandic departed Sydney on 7 June to continue its outward voyage to New Zealand ports. This vessel made one further voyage to Australia and New Zealand with migrants later in 1912.

The other three vessels also made voyages to Australia with migrants during 1912, under charter to White Star Line. *Waimana* departed Liverpool on 16 July with 1,025 passengers on board, arriving in Sydney on 29 August, and leaving for New Zealand the next day. *Rangatira* arrived in Melbourne on 8 September and Sydney two days later, with about 1,000 migrants.

Pakeha arrived in Sydney on 4 October from London

with over 1,000 migrants on board, and it was reported that during the voyage there were three deaths on board, and one birth.

On 22 January 1913, *Zealandic* departed New Zealand with the largest wool cargo yet transported to Britain by a single vessel. Later in 1913, *Zealandic* was chartered by the Government of Western Australia to bring migrants from Britain to Fremantle, where it arrived on 8 November carrying 1,067 passengers, all of whom disembarked there. *Zealandic* then continued to New Zealand to load a full cargo.

When war broke out in August 1914, *Waimana* was in New Zealand waters, being requisitioned by the New Zealand Government to take part in the first ANZAC convoy to be sent overseas. After embarking their troops at various New Zealand ports, the ten vessels steamed to King George Sound, near Albany in Western Australia, where they linked up with the vessels carrying Australian troops.

In September 1914 *Rangatira* was taken over by the Australian Government and converted to an auxiliary troop transport at Sydney and designated A22. On 29 September 1914 the 3rd Field Artillery Brigade and the 1st Division of the 3rd Field Ambulance Corps departed Brisbane aboard the *Rangatira* for King George Sound.

Departing on 1 November 1914, the convoy was stopped at Alexandria, where the troops disembarked. *Waimana* and *Rangatira* went on to Britain, and along with *Pakeha* and *Zealandic* continued to trade from Britain to Australia and New Zealand, though only carrying cargo.

In July 1915 *Zealandic* was chased by a German submarine while passing through the English Channel, but was able to escape. In April 1916 *Rangatira* left Britain on a voyage to Hobart and Wellington, carrying only general cargo and no migrants. As the vessel was approaching Cape Town on 31 March, the vessel ran aground on Robben Island at the entrance to Table Bay. The ship could not be refloated, but most of the cargo was recovered before the vessel was smashed to pieces by heavy seas.

In 1917, *Zealandic*, *Pakeha* and *Waimana* were requisitioned for military service as cargo carriers. *Zealandic* was returned to White Star Line in 1919, and resumed trading to New Zealand for White Star Line, as did *Pakeha* and *Waimana* for Shaw Savill Line, though now they made the voyage through the Panama Canal.

However, on 4 December 1920 *Zealandic* departed Liverpool on a voyage to Australia via Cape Town, carrying 350 former British servicemen and their families, the first group to be sent out under the Overseas Settlement Scheme, arriving in Sydney on 29 January 1921.

Later in 1921, the New Zealand Government began offering assisted passages to British migrants, which resulted in a huge increase in demand for migrant berths. *Zealandic*, *Pakeha* and *Waimana* were again fitted out to carry about 1,000 migrants in temporary accommodation, the route being from Liverpool through the Panama Canal to New Zealand. On the return voyage to Britain, the vessels sometimes called at Australian ports

Another company associated with White Star Line was the Aberdeen Line, which operated a migrant service to Australia, but by 1926 it was not doing very well. In June 1926 it was arranged that the two newest Aberdeen Line ships, *Sophocles* and *Diogenes*, would be transferred to Shaw Savill Line, and to replace them, *Zealandic* and *Waimana*, would join the Aberdeen Line.

Zealandic was renamed *Mamilius* while *Waimana* became *Herminius*, and they began operating a regular cargo service from Britain via South Africa to Australia, but did not carry any passengers.

In November 1926 the White Star Line, Shaw Savill Line and the Aberdeen Line all became part of the Kylsant Group of shipping companies, but the ships continued to operate as before. However, in 1932 the Kylsant Group suffered a total financial collapse, which resulted in the Aberdeen Line being wound up, and its ships transferred to the ownership of Shaw Savill Line.

Zealandic was included in this arrangement, and became *Mamari* in the Shaw Savill fleet, and *Waimana* regained its original name, but they continued to operate only as cargo ships. Throughout this period *Pakeha* had remained in the Shaw Savill fleet, but after 1926 only carried cargo.

When war came in September 1939, *Mamari*, *Pakeha* and *Waimana* were sold to the British Admiralty. *Mamari* was given a major conversion to resemble the aircraft carrier HMS *Hermes*, while *Pakeha* was rebuilt to resemble the battleship HMS *Revenge*, and *Waimana* altered to look like the battleship HMS *Resolution*. The vessels were then anchored at various British naval bases, hopefully to fool German air reconnaissance that the real aircraft carrier and battleships were there. They served in this unusual role until the middle of 1941, when it was decided they were no longer needed, especially after the real *Hermes* was sunk in March 1941.

On 4 June 1941 *Mamari* was on the way to Chatham to be converted back to a cargo ship when it was attacked by German bombers near Cromer. In trying to avoid the falling bombs, the vessel hit the wreck of the tanker *Ahamo*, and was beached to prevent it sinking. Before it could be refloated, a German E-boat managed to put a torpedo into the grounded vessel, which subsequently sank.

The other two were converted back to cargo ships, to be operated by the Ministry of War Transport, under Shaw Savill management. Their names were amended to *Empire Pakeha* and *Empire Waimana*, and they served as such for the remainder of the war.

In 1946 both vessels were bought back by Shaw Savill Line, and regained their original names yet again. They served as cargo ships on the trade between Britain and New Zealand for several more years. *Pakeha* was withdrawn in May 1950 and sold to shipbreakers at Briton Ferry, while *Waimana* continued in service until the end of 1951, and in January 1952 arrived at Milford Haven to be broken up.

THE FIRST P&O B CLASS

BALLARAT BELTANA BENALLA BERRIMA BORDA
Built: 1911/12/12/13/13 by Caird & Co., Greenock
Gross tonnage: 11,120
Dimensions: 515 x 63 ft/157 x 19 m
Service speed: 14 knots
Propulsion: Quadruple expansion/twin propellers

In January 1910 the P&O Line purchased the fleet and goodwill of the Blue Anchor Line, which had been involved in the migrant trade to Australia for thirty years. There were five ships in the Blue Anchor fleet, and for a short period P&O retained that name for the service, but in June 1910 it was renamed the P&O Branch Line, and five new ships were ordered, designed as the best migrant ships on the Australian route.

The first to be launched was *Ballarat*, on 23 September 1911, making its maiden departure from London on 30 November. *Ballarat* arrived in Adelaide 37 days after leaving London, which was a record passage for the Cape route, going on to Melbourne and then Sydney, where it arrived on 10 January 1912. Next day a description of the vessel appeared in the *Sydney Morning Herald*:

> An interesting arrival in Port Jackson yesterday was the new P&O Branch Service steamer *Ballarat*, 11,122 tons, which fully loaded with immigrants berthed at Brown's Wharf, Woolloomooloo Bay. The vessel is divided into nine watertight compartments and has a cellular bottom extending her full length. She is fitted with wireless, beside all other modern innovations for safety at sea.
>
> The chief passenger accommodation is placed in the

upper and bridge decks amidships, and although 300 passengers are berthed here, practically every cabin in this part of the ship has direct light and air provided by a port. There is a spacious dining saloon on the upper deck and all the passengers berthed amidships are able to dine together. On the forward part of the bridge deck is a very comfortable lounge for the use of ladies, with piano, library etc. The smoking room is a particularly fine apartment situated in the after end of the boat deck and leading out of this room is a verandah fitted with seats and tables and so enclosed as to render it a comfortable lounge in wet weather. The promenade decks are unusually spacious. In addition to accommodating some 1,100 passengers, the steamer is capable of carrying about 10,000 tons of cargo (including some 5,000 tons of frozen cargo) and is fitted with the latest appliances for the handling of such a large freight. She is what is termed a one-class vessel, fares approximately equivalent to third class being charged. Externally she is somewhat of a disappointment for instead of following general P&O lines, she is more of the earlier Lund type of boat, her masts and funnel being perpendicular. Her funnel is also painted in the old Lund colours or black with broad white stripe, on which is a blue anchor, instead of the P&O black.

On 24 January 1912 the second ship was launched, and named *Beltana*, entering service in May, while on 21 October 1912 the third member of the group, *Benalla*, was launched, making its maiden voyage from London in March 1913.

All three vessels were given the funnel colours of the Blue Anchor Line, but at the end of 1913 it was decided to repaint their funnels black, as with all other

Ballarat with Blue Anchor funnel.

Benalla

P&O vessels. Thus the fourth vessel, *Berrima*, which had been launched on 15 April 1913, entered service in December 1913 with a plain black funnel, as did the final ship, *Borda*, which was launched on 17 December 1913 and placed in service in March 1914.

All five ships offered accommodation for 1,100 passengers in third class only, with the standard of amenities better than that of any opposing companies. With the assistance of *Commonwealth* and *Geelong* from the old Blue Anchor Line, the Branch Line was able to offer a sailing from London every three weeks.

When war broke out in August 1914, the five B ships were requisitioned for military duty. *Berrima* was taken over by the Australian Government on 12 August in Sydney, and quickly converted into a troop transport, carrying some 1,500 troops to capture Rabaul in German New Guinea, returning to Sydney in early October.

Benalla became transport A24, being fitted out to carry 50 officers and 1,200 other ranks in the first convoy to carry Australian and New Zealand troops overseas in World War I, departing Albany on 1 November and disembarking them in Egypt.

Borda was given the number A30 and fitted out to carry 26 officers, 550 other ranks and 260 horses, while *Berrima*, number A35, carried 60 officers and 1,500 other ranks. Both these ships were involved in the second convoy to carry Australian troops overseas, which departed Albany on 31 December 1914. Later *Ballarat* became A70 and *Beltana* A72, both being equipped to carry some 48 officers and 1,580 other ranks.

On 3 December 1915 *Benalla* was attacked by gunfire from a surfaced submarine when passing through the Mediterranean, but was able to escape. On 18 February 1917 *Berrima* was passing through the English Channel when it was torpedoed, but the vessel remained afloat and was beached on Portland Bill. *Berrima* returned to service after repairs had been completed.

This luck was not to continue, however. On 19 February 1917, *Ballarat* left Melbourne with 1,752 persons on board, including 1,600 troops, bound for Britain. Bunkering at Cape Town was done with poor quality coal, which reduced speed to 9 knots. Approaching England, *Ballarat* was being escorted by HMS *Phoenix* at 8 knots when it was struck by a torpedo in the early afternoon of 25 April, south-west of Wolf Rock at the entrance to the English Channel. All on board were rescued, and an attempt began to tow the stricken vessel into shallow water, but on 26 April *Ballarat* sank.

The other four B ships survived the war, and during 1919 they were handed back to P&O and given extensive refits. The Branch Line service was reopened with the sailing of *Commonwealth* from London in October 1919, and over the next six months the four B ships all returned to the route.

The return of *Berrima* was delayed several weeks, as on 24 March 1920 the vessel was despatched from London under charter to the British India Line, another P&O subsidiary, for a single voyage through the Suez Canal to Australian ports and return, this being the only time any of these five ships would pass through the canal.

With the Branch Line fleet reduced to just four B ships and *Commonwealth*, a new schedule of four-weekly departures was established. However, P&O anticipated that in the post-war period there would be

Beltana

an increase in the demand for migration from Britain to Australia, and placed orders for a new series of five ships for the Branch Line, which would be of a similar basic design to the original quintet but larger.

The first of these ships was delivered in 1921 and named *Ballarat*, thus reviving the name of the first of the original B class ships and the only one to become a casualty of the war. After the final new B ship entered service in 1923, the P&O Branch Line was able to operate a schedule of three weekly departures from London, using nine ships of similar design and capacity.

For a couple of years the foresight of P&O in building the new migrant ships appeared to have been correct, as there was a steady demand for passages, although in 1922 serious competition appeared when the Australian Government placed their five new Bay ships in service (page 154).

For a brief period there were enough passengers to keep all the ships full, but by 1926 it was clear that the migrant boom was beginning to collapse, as demand for passages fell off considerably. In an effort to attract what third class passengers there still were to their ships, P&O began routing some of their newer Branch Line vessel through the Mediterranean, with a call at Malta before passing through the Suez Canal, then going on by way of Aden and Colombo to Australia, which reduced passage time, but the older ships continued to make the voyage around South Africa.

Over the next three years the situation deteriorated further, and *Berrima* was laid up during 1928. In July 1929 the P&O Branch Line came to an end when the service around South Africa was abandoned altogether. The immediate result of this decision was the withdrawal of the last three of the original B class ships, and all four vessels were offered for sale.

With the depression beginning to affect many countries, it was not surprising that few buyers came forward for the laid up ships. *Benalla, Berrima* and *Borda* were all sold in May 1930 to Japanese shipbreakers, but *Beltana* was sold during the same year to Toya Hogei KK, a Japanese firm based at Osaka. They planned to rebuild the ship as a whaling mothership, but following its arrival in Japan the vessel was laid up. *Beltana* remained afloat a further three years, but in the end the conversion plans were abandoned, and the vessel was sold to shipbreakers in Japan in 1933.

BELGIC

Built: 1903 by New York Shipbuilding Co., Camden
Gross tonnage: 10,151
Dimensions: 510 x 58 ft/155.4 x 17.7 m
Service speed: 14 knots
Propulsion: Triple expansion/twin propellers

By the time this vessel began operating to Australia it was under its third name and ownership. Built for an American company, the Atlantic Transport Line, it was named *Mississippi* when launched on 15 December 1902, being completed in April 1903. The vessel had been designed as one of four 7,913 gross ton cargo ships with accommodation for about 1,900 migrants on the voyage from Europe to America, the other three being named *Maine*, *Missouri* and *Massachusetts*.

In 1902 Atlantic Transport Line was purchased by the International Mercantile Marine Company, which also owned the Red Star Line. In July 1906 *Mississippi* was transferred to Red Star, renamed *Samland*, and placed on a regular service between Philadelphia and Antwerp.

In December 1909 *Samland* was transferred to Belgian registry, though still under the ownership of Red Star Line, and from January 1910 began operating between Antwerp and New York. In April 1911 *Samland* was transferred to a service from Hamburg to Montreal.

On 30 August 1911, *Samland* was transferred to White Star Line, another company within the International Mercantile Marine Company group. The vessel was renamed *Belgic*, but remained under the Belgian flag, and was placed on the service from Britain to Australia.

By this time the superstructure of the vessel had been enlarged, but it was still basically a cargo ship with quarters for about 1,000 migrants on the voyage from Liverpool to Australia via South Africa.

On its first voyage for White Star Line, *Belgic* departed Liverpool on 25 September, taking almost four weeks to reach Cape Town, on 21 October. *Belgic* arrived in Fremantle on 12 November 1911, continuing to Adelaide on 20 November and Melbourne three days later, berthing in Sydney on 26 November.

On its second voyage to Australia *Belgic* arrived in Fremantle on 11 June 1912, returning on 23 November the same year. On 27 November the *Sydney Morning Herald* carried the following report from their Perth correspondent:

> The *Belgic*, which arrived on Saturday, brought 640 new settlers to Western Australia. The new arrivals, particularly those travelling on assisted passages, appear to be a bright, healthy lot, of the right type. All told, there were 1,450 souls who came to swell Australia's population. About 10 percent of them are assisted, and hail from the lowlands of Scotland and the English provinces.

The next stop for the *Belgic* was Adelaide, from where it was reported on 4 December that 'during the voyage of the steamer *Belgic* from Liverpool to Adelaide two births and the death of one infant occurred.' *Belgic* continued its voyage to Melbourne and Sydney, disembarking migrants at each port. The fourth and final voyage by *Belgic* reached Fremantle on 3 July 1913, and also went on to Melbourne and Sydney.

In December 1913, *Belgic* was transferred back to Red Star Line, regained the name *Samland*, and returned to the trade between Antwerp and New York. From October 1914 *Samland* operated from London to New York, then in March 1916 was placed on a service from New York to Rotterdam until the war ended.

In February 1919, *Samland* returned to the route from Antwerp to New York, on which it served until 1931, when it was sold to shipbreakers at Ghent in Belgium.

Belgic (Western Australia Maritime Museum)

ORAMA

Built: 1911 by John Brown, Clydebank
Gross tonnage: 12,927
Dimensions: 569 x 64 ft/173.4 x 19.6 m
Service speed: 18 knots
Propulsion: Triple expansion/triple propellers

An enlarged version of the Orsova class built in 1909, *Orama* was launched on 28 June 1911, and handed over to the Orient Line on 5 November 1911. *Orama* provided accommodation for 293 first class, 145 second class and 867 third class passengers, much the same as the earlier ships, but was powered by combination machinery driving three propellers. This comprised triple expansion engines driving the two wing shafts, with the exhaust from these engines driving a low pressure turbine on the centre shaft. *Orama* was to be the only Orient Line vessel to be given this type of propulsion, although it was originally proposed for *Ormonde*, and the only triple screw vessel ever operated by the company.

Orama left London on its maiden voyage on 10 November 1911, arriving in Sydney on 21 December, on which day the *Sydney Morning Herald* reported:

> This morning the latest addition to the Orient Royal Mail line of steamers, the RMS *Orama*, will make her appearance in Port Jackson. She closely resembles her five predecessors of the same fleet, over each of which, however, she has a considerable advantage in size.
>
> In the construction of the *Orama* attention was bestowed to all modern improvements…She is also the first liner built for the Commonwealth mail line in which turbines

are employed. Her propelling machinery consists of two independent sets of reciprocating triple expansion engines, working in conjunction with a low-pressure Parsons turbine.

She has accommodation for 450 first and second saloon passengers, and about 800 third class passengers. As in the other new vessels of the Orient Line, a special feature is the provision of a large number of rooms for one only. The dining saloons, lounge, music and smoking rooms are large and lofty. Special attention has been given to the third-class sleeping-rooms, dining rooms, and promenade decks, which are fitted up to give thorough comfort. The two third-class promenade decks are on the bridge deck and shelter deck respectively. The smoking and music rooms in this class are on the shelter deck, while the sleeping berths are on the main and upper decks. Electric lifts and a laundry are prominent features.

In November 1913 *Orama* was berthing in the Brisbane River at the end of a voyage from Britain when it ran aground in mud. It was not until all the cargo had been discharged into lighters that the vessel could be refloated the next day with the assistance of several tugs. Fortunately no damage was suffered, and *Orama* left on its return trip on schedule.

On 22 May 1914 *Orama* left London on what was destined to be its final voyage to Australia. After arriving back in London, *Orama* was converted into an armed merchant cruiser. On 19 October 1917 *Orama* was torpedoed while escorting a convoy south of Ireland. All on board were saved, but *Orama* sank four hours after being hit.

Orama

INDRAPURA, MAKARINI and HAWKES BAY

INDRAPURA

Built: 1911 by Swan, Hunter & Wigham Richardson, Newcastle
Tonnage: 10,286 gross
Dimensions: 508 x 61 ft/154.9 x 18.7 m
Service speed: 13 knots
Propulsion: Triple expansion/twin propellers

MAKARINI HAWKES BAY

Built: 1912 by Workman, Clark & Co., Belfast
Tonnage: 10,624/10,641 gross
Dimensions: 508 x 61 ft/154.9 x 18.7 m
Service speed: 13 knots
Propulsion: Triple expansion/twin propellers

Although owned by two different companies, G. D. Tyser & Co. and the Indra Line, these three ships were almost identical, being essentially cargo ships that could also carry migrants to Australia.

Indrapura was launched on 10 October 1911, and entered service for the Indra Line two months later with a voyage from London to Australia and New Zealand via Cape Town, berthing in Melbourne on 1 February and Sydney on 12 February 1912. On this voyage only cargo was carried, but the vessel merited mention in the shipping section of the *Sydney Morning Herald* on 13 February, which said in part:

The new 'Indra' liner, the twin-screw steamer *Indrapura*, now in Sydney on her maiden voyage from London to Melbourne, Sydney and New Zealand ports, is discharging at the Tyser Wharf, Miller's Point. Like other ships of this line, she will be employed in carrying refrigerated cargoes from New Zealand and Australia to London. Three of the

holds and 'tween decks are insulated for this purpose. The living accommodation for both the officers and crew has been carefully planned and well ventilated, making these quarters more roomy and comfortable than is often the case. There are also comfortable cabins for a dozen first-class passengers.

On 23 January 1912 the Victorian Government had signed a contract with Tyser & Co. and Wm Milburn & Co. to carry some 24,000 migrants from Britain to Melbourne over the next three years. In order to meet this contract, *Indrapura* would be used by Tysers, and have passenger accommodation fitted, as would two cargo ships then under construction for Tysers. Temporary cabins and dormitories would be provided on the shelter deck, all fitted with iron beds and a washbasin. There would be a 500-seat dining room, smoking and sitting rooms, and additional toilet and ablution facilities, all of which could be disassembled for the voyage back to Britain with cargo.

The first of the pair being built for Tysers, *Makarini*, was launched on 3 February 1912, and left Plymouth on 12 June, with about 800 migrants on board, voyaging by way of South Africa. On 8 June 1912, the *Sydney Morning Herald* reported:

The new Tyser liner *Makarini*, now making her maiden voyage to Melbourne, Sydney and New Zealand ports, is a vessel of the shelter-deck type, and has been constructed for the highest class in Lloyd's Register. She has been specially designed for the carriage of frozen meat, three of the five holds being insulated. Accommodation for about 850 steerage passengers is provided in rooms on the upper

Makarini, shown here as *Port Nicholson*.

Hawkes Bay, shown later as Port Napier.

'tween decks, the rooms being large, well lighted and ventilated, and fitted with wash basins.

Makarini arrived in Melbourne in the late evening of 21 July, remaining in port for five days before continuing to Sydney, where it berthed on 28 July. The second vessel to depart under the Victorian contract was *Indrapura* from London on 2 October 1912, carrying about 300 men and 700 women and children bound for Melbourne.

Hawkes Bay was launched on 27 September 1912, and delivered to Tyser's at the end of December, departing London in early January 1913 on its first voyage to Australia, arriving in Melbourne on 20 February. The next day the *Sydney Morning Herald* included two small items from Melbourne referring to the vessel, the first sent on the day it arrived in Melbourne:

The Tyser liner *Hawkes Bay* arrived from London today, having on board 531 newcomers for Victoria.

Messrs Tyser and Company's new steamer *Hawkes Bay* arrived at Melbourne yesterday morning from London, via ports. The *Hawkes Bay* is a twin-screw steamer, and contains five holds, three of which are specially insulated and cooled by an installation of refrigerating machinery, being intended for the carriage of frozen meat. Accommodation is also provided for 750 steerage passengers, with a dining saloon providing accommodation for the same number at one sitting.

Hawkes Bay arrived in Sydney on 28 February, and after disembarking passengers and discharging cargo, departed for Auckland on 6 March.

Early in 1914 four British firms, G. D. Tyser & Co., the Indra Line, James P. Corry & Co. and the Anglo-Australasian S. N. Co. merged to form Commonwealth & Dominion Line, but the ships continued to operate under their original names, though all carrying the same hull and funnel colours.

With the outbreak of war in 1914, *Hawkes Bay* was one of ten vessels requisitioned by the New Zealand Government to carry troops in the first convoy to be sent overseas. They joined up with twenty-six vessels carrying Australian troops and horses, and on 1 November the full convoy departed Albany, disembarking their troops in Egypt.

In 1916 the three ships were given new names, *Indrapura* changing to *Port Adelaide*, *Makarini* becoming *Port Nicholson* and *Hawkes Bay* being renamed *Port Napier*. Later in 1916 the Commonwealth & Dominion Line was acquired by the Cunard Line, and the company became better known as the Port Line.

On 15 January 1917 *Port Nicholson* hit a mine in the English Channel off Dunkirk, and sank. *Port Adelaide* was torpedoed 180 miles (290 km) south-west of Fastnet on 3 February 1917, and also sank. The former *Hawkes Bay* served in the Port Line fleet as *Port Napier*, carrying cargo only, until 1936, when it was sold to another British company, T. & J. Brocklebank, being renamed *Martand*.

In 1938 the vessel was sold again, to A. Zanchi of Genoa, being renamed *Martano*, which was soon changed to *Mar Bianco*. In September 1943 it was seized by the German Navy after the Italian capitulation. This did not last long however, as on 7 December 1943 the vessel was sunk by Allied bombers during an attack on Zadar in Yugoslavia.

ARGYLLSHIRE, SHROPSHIRE and WILTSHIRE

Built: 1911/1911/1912 by John Brown, Clydebank
Gross tonnage: 10,392/11,911/10,390
Dimensions: 544 x 61 ft/165.8 x 18.7 m
Service speed: 14 knots
Propulsion: Quadruple expansion/twin propellers

These three vessels were owned by two companies, Scottish Shire Line and the Federal Steam Navigation Company. The Scottish Shire ship was the first to be launched, on 27 February 1911, being named *Argyllshire*. On Saturday, 5 August the vessel sailed from Liverpool, under the command of Captain Chicken, to inaugurate the new service to Australia, going by way of Cape Town and calling at Adelaide, Melbourne, Sydney and Brisbane.

Accommodation was provided for 131 first class passengers, and temporary berths could be installed in the holds for about five hundred migrants from Britain to Australia.

On 21 September, the following item, under the headline 'New Five-Masted Liner' appeared in the *Sydney Morning Herald*:

> Specially designed for passengers as well as cargo, the *Argyllshire* is provided with all the latest improvements for comfort at sea. The dining room can seat 132 persons — practically the whole of the first-class complement — at the same time being a most commodious apartment, extending the full width of the ship. A lounge about 40ft square is a striking feature of the accommodation, whilst all the state rooms have the great advantage of being on deck. These cabins are very spacious; and indeed throughout the ship there is a roominess which should commend the liner to voyagers.

The first of the Federal Line pair was named *Shropshire* when launched on 27 April 1911, departing Liverpool on 28 October on its maiden voyage to Australia. The last member of the trio was launched on 19 December 1911 and named *Wiltshire*, being handed over to the Federal Line on 15 February 1912. *Wiltshire* left Liverpool on 16 March at the start of its maiden voyage, and with the three ships now in service it was possible to operate regular four-weekly departures.

These three ships had a unique appearance, with five masts and a single tall funnel. The only outward difference between the *Argyllshire* and the Federal ships was the funnel colours, as each ship carried the markings of its owner.

Although the terminal port for the service was Liverpool, the ships regularly used the Manchester Ship Canal as well. To enable them to pass under the numerous bridges, the topmasts were telescopic and the top section of the funnel was detached by a crane and left on the wharf at the start of the canal until the ships returned.

This was the first major venture by both companies into the passenger trade, and it did not meet with the anticipated success. After *Wiltshire* had made only one voyage, the accommodation on all three ships was

Argyllshire

Shropshire

reduced to 66 first class only.

In January 1912 the Federal Steam Navigation Company was taken over by the New Zealand Shipping Company, but this had no effect on the operation of the *Shropshire* and *Wiltshire*. Four months later the New Zealand Shipping Company acquired the Australian and New Zealand interests of Houlder Bros, and from May 1912 the joint service became known as the Federal & Shire Line.

At the time of the change of ownership, the three vessels had their accommodation altered, being fitted with what was described as 'superior third class accommodation', with cabins containing either two or four berths. *Shropshire* made the first departure in this new guise from Liverpool on 11 May 1912, arriving in Melbourne on 21 June and Sydney two days later.

Shortly after the outbreak of war in 1914 the three ships were requisitioned by the Australian Government for service as troop transports. *Argyllshire* was allocated pennant number A8, and fitted out to carry 100 officers, 1,000 other ranks and 397 horses. *Shropshire* became A9, being converted to transport 57 officers, 878 other ranks and 461 horses, while *Wiltshire*, as A18, could carry 36 officers, 720 other ranks and 505 horses. All three were included in the first convoy carrying Australian and New Zealand troops overseas that left Albany on 1 November 1914.

Crossing the Arabian Sea, *Shropshire* was rammed in the stern by *Ascanius*, and the ships remained locked together for a short time. The troops on board both ships were sent to their evacuation stations, but there was no panic and lifeboats were not lowered. When the two ships separated, *Ascanius* managed to strike *Shropshire* a second time, leaving *Shropshire* with a badly damaged stern, while *Ascanius* had a hole in the bow, but neither ship was in any danger, and continued their voyage, eventually arriving at Alexandria in the first days of December.

The three ships served as troop carriers for most of the war, though *Shropshire* was transferred to the Shipping Controller in August 1917 and returned to the Australian trade, where its huge cargo capacity was needed to bring supplies to Britain.

Argyllshire was the only one of the trio to be damaged in the war. A fortunate escape during May 1915, when two torpedoes missed the ship was followed by near disaster in February 1917, when the vessel was hit by a torpedo off Start Point. Fortunately the damaged vessel was able to make port safely, but was out of service for some time while repairs were completed, after which it continued in its trooping role until the war ended.

All three ships survived the war, but the joint service was not to be revived in the post-war years. The reason for this stemmed from the takeover of the New Zealand Shipping Company, and hence the Federal Steam Navigation Company as well, by the P&O Group in July 1916.

With *Argyllshire* now owned by a different company to the other pair, the Federal & Shire Line ceased to exist. In 1917 the Scottish Shire Line had been purchased by Cayzer, Irvine & Co., who operated as the Clan Line, although Scottish Shire Line continued as a separate entity.

After an extensive refit, during which the passenger

accommodation was altered to 133 first class and 76 third class, in 1920 *Argyllshire* was placed on a new service, from Britain to Australia and New Zealand via the Cape.

Shropshire and *Wiltshire* had been handed back to the Federal Line after the war, but when they returned to service in 1920 on a route from Liverpool to New Zealand by way of the Panama Canal it was as cargo ships.

During 1921 *Shropshire* went to Falmouth for further work, and while there a fire broke out on 28 October, causing serious damage to the vessel. On 11 November 1921, after a second outbreak of fire had caused more damage, the vessel was laid up at Falmouth..

On 31 May 1922, *Wiltshire* was approaching Auckland in bad weather and ran aground in Rosalie Bay, near Great Barrier Island. With the bow held fast and the stern in deep water, the ship could not be refloated, and soon afterward broke in two directly under the bridge, becoming a total loss.

It was also during 1922 that *Shropshire* was chartered to the New Zealand Shipping Company, and extensively rebuilt with accommodation for 131 first class, 270 second class and 270 third class passengers. Renamed *Rotorua*, on 23 March 1923 the vessel departed Southampton, called at Plymouth the next day, then voyaged via the Panama Canal to New Zealand, to commence the most successful phase of its career.

Unfortunately, *Argyllshire* was not enjoying much success, so in 1926 it was taken out of service and laid up. In 1928 the vessel was reactivated to make two voyages, the second of which left Liverpool on 17 November 1928, going via Cape Town to Australian and New Zealand ports and returning through the Panama Canal, then was laid up in the Gareloch. In November 1932 *Argyllshire* was transferred to the Clan Line, and following a refit, during which the former passenger accommodation was removed, the ship was renamed *Clan Urquhart*, and returned to service operating to South and East Africa until 1936, when it was sold to T. W. Ward and broken up by them at Briton Ferry.

Rotorua operated for the New Zealand Shipping Company from London to New Zealand via the Panama Canal through the 1920s, but from 1929 was mostly used on a secondary service from other British ports. In 1933 *Rotorua* was refitted to carry 400 tourist class passengers only: in 1934 the top section of the second mast was knocked off by a crane in New Zealand, and never replaced.

When war broke out again in 1939, *Rotorua* remained on her regular trade. In October 1940 the vessel departed Lyttelton with a full cargo of meat and dairy products bound for Avonmouth via the Panama Canal. At Halifax *Rotorua* joined a convoy for the crossing of the Atlantic, but when it was 110 miles (175 km) west of St Kilda, off the north of Scotland, *Rotorua* was struck by a torpedo fired by the German submarine *U96*. *Rotorua* sank in twenty minutes, with nineteen fatalities, though 106 persons survived.

Rorotua, formerly *Shropshire.*

THEMISTOCLES and DEMOSTHENES

THEMISTOCLES
Built: 1911 by Harland & Wolff, Belfast
Gross tonnage: 11,231
Dimensions: 517 x 62 ft/157.6 x 19 m
Service speed: 14 knots
Propulsion: Quadruple expansion/twin propellers

DEMOSTHENES
Built: 1911 by Harland & Wolff, Belfast
Gross tonnage: 11,233
Dimensions: 517 x 62 ft/157.6 x 19 m
Service speed: 14 knots
Propulsion: Triple expansion/triple propellers

Built for the Aberdeen Line, the first of this pair to be launched was *Themistocles*, on 22 September 1910, being handed over to the Aberdeen Line on 14 January 1911. On 16 February *Themistocles* left London for Cape Town, Melbourne and Sydney, where it arrived on 2 April. Next day the *Sydney Morning Herald* reported:

The new Aberdeen liner *Themistocles* reached Sydney yesterday, after a successful maiden voyage from London, via Capetown, of 45 days. She covered the distance to Melbourne in 40 days, which was but two days longer than is taken by the mailboats via Suez. She has most superior accommodation for 100 first-class and nearly 800 third-class passengers. While the demand nowadays for single-berth staterooms is a marked feature of ocean travel, this vessel possesses a larger proportion of cabins of this type,

one complete deck being allocated. The public apartments are spacious in size and artistic in decoration.

Situated on the bridge deck forward are the library and the lounge. On the same deck aft will be found the smoke-room, also a delightful verandah cafe. The single-berth staterooms are all located on the bridge deck, whilst on the awning deck below are those for two or three persons, the rooms all being provided with wardrobes. The surgery, barber's shop, and nursery are also on the awning deck. In the handsome dining saloon on the main deck meals are served at small tables, seating from four to eight passengers, on the restaurant principle. There is a wealth of bathroom accommodation. The width of the alleyways, the loftiness of the cosy staterooms, and the spacious expanse of the promenade decks, all unite in making her an ideal ship.

The third-class quarters also attain a high degree of excellence. On the awning deck there is an excellent smoke-room, also a general room with a piano, where passengers of either sex may foregather. Some of the two-berth staterooms are situated on the same deck, which is also provided with numerous bathrooms. Below, on the main deck, is a spacious dining saloon, in addition to the major portion of the sleeping accommodation, consisting principally of commodious two and four berth cabins also. Altogether the third-class quarters are unusually attractive.

On 28 February 1911, *Demosthenes* was launched, and completed six months later. *Themistocles* and *Demosthenes* provided accommodation for 103 first

Themistocles (David Finch collection)

Demosthenes (David Finch collection)

class and 256 third class passengers in permanent berths. The ships also had seven holds, in which an extra 500 third class passengers could be accommodated in temporary quarters on outward voyages from Britain.

Themistocles was given standard quadruple expansion machinery driving twin screws, but *Demosthenes* had triple expansion engines driving two outer propellers, with the exhaust steam being fed into a low-pressure turbine engine which drove a centre shaft.

Demosthenes left London on 31 August on its maiden voyage, calling at Plymouth before going around South Africa, arriving in Melbourne on 9 October and Sydney on 14 October, on which day the *Sydney Morning Herald* reported:

The new Aberdeen liner *Demosthenes*, 11,200 tons, which is due to arrive in Sydney this morning from London, via Capetown and Melbourne, is not only the first triple-screw vessel in the Aberdeen Line, but the first vessel engined on the combination principle of reciprocating and turbine machinery to enter the Australian trade.

The public apartments are spacious in size and artistic in decoration. These comprise a library and lounge situated forward on the bridge deck, while the smoke room and a delightful verandah café are situated aft on the same deck. The single-berth staterooms are located on the bridge deck, whilst on the awning deck below are two and three berthed rooms. The dining saloon is situated on the main deck, the tables there seating from four to eight passengers on the restaurant principle.

The third class quarters are said to attain a high degree of excellence. A smoke room and general room are situated on the awning deck, where also are a few two-berth staterooms, while the dining room and the major portion of the sleeping accommodation, comprising mostly single, two, three and four berth rooms, are situated on the main deck.

More details of the ship and its voyage were reported the following day:

The new Aberdeen liner *Demosthenes*, first triple-screw turbine steamer to visit Australia, arrived in Sydney early on Saturday morning. The vessel has brought the largest number of passengers to arrive in one bottom.

On boarding the vessel one is at once struck with the comfortable lounge and reading room. Then you come to the large and splendidly appointed single-berth rooms, and work aft to the smoke room and verandah café. Below this, on the upper deck, are the bibby cabins and two-berth rooms, also a children's nursery. Proceeding down on to the main deck one comes to the magnificently appointed dining-room.

Themistocles and *Demosthenes* remained on the regular service to Australia until *Themistocles* arrived from Britain in October 1914 and was taken over by the Australian Government. Designated as troop transport A32, the vessel carried troops to Egypt in the second convoy that departed Albany on 31 December. *Demosthenes* was requisitioned early in 1915, becoming Australian troop transport A64, and carried Australian troops until 16 March 1916, then was passed on to the British Government. *Demosthenes* made numerous voyages with South African and Canadian troops, being joined under British control by *Themistocles* on 20 October 1917. In 1918 they were both used to carry American

124

troops across the Atlantic to Europe. During their war service the ships steamed over 200,000 miles each, and carried more than 50,000 troops.

On 21 December 1918, *Themistocles* departed London with troops returning to India, coming through the Suez Canal to Bombay, and then steaming non-stop to Sydney, where it arrived on 5 February 1919. *Demosthenes* picked up 550 Australian troops in Palestine and brought them directly to Sydney, but on arrival on 3 March was put into quarantine, with no one allowed ashore for three days. *Demosthenes* then went on to Newcastle and Melbourne before returning to Sydney, and then making a voyage back to Britain.

Themistocles departed London on 13 June 1919 with 1,500 troops returning to Australia, and left Cape Town on 3 July to continue the voyage. Late the same night in thick fog, *Themistocles* collided with the Norwegian sailing vessel *Edderside*, which sank with the loss of seven lives. With the port propeller damaged, *Themistocles* had to put back to Cape Town, and did not leave again until 20 July.

Late in 1919, *Themistocles* and *Demosthenes* were returned to their owners, and refitted for commercial service. On 20 July 1920 *Themistocles* made its first post-war sailing, with *Demosthenes* departing London on 19 August 1920.

From April 1923 the Plymouth call was dropped, and Southampton substituted on the return voyage only. In November 1926 the Aberdeen Line became part of the Kylsant Group, but the two liners were not affected until September 1928, when their home port was changed to Liverpool, and they passed into the management of White Star Line. They retained their Aberdeen Line hull and funnel colours, but wore the White Star house flag.

Themistocles took its first departure from Liverpool during September 1928, while *Demosthenes* did not make its first sailing from the west coast port until 2 February 1929. However, on 6 February 1931 *Demosthenes* left Liverpool on its final voyage to Australia, and was then laid up. Later in 1931 the Kylsant shipping empire collapsed, and *Demosthenes* was sold to Hughes, Bolckow & Co. for breaking up at Newcastle.

Themistocles was purchased by Shaw Savill & Albion, and retained its name, though being repainted in Shaw Savill colours, and refitted to carry 103 first class and 254 third class passengers. The only Shaw Savill & Albion vessel to be employed on the Australian trade at that time, *Themistocles* departed Liverpool on 30 June 1932 on its first voyage under the new colours, still going via Cape Town to Australia.

Themistocles was not requisitioned when war broke out in 1939, and remained on the regular trade. In July 1943 the vessel was the target for a group of German dive-bombers that attacked a convoy, but escaped without damage.

Themistocles survived the war, but was laid up in the River Blackwater in 1946, remaining there until 21 August 1947, when the old vessel was towed away to Dalmuir, arriving on 24 August, and being broken up shortly afterwards.

Themistocles in Shaw Savill colours.

CASSEL and CHEMNITZ

Built: 1901 by J. C. Tecklenborg, Geestemunde
Gross tonnage: 7,542
Dimensions: 428 x 54 ft/ 130.5 x 16.6 m
Service speed: 13 knots
Propulsion: Triple expansion/twin propellers

These two vessels and two sisters, *Brandenburg* and *Breslau*, were built for North German Lloyd to operate various secondary services across the North Atlantic, mostly serving on the route from Bremen to Baltimore, with occasional voyages from Bremen to New York, Philadelphia and Galveston.

Cassel was launched on 31 July 1901 under the name *Breslau*, being renamed prior to being completed three months later, departing Bremen on its maiden voyage to New York on 26 October 1901. *Chemnitz* was launched on 27 November 1901, leaving Bremen on 21 March 1902 on its maiden voyage, going to Baltimore.

They were basically large cargo ships fitted with cabins for 129 second class passengers, and could also carry up to 1,935 migrants in temporary steerage quarters on the westbound voyage.

On 7 October 1911 *Cassel* departed Bremen on the first of three voyages to Australia. The vessel called first at Antwerp and then Southampton to embark more passengers, arriving in Fremantle on 21 November.

Cassel went on to Melbourne, arriving on 1 December, carrying some 700 passengers, most of them migrants who disembarked there. *Cassel* continued to Sydney, arriving on 4 December, and on to Brisbane.

The second voyage made by *Cassel* arrived in Fremantle on 2 May 1912, Melbourne on 8 May and Sydney on 13 May, and the third voyage reached Melbourne on 21 October 1912 and Sydney nine days later, both trips continuing on to Brisbane.

On 25 August 1912 *Chemnitz* departed Antwerp carrying 800 migrants, arriving on 8 October 1912 in Melbourne, where most of the migrants disembarked. The vessel reached Sydney on 14 October and Brisbane on 18 October. This was destined to be the only time this vessel would be seen in Australian waters under the German flag, and it went back to the North Atlantic trades after returning from Australia.

Both these vessels were in Bremen when the war started in August 1914, and remained laid up there throughout the conflict. In 1919 they were seized by the victors as war prizes.

Cassel went to the French Government and was sold to Messageries Maritimes, by whom it was renamed *Marechal Gallieni*, serving under this name until being sold to shipbreakers at La Seyne, arriving there on 23 June 1926.

Chemnitz went to the British Government, and in 1920 made a voyage to Australia from Bombay, arriving in Melbourne on 7 May and Sydney on 9 May, then proceeding to Newcastle before returning to Britain.

Soon after arriving back in Britain *Chemnitz* was sold to the Ellerman Wilson Line, but not renamed. Its service for the new owners was quite brief, as on 8 December 1923 *Chemnitz* arrived in Rotterdam to be delivered to shipbreakers there.

Chemnitz

PORT LINCOLN and PORT MACQUARIE

Built: 1912 by Hawthorn Leslie, Newcastle
Tonnage: 7,243/7,236 gross
Dimensions: 426 x 54 ft/129.8 x 16.6 m
Service speed: 13 knots
Propulsion: Quadruple expansion/single propeller

Built for William Milburn & Co., better known as the Anglo-Australasian Steam Navigation Company, *Port Lincoln* was launched on 3 April 1912, being completed two months later. It was followed by *Port Macquarie*, which was launched in July 1912, and entered service in September.

Port Lincoln departed London in early August 1912 on its maiden voyage to Australia. On Saturday, 14 September 1912, the *Sydney Morning Herald* reported:

> The new steamer *Port Lincoln* (Messrs William Milburn and Co.'s new liner), the first of two sister vessels constructed by Hawthorn, Leslie and Co. Limited, is due to arrive at Sydney on Tuesday on completion of her maiden voyage from London. She is carrying passengers and general cargo. The cargo capacity is about 9,500 tons. Cabins with electric light and all the most modern conveniences are provided for 600 emigrants, and with the officers, doctors, stewards etc, the total number of persons carried can be about 740.

Port Macquarie departed London on 9 October 1912 on its maiden voyage, carrying 650 migrants to Melbourne and Sydney.

In January 1914 William Milburn & Co. amalgamated their operation with three other British firms to form the Commonwealth & Dominion Line, but there was no change in the service of the ships.

Shortly after war broke out in August 1914, *Port Lincoln* was requisitioned by the Australian Government, refitted to carry 25 officers, 370 troops and 371 horses overseas as transport A17, and left Albany on 1 November in the first convoy.

In December 1914 *Port Macquarie* was also taken over by the Australian Government, as transport A39, refitted to carry 25 officers, 371 troops and 456 horses, and joined the second convoy, which departed Albany on 28 December.

In 1916 the Commonwealth & Dominion Line was purchased by the Cunard Steamship Company. At first the company was known as the Cunard Line Australasian Service, but this was later changed to the Port Line.

After the war *Port Lincoln* and *Port Macquarie* continued to operate to Australia and New Zealand, but only as cargo ships, and in 1927 they were sold to the William Thomas Shipping Company. *Port Lincoln* was renamed *Cambrian Baroness*, while *Port Macquarie* became *Cambrian Marchioness*.

In 1929 *Cambrian Baroness* was sold to the Clan Line, and renamed *Clan Graham*. In 1938 the vessel was sold to another British firm, Neil & Pandelis, and renamed *Maritima*. *Cambrian Marchioness* remained in the William Thomas fleet until 1939, when it was sold to the Stanhope Shipping Co., of London, being renamed *Stangrant*, but on 13 October 1940 was torpedoed and sunk by the German submarine U37 in the North Atlantic, with the loss of eight lives. On 2 November 1942 *Maritima* was torpedoed and sunk by *U522*, also in the North Atlantic.

Port Macquarie

CERAMIC

Built: 1913 by Harland & Wolff, Belfast
Gross tonnage: 18,481
Dimensions: 679 x 69 ft/207 x 21.1 m
Service speed: 15 knots
Propulsion: Triple expansion/triple propellers

Ceramic was the longest liner operating on the route from Britain to Australia and New Zealand via Cape Town throughout its career. Launched on 11 December 1912, and completed in July 1913, *Ceramic* was a most impressive-looking vessel, its great size being offset by a low superstructure and long, sleek hull containing seven holds, being 19,590 tons deadweight, and 34,520 tons displacement. The bridge deck was 395 feet long, and the boat deck above 210 feet in length. The hull was subdivided by twelve watertight bulkheads.

Propulsion was by three propellers, with triple expansion engines on the two outer shafts and a low pressure direct drive turbine on the centre shaft powered by the exhaust steam of the wing engines.

Only third class accommodation for 600 passengers was provided, though an extra 220 could be carried in temporary berths if necessary. The accommodation consisted mostly of two and four berth cabins, located on the upper and middle decks, with the main restaurant also on the middle deck.

Leaving Liverpool on 24 July 1913, *Ceramic* proceeded first to Cape Town, and then across the Indian Ocean to Albany, Adelaide, Melbourne and Sydney, arriving there on 9 September. The *Sydney Morning Herald* reported on 10 September 1913:

The huge White Star liner *Ceramic*, by far the largest vessel to enter Port Jackson, steamed up the harbour early yesterday morning, amidst the noisy greetings of the small harbour craft. The *Ceramic* is a vessel of 18,481 tons gross, and she looked every ounce of it, as she loomed above the wharf and sheds at Miller's Point yesterday.

An inspection showed that the *Ceramic*, though of tremendous size, cannot be described as a floating palace. This is due to the fact that she carries only third class passengers. Her cabins are neat, but plain, and no unnecessary fittings are installed. In the dining saloon the visitor is again impressed more with the vastness of the vessel than with her decorations. Rows of long narrow tables hemmed in between further rows of swinging chairs stretch away on either side. No fewer than 500 seats are provided in this room, and there is still a good deal of space left for passageways for the stewards.

Her decks are wide and roomy, the saloon decks giving a free run of 500ft, and for the athlete, who is not satisfied with pacing them, there are provided a well-equipped gymnasium and a couple of large swimming baths.

Ceramic arrived in Australian waters from Britain in November 1914, and was taken over by the Australian Government for service as a transport in the second convoy carrying the Australian Expeditionary Force overseas. Allocated pennant number A40, *Ceramic* was refitted to carry 2,800 troops, the most to be carried from Australia in one vessel throughout the war. Departing Albany on 31 December 1914, the convoy reached Alexandria on 1 February 1915. After the troops disembarked, *Ceramic* continued to Britain.

Ceramic served the rest of the war under British control, and in May 1916 had a narrow escape from submarine attack in the Mediterranean. With 2,500 troops on board, the vessel was fired at about midnight by an unseen assailant, thought to have been a surfaced U-boat. The stern gun on *Ceramic* jammed after firing a few rounds, but the vessel managed to get away.

When the war ended, *Ceramic* returned to its pre-war route, which was being operated jointly by vessels of White Star, Shaw Savill, Blue Funnel and the Aberdeen Line. In 1926 the Kylsant Group took over three of the companies, White Star, Shaw Savill and the Aberdeen Line. *Ceramic* then ran under the banner of the White Star-Aberdeen Line, operating a joint service with Blue Funnel Line. The vessel subsequently made two round trips a year to Australia, departing Liverpool in January and August. In 1934 *Ceramic* was integrated into the Shaw Savill Line fleet, and the accommodation was reduced to 411 in third class, but it continued to make two round trips a year as before.

In 1936 the vessel was sent to

Ceramic as built.

the Govan yard of Harland & Wolff for an extensive refit, which lasted three months. The interior was completely stripped out, a new range of cabins being constructed in the modern style, many being single berth, some having private facilities, and all fitted with wash basins and hot and cold water. The Bibby tandem cabin system was also incorporated to increase the number of cabins with a porthole. As the passenger capacity was reduced to 336, several lifeboats were removed. The public rooms were redecorated, the forward end of the promenade deck glassed-in, and a verandah café added at the after end of the superstructure.

The engines were overhauled, modern condensers being installed, and two new bronze propellers along with a streamlined rudder were fitted. On running trials after the completion of the work, *Ceramic* was able to maintain 16 knots, and the gross tonnage had risen to 18,750.

On 15 August 1936 the vessel left Liverpool for Australia once again, still voyaging by way of Cape Town to Australia. When war was declared in 1939 *Ceramic* was outward bound from Britain, but was not called up for military duties, and continued to operate a regular service to Australia and New Zealand. From February 1940 the vessel came under the Shipping Controller, and the accommodation was usually taken up by service personnel, though when space permitted commercial passengers were carried as well.

On 20 July 1940 *Ceramic* departed Liverpool under the command of Captain G. Williams, bound for Australia, carrying 270 passengers and over 9,000 tons of general cargo. At 2.30 am on 11 August, when the vessel was off the coast of South West Africa, it collided almost head-on with the British cargo vessel *Testbank*, travelling in the opposite direction. The bow of the cargo vessel crashed into the starboard bow of *Ceramic*, causing a large hole above the water line. Fortunately the British liner *Viceroy of India*, which was serving as a troopship, was close by, and the passengers from *Ceramic* were transferred to it in lifeboats and taken to Cape Town. They were later embarked on another vessel to complete their journey to Australia.

Ceramic had to be towed stern first to Walvis Bay, arriving there on 16 August. After basic repairs had been made, the vessel left Walvis Bay under tow on 24 September, arriving in Cape Town on 1 October, where further repairs were completed. *Ceramic* finally departed Cape Town on 12 December to complete its voyage to Australia via Durban and Fremantle, arriving in Sydney on 18 January 1941. An inquiry held into the collision found the officer on watch aboard *Ceramic* was responsible as there had been insufficient lookouts on duty.

In October 1942 *Ceramic* was given a refit at Liverpool, and on 23 November left that port for Australia, carrying 378 passengers and 150 crew, and disappeared. After the war it became known that on 6 December 1942 *Ceramic* was torpedoed and sunk by a German submarine in the Atlantic. There was only one survivor, who was picked up by the submarine, and spent the rest of the war in a prison camp. It was not until he was released that the fate of *Ceramic* became known.

Ceramic after alterations in 1932.

NESTOR and ULYSSES

Built: 1913 by Workman, Clark & Co., Belfast
Gross tonnage: 14,501/14,499
Dimensions: 580 x 68 ft/176.8 x 20.8 m
Service speed: 14 knots
Propulsion: Triple expansion/twin propellers

Built for the Blue Funnel Line, *Ulysses* was the fourth vessel in the fleet to bear that name, and *Nestor* the third. Launched on 7 December 1912, *Nestor* ran trials on 28 April 1913, and departed Liverpool on its maiden voyage on 19 May, going by way of Cape Town to the main Australian ports. On 10 June, the *Sydney Morning Herald* reported:

> The *Nestor* will be the largest liner which has ever visited Australia, having a gross tonnage of 14,500 and a loaded displacement of about 26,900 tons. She has accommodation for 340 first-class passengers, occupying the midships portion of three decks. A large number of cabins have single berths, though the majority of rooms are arranged for two, three and four persons.
>
> The dining saloon on the main deck extends the full width of the vessel, and contains small tables and moveable chairs. A room adjoining the dining-room is provided for children. A broad oak staircase leads from the dining saloon to the entrance hall on the promenade deck. The music saloon opens off the main entrance hall, and has a raised central roof giving it a lofty appearance.
>
> A social lounge and smokeroom are also prominent features. A system of steam heating has been arranged throughout the vessel, and each section is under separate control. The vessel is lighted throughout with electricity, and electric call bells are fitted in all staterooms and public rooms.
>
> There are seven holds for cargo, one of which has been insulated, as are also the after 'tween decks. Each hold is provided with steam winches and special gear for handling cargo. A system of steam pipes for extinguishing fires has been arranged to each hold and 'tween decks. The propelling machinery consists of two independent sets of triple-expansion engines.

For a few weeks *Nestor* was the largest vessel on the Australian service, being eclipsed by *Ceramic* in July 1913. *Ulysses* was launched on 5 July 1913, handed over to Blue Funnel Line on 22 October, and departing soon afterward on its maiden voyage to Australia.

Both ships originally had accommodation for 275 first class passengers only, spread over three decks amidships, being spacious and comfortable without luxury. The most notable feature of the pair was their single tall funnel, which rose 75 ft/22.8 m above the

Nestor

Ulysses

boat deck, and was one of the highest ever fitted on a ship. They were notably steady, and the fact that the accommodation was one class increased their popularity, and it was soon increased to cater for 338 passengers.

In November 1914, *Ulysses* was requisitioned by the Australian Government as transport A38, fitted out to carry 100 officers and 2,000 other ranks, and included in the second convoy to depart Australia, leaving Albany on 31 December, with the troops being landed at Alexandria. In September 1915 *Nestor* was also requisitioned by the Australian Government, becoming troopship A71, with accommodation for 90 officers and 2,149 other ranks. *Nestor* made several trips with Australians to the Dardanelles, and although attacked on occasions by Turkish shore batteries, escaped unscathed.

In January 1916 *Nestor* was a member of a huge troop convoy that left Plymouth to travel by way of South Africa to East Africa, India and Mesopotamia. In the middle of 1917 *Nestor* was released from its troop carrying role and returned to the Australian route.

From April 1918 *Nestor* made five round trips between Britain and America, bringing back essential foodstuffs and armaments. This ended in November 1918, at which time it was released from Government control, given a quick refit and in December resumed the Australian service. *Ulysses* did not resume commercial service until September 1920, with a voyage from Glasgow to Australia.

Once the immediate post-war rush had subsided, *Nestor* was given a more complete refit, which included the addition of a lounge and smoke room at the after end of the boat deck. In 1921 super-heaters were fitted to the engines of both vessels to improve economy.

In 1926 the route was suffering the early effects of the coming Great Depression, and Blue Funnel began a joint service with Shaw Savill and the White Star Line to avoid cut-throat competition. When Shaw Savill took over both White Star and the Aberdeen Line, the service was known as the Blue Funnel-Shaw Savill Line, with four ships in operation from each company.

In 1935 alterations were made to the accommodation of *Ulysses* and *Nestor*, which was reduced to 175 in first class only by converting many two berth cabins into singles, and the addition of some special cabins on the boat deck. When war broke out again in 1939, *Nestor* and *Ulysses* were left on the Australian run, and at one time *Nestor* was used to evacuate British children to Australia.

Apart from one voyage to the Far East, *Nestor* remained on the Australian route throughout the conflict, during which time its passenger capacity was raised again to 250. *Nestor* survived the war without incident, but *Ulysses* was not so fortunate.

In April 1942 *Ulysses* was en route from Australia to Britain through the Panama Canal, and in the Caribbean collided with a tanker. *Ulysses* was ordered to make for an American port, but was hit by a torpedo from a German submarine and sunk on 10 April 1942 off Palm Beach in Florida.

After the war *Nestor* had its passenger complement reduced to 175 again, and remained on the service to Australia. On 23 December 1949 *Nestor* left Liverpool on its final voyage and on returning to Britain was sold to shipbreakers.

EURIPIDES

Built: 1914 by Harland & Wolff, Belfast
Gross tonnage: 14,947
Dimensions: 570 x 67 ft/173.6 x 20.5 m
Service speed: 15 knots
Propulsion: Triple expansion/triple propellers

Built for the Aberdeen Line, *Euripides* was launched on 29 January 1914, being completed six months later. The propulsion of the ship comprised triple expansion engines driving the two outer propellers while the centre propeller was turned by a low pressure turbine powered by the exhaust steam from the wing engines. There were five boilers burning coal, with a bunker capacity for 2,685 tons burnt at 90 tons per day at full speed.

Accommodation was provided for 140 first class and 334 third class passengers, but areas of the 'tween decks could be used by a further 800 third class or migrants. *Euripides* departed London on 1 July 1914, going by way of Cape Town to arrive in Sydney on 16 August. Next day the *Daily Telegraph* reported:

> The *Euripides*, the latest acquisition to the Aberdeen Line, a strikingly handsome liner, is berthed at Dalgety's Wharf after her maiden run from London.
>
> The *Euripides* has been designed and constructed with a view to ensuring the utmost strength of structure and the greatest margin of safety. The double bottom extends right fore and aft, and there are 11 watertight bulkheads carried up to the awning deck.

> The *Euripides* has excellent accommodation for 1350 passengers. As usual with the Aberdeen Line, two classes only are carried – first and third – which enables the greatest advantage to be taken of the space available in arranging the accommodation for the respective classes. The first-class dining saloon on the main deck forward extends right across the ship, and is arranged to seat 112 passengers. It is Georgian in design, and exceptionally large and commodious, as, indeed, are all the public rooms. The sidelights are of large diameter, and the room has a very handsome and pleasant appearance. The nursery is on the awning deck, panelled and framed in pine, finished white, with mahogany furniture.

> The first-class smoke-room, on the boat deck, is panelled and framed in oak, relieved with carvings. The furniture is oak. At the after end is a verandah. The library and lounge, on the bridge deck is panelled and framed in sycamore. This compartment has parquetry flooring, and contains bookcase, small tables, writing tables, settees, and easy chairs. The gymnasium will be appreciated by passengers.

> The staterooms are situated on the bridge and awning decks, and are arranged as two and three berth-rooms. Cot beds are fitted to eight rooms on the awning deck, and one room can be converted into a sitting room. Each room is fitted with a single or double folding lavatory and wardrobe. A large number of the rooms on the bridge deck are intercommunicable.

Euripides (David Finch collection)

On the awning deck the rooms are arranged on the tandem principle. All the cabins are of good height, those on the awning deck being 8 ft 9 in, and those on the bridge deck 9 ft. Every cabin has a porthole to itself.

Like the other vessels of the line, the *Euripides* has superior accommodation for third-class passengers. The third-class dining saloon, on the main deck, will seat 274 persons.

Euripides arrived in Brisbane on 24 August, and two days later was requisitioned by the Australian Government, becoming transport A14. *Euripides* was included in the first convoy that left Albany on 1 November 1914, disembarking troops on 3 December at Alexandria, then continuing on to Britain to unload cargo.

Euripides remained on the Australian service, returning to Britain with troops, carrying over 38,000 men in the first six months of the war. In 1918 *Euripides* was diverted to New York, from where American troops were carried to Britain, and for some time the vessel was employed on the North Atlantic troop service. By the time the war ended in November 1918, *Euripides* had steamed over 900,000 miles in Government service.

Euripides left London on 3 March 1919 with Australian troops returning home, going through the Suez Canal and calling at Colombo. After calls at Fremantle, Adelaide and Melbourne, *Euripides* arrived in Sydney on 22 April and was put in Quarantine for three days before the troops disembarked.

Later in 1919 *Euripides* was returned to full commercial service. A minor change to the route occurred in March 1923, when the call at Plymouth on the homeward bound voyage was dropped, and Southampton substituted. By 1926 passenger traffic was slumping, and in 1927 *Euripides* was laid up in the Gareloch.

In 1928 the Aberdeen Line ceased to exist as a separate entity in the Kylsant Group, being renamed the White Star Aberdeen Line. *Euripides* was transferred to the new company, and began operating from Liverpool alongside ships of the White Star Line. In 1931 *Euripides* was transferred to Shaw Savill Line, and completed its final voyage in Aberdeen Line colours at Liverpool in July 1932. The vessel was then refitted by Hawthorn Leslie for the New Zealand trade.

The boilers were converted to oil firing, which also increased speed to 15 knots, and the accommodation was completely rebuilt to cater for 200 cabin class passengers only. New amenities provided included a swimming pool, gymnasium and a verandah cafe atop the after end of the superstructure, a feature of all Shaw Savill ships.

The vessel was renamed *Akaroa*, and departed London on 30 December 1932 on its first voyage to New Zealand, going via the Panama Canal in both directions. When war broke out in 1939, *Akaroa* was left on its regular service, and also made some voyages to Australia. For a while *Akaroa* was based at Southampton, but eventually operated out of Avonmouth.

Akaroa was sent to the Tyne for an extensive refit in 1946. The accommodation was reduced to carry only 190 cabin class passengers, and in 1947 *Akaroa* resumed her service to New Zealand.

On 28 April 1954 *Akaroa* arrived in Southampton at the end of its last voyage, and shortly after was sold to shipbreakers.

Akaroa.

THE P&O K SHIPS

KHYBER   KARMALA KHIVA KALYAN
Built: 1914/14/14/15 by Cammell Laird, Birkenhead
Gross tonnage: 9,114/9,128/8,947/9,144
Dimensions: 480 x 58ft/144 x 17.4 m
Service speed: 14 knots
Propulsion: Quadruple expansion/twin propellers

KASHGAR   KASHMIR
Built: 1914/15 by Caird, Greenock
Gross tonnage: 9,005/8,985
Dimensions: 480 x 58ft/144 x 17.4 m
Service speed: 14 knots
Propulsion: Quadruple expansion/twin propellers

These vessels were ordered for the service from London to Japan, and two were still being built when the war started in August 1914. Five were used on the Australian trade in the early years of the war, though they could only accommodate 79 first class and 68 second class passengers.

The first vessel to be launched was *Khiva*, on 19 September 1913, which departed London on 7 January 1914 on its maiden voyage to Japan. *Khyber* joined the Japanese trade in April 1914, followed a month later by *Kashmir*, and *Karmala* in June. *Kashgar* was completed in December 1914, and also joined the Japan service, but *Kalyan*, which was launched on 24 September 1914, went straight into military service when completed in April 1915.

The first voyage to Australia, leaving London on 5 September 1914, was taken by *Khyber*, which made four round trips. *Karmala* also made four round trips, the first departing on 27 November 1915, followed on 5 February 1916 by *Khiva*, which made two voyages. *Kashgar* made three voyages, the first departing on 4 March 1916, while *Kashmir* left London on 22 December 1916 on the first of two trips.

Kashgar, *Karmala* and *Kashmir* were all taken over for military duty between 1916 and 1918, mostly serving as troopships, while *Kalyan* later became a hospital ship.

All six ships survived the war, and most were returned to the Far East trade, but two were placed on the Australian route briefly. *Karmala* left London on 19 June 1919 on a single round trip to Sydney, carrying Government-sponsored passengers only, while *Khyber* made a 15 May 1920 departure from London, and remained on the route for a further four round trips.

On 23 June 1922 *Khiva* left London on a single voyage to Australia, while *Kalyan* made its first appearance on the route when it left London on 22 December 1922 for a single round trip. *Khiva* made one further trip to Australia from London on 27 February 1925, while the last voyage to Australia by these ships was that by *Karmala* from London on 17 May 1928.

Khiva was severely damaged by a fire during 1931 and sold to shipbreakers, while *Khyber* and *Kalyan* also went to the breakers' yard the same year. *Karmala*, *Kashgar* and *Kashmir* followed to the breakers' yard in 1932.

Karmala

134

HORORATA

Built: 1914 by Wm Denny & Bros, Dumbarton
Gross tonnage: 9,178
Dimensions: 510 x 64 ft/155.4 x 19.5 m
Service speed: 13 knots
Propulsion: Quadruple expansion/twin propellers

Basically designed as a large cargo ship for the New Zealand Shipping Company, *Hororata* was launched on 29 December 1913, but fitting out was delayed by a riveters' strike, and then the after deck was strengthened to enable two 4.7 inch guns to be fitted in the event of war. It was not until 23 May 1914 that *Hororata* was delivered to the NZSC.

In addition to a large cargo capacity, *Hororata* was fitted with cabin accommodation for five first class passengers, and temporary accommodation for up to 1,066 migrants erected in the 'tween decks.

Hororata departed London on its maiden voyage in June 1914, but on reaching Australia was requisitioned by the Australian Government and converted into a troopship in Brisbane and allocated pennant number A20. *Hororata* embarked troops in Melbourne and steamed to Albany in Western Australia, where the first convoy to be sent overseas from Australia was being assembled. The convoy departed on 1 November 1914, with the troops being landed at Alexandria in Egypt in early December. *Hororata* continued on to Britain, and remained under Australian control until August 1917, when the Shipping Controller took over.

After the war *Horarata* was refitted to again carry migrants, and began operating a regular service between Britain and New Zealand via the Panama Canal. *Hororata* continued in this trade until May 1939, when it was transferred within the P&O Group to British India Line, being renamed *Waroonga*. The vessel was employed on a service from British ports to Australia, and remained on this trade after war broke out in September 1939 being used to transport troops and supplies between Australia and Britain.

In April 1943 *Waroonga*, carrying a full cargo of foodstuffs from Australia to Britain, including butter and cheese, joined a large convoy proceeding from New York to Liverpool. The convoy was detected by a wolf-pack of U-boats four days out on its voyage, and during the night of 4–5 April the wolf pack attacked, and *Waroonga* was one of several ships hit by torpedoes.

With No. 4 hold flooded, the vessel was able to remain afloat through the night, and at daylight it was hoped it could be saved. Throughout the day *Waroonga* made its way slowly eastward, awaiting the arrival of a rescue tug, but during the next night the engine-room bulkhead began leaking. On the morning of 6 April the situation had deteriorated to the point where, shortly before dawn, the captain gave the order to abandon ship. By now the weather had also turned bad, with strong winds whipping up high seas, and it was also very cold. Lifeboats were launched, but one containing thirteen crewmen and the Chief Officer turned over, and all were lost. The rest of the crew was able to reach a rescue ship, and *Waroonga* then sank slowly by the stern, the bow pointing almost vertically into the air before it slipped beneath the waves.

Hororata

STAR OF VICTORIA and STAR OF ENGLAND

Built: 1914 by Workman, Clarke & Co., Belfast
Tonnage: 9,152/9,136 gross
Dimensions: 501 x 64 ft/152.7 x 19.3 m
Service speed: 13 knots
Propulsion: Triple expansion/single propeller

In 1913 the Belfast firm of James P. Corry & Co. secured a contract from the Government of Victoria to transport migrants, and ordered two vessels for this trade. They would essentially be cargo ships, but on the outward voyage to Melbourne temporary quarters would be erected in the holds for several hundred migrants. The first, *Star of Victoria*, was launched on 13 November 1913, and handed over to James P. Corry & Co on 10 January 1914.

In January 1914, Corry & Co. merged with G. D. Tyser & Co., the Indra Line and the Anglo-Australasian Steam Navigation Co. to form a new company, Commonwealth & Dominion Line Ltd. On 23 January 1914, *Star of Victoria* was transferred to the ownership of the Commonwealth & Dominion Line, and repainted in their colours.

On 1 February 1914 *Star of Victoria* departed London on its first voyage to Australia, via Cape Town, arriving in Melbourne on 11 March, and Sydney on 16 March. The vessel departed Sydney on 20 March for Auckland and Wellington, then voyaged back to Britain around Cape Horn, returning to London on 21 June.

The second vessel was launched on 16 February 1914 as *Star of England*, being delivered in April to Commonwealth & Dominion Line, who also took over the payments for the vessel. *Star of England* left London on 14 May 1914 on its first voyage to Australia, arriving in Melbourne on 23 June and Sydney on 29 June.

After war broke out in August 1914, both vessels were requisitioned when they arrived in Australian waters from Britain, *Star of England* becoming Australian transport A15, while *Star of Victoria* became A16. *Star of England* was fitted out to carry 29 officers, 499 troops and 476 horses, while *Star of Victoria* could carry 30 officers, 511 troops and 537 horses. The two ships joined the first convoy of Australian and New Zealand troops to be sent overseas, departing Albany on 1 November 1914, disembarking their troops and horses at Alexandria some five weeks later.

Star of Victoria and *Star of England* were then released by the Australian Government, but for the rest of the war were controlled by the British Government, and continued to operate to Australia and New Zealand carrying valuable foodstuffs back to Britain in their refrigerated holds.

In 1916 the Commonwealth & Dominion Line was acquired by the Cunard Line, and *Star of Victoria* was renamed *Port Melbourne*, while *Star of England* became *Port Sydney*. After the war the ships had their funnels repainted in Cunard colours, with a grey hull. For some years the company was known as the Cunard Line Australasian Service, but eventually became known as the Port Line.

Port Melbourne and *Port Sydney* continued to operate to Australia and New Zealand, but only carried a maximum of twelve passengers. Both survived World War II, and continued trading for a couple of years after it ended. *Port Melbourne* arrived at Blyth on 18 May 1948 to be broken up, while *Port Sydney* was broken up at Preston during the same year.

Star of England as Australian transport A15 in World War I.

KAISAR-I-HIND

Built: 1914 by Caird & Co., Greenock
Gross tonnage: 11,430
Dimensions: 540 x 61 ft/164.6 x 18.6 m
Service speed: 16 knots
Propulsion: Quadruple expansion/Twin propellers

This liner, the second to carry the name, was built to operate on the P&O mail service between London and Bombay, *Kaisar-I-Hind* being Hindi for 'Empress of India'. Launched on 28 June 1914, the vessel was still being completed when war broke out two months later. Despite this the work continued, and the vessel was handed over to P&O on 1 October 1914.

On 24 October *Kaisar-I-Hind* departed London on its maiden voyage to Bombay as scheduled, setting a new record for the voyage of just under 21 days. Accommodation was provided for 315 first class and 233 second class passengers, and there was very little cargo space. *Kaisar-I-Hind* operated regular voyages to India for almost two years,

During World War I most of the passenger liners owned by the P&O Line were taken over for military duty, and the company also suffered the loss of several of the ships it was using to maintain its regular services to India and Australia. It was under these conditions that *Kaisar-I-Hind* made several voyages to Australia.

On 9 June 1916 the vessel departed London on its first voyage to Australia, via Bombay and Colombo, passing through Adelaide on 19 July and Melbourne on 21 July, arriving in Sydney on 24 July. A second voyage to Australia left London in October 1916, reaching Sydney on 30 November.

The third voyage to Australia by *Kaisar-I-Hind* departed London on 16 February 1917, arriving in Sydney on 18 April. Soon after returning to Britain *Kaisar-I-Hind* was taken over for duty as a troop transport. The vessel managed to escape five torpedo attacks during the war, including one incident in September 1918 when a torpedo fired by a U-boat actually hit the ship, but failed to explode, only denting several plates.

On 6 May 1919 *Kaisar-I-Hind* departed Britain on another voyage to Australia, this time bringing home troops as well as carrying fare-paying passengers, arriving in Fremantle on 9 June, Melbourne on 16 June and Sydney on 18 June.

After returning to Britain the vessel was given a quick refit, and on 10 October 1919 departed London on its first post-war voyage to Bombay.

In 1921 *Kaisar-I-Hind* was chartered to Cunard Line, and under the name *Emperor of India* departed Southampton on 21 June on the first of four round trips to New York. On being returned to P&O it reverted to its original name.

Kaisar-I-Hind remained on the service to Bombay until 1929, when it began extending its voyages to the Far East. On 22 April 1938 the vessel arrived in London for the last time, and was sold soon after to shipbreakers at Blyth.

Kaisar-I-Hind berthed in Sydney.

GANGE, LOUQSOR and EL KANTARA

Built: 1905 by Soc. Provencale de Cons Nav., La Ciotat
Gross tonnage: 6,886
Dimensions: 447 x 52 ft/136.3 x 15.8 m
Service speed: 13 knots
Propulsion: Triple expansion/single propeller

This trio, along with another sister, *Euphrate*, were built as cargo/passenger ships for Messageries Maritimes to operate on their route from French ports to French colonies in the Far East, terminating at Haiphong in Vietnam. Accommodation was provided for 40 first class and 54 second class passengers, and up to 1,200 troops could be transported using hammocks and temporary quarters erected in the holds.

Louqsor was launched on 9 April 1904, departing Dunkirk on 27 January 1905 on its maiden voyage. *El Kantara* was launched on 4 August 1904, entering service in March 1905. *Gange*, the last member of the group to be built, was launched on 6 August 1905, entering service by the end of that year.

For ten years the three vessels remained on the Far East trade, but in August 1914 they were taken over for military duty, initially serving as troopships. In April and May of 1915 Gange was involved in the landings at Gallipoli. On 18 December 1916 *Louqsor* became a hospital ship, serving in this role until 12 July 1917 then reverting to trooping duties again.

In early September 1916, *Gange* left Marseilles on a voyage to Melbourne and Noumea via the Suez Canal.

The vessel first called at Malta to embark a group of 214 young men who had been granted visas by the British Colonial Office to migrate to Australia at their own expense to find work.

Meanwhile, in Australia the Prime Minister, Billy Hughes, was actively promoting a 'yes' vote in a referendum about to be held on the introduction of conscription. There was uproar throughout the country when another ship, the P&O liner *Arabia*, arrived in Sydney in September 1916 and disembarked 97 men from Malta who had paid their own fares to migrate to Australia to find work. The unions branded these Maltese migrants 'cheap labour' who would steal jobs from Australian men sent overseas to fight in the war.

Prime Minister Hughes promised that no more foreign workers would be allowed to enter the country, and demanded that the British Colonial Office not grant any more Maltese men permission to travel to Australia, but by then the *Gange* was on its way.

Hughes then discovered that *Gange* was due to arrive in Melbourne on 29 October, the same day voting would be held on the referendum. In desperation, he slapped a media embargo on news about the *Gange* and its migrants, and tried to have the ship prevented from berthing in Melbourne. However, word leaked out about the Maltese men who would be arriving on the *Gange*. Soon it was common knowledge around the country, and Hughes, a strong supporter of conscription, knew it could kill the referendum.

When the *Gange* berthed in Melbourne, troops were

El Kantara

Louqsor

called in to prevent the Maltese men landing. They were forced to sit a dictation test, given to them in Dutch, which they naturally failed, and on that basis were declared prohibited immigrants. The men remained on board the *Gange* when it left Melbourne on 3 November for Noumea, where they disembarked, and were housed in a disused hall at Australian Government expense.

The referendum to introduce conscription was defeated, and after two months Billy Hughes reluctantly allowed the Maltese migrants to be brought to Sydney, but they were imprisoned on an old hulk in Berry's Bay until 9 March 1917, when they were finally freed.

Ironically, many of the men later returned to Malta, but a few settled in Australia. One, Emanuel Attard, joined the Australian army, and ended up fighting in France. After the war he returned to Australia, where he spent the rest of his life.

Meanwhile, *Gange* had embarked troops in Noumea to be taken to France, arriving at Marseilles on 12 February 1917. Two months later the vessel was entering the port of Bizerta on 14 April 1917 when it hit a mine and was sunk.

The three sisters of *Gange* all survived the war, and were handed back to Messageries Maritimes. In 1919 *El Kantara* carried troops home from Marseilles to Tahiti and New Caledonia, and on this voyage became the first French flag ship to pass through the Panama Canal, in May 1919.

In March 1920 *El Kantara* was placed on the trade from Marseilles to Colombo, Australian ports and Noumea, passing through Fremantle on 3 April. This was followed by a second voyage at the end of 1920, and a third voyage passing through Fremantle on 14 August 1921. The final voyage to Australia by *El Kantara* arrived in Fremantle on 25 April 1922.

It was not until June 1922 that *Louqsor* made its first voyage to Australia. *Louqsor* made only two trips on the route, the second reaching Fremantle on 24 April 1923. The use of these two ships on the Australian trade was only a stopgap measure until better vessels were available. They had permanent accommodation for 40 first class and 54 second class passengers, while temporary quarters for a large number of migrants could be erected in the holds on the outward voyages.

Both vessels were transferred to the service from France to Tahiti and Noumea via the Panama Canal, with *El Kantara* leaving Marseilles on 24 April on its first voyage on this route. In December 1926 *El Kantara* was sold to shipbreakers at Dunkirk. *Louqsor* remained in service for a further three years, then was sold to shipbreakers in Belgium in March 1930. The fourth sister, *Euphrate*, survived through the Second World War too, and served until September 1951, when it was wrecked at Socotra.

NALDERA and NARKUNDA

NALDERA

Built: 1920 by Caird & Co., Greenock
Gross tonnage: 15,825
Dimensions: 605 x 67 ft/184.4 x 20.5 m
Service speed: 17 knots
Propulsion: Quadruple expansion/twin propellers

NARKUNDA

Built: 1920 by Harland & Wolff, Belfast
Gross tonnage: 16,118
Dimensions: 606 x 70 ft/184.7 x 21.4 m
Service speed: 17 knots
Propulsion: Quadruple expansion/twin propellers

These vessels were laid down in 1914, but work stopped when the war started. For three years the hulls sat on the slips, but in 1917 all incomplete merchant vessels were ordered to be finished as quickly as possible, and pressed into military service.

Naldera was launched on 29 December 1917, followed by *Narkunda* on 25 April 1918, but neither was completed when the war ended, and P&O gained control of them late in 1918.

Naldera and *Narkunda* were the last coal-fired liners to be built for P&O, having a bunker capacity of 1,895 tons of coal burned at a rate of 200 tons per day at 17.5 knots. The new ships were the first in the company to be given three funnels and cruiser sterns.

The two ships were easily distinguishable, as *Narkunda* was given a rather ugly forecastle. Only the forward pair of funnels served the boilers, the aft funnel acting as a ventilator for the engine room. Both ships provided accommodation for 426 first class and 247 second class passengers.

Naldera was the first to be handed over to P&O, on 24 March 1920, and on 10 April left Tilbury on its maiden voyage to Australia. *Narkunda* was handed over to P&O on 30 March 1920, but its maiden voyage from Tilbury on 24 April was on the Indian service, being a return voyage to Bombay. On 9 July the vessel left Tilbury on its first voyage to Australia.

For their first couple of years on the Australian trade a call was made at Bombay on alternate outward voyages. *Naldera* and *Narkunda* gave efficient if unspectacular service to P&O, but being coal burners was a drawback.

On 2 April 1931 *Naldera* left Tilbury on its last regular voyage to Australia and was then transferred to the service from London to Bombay and on to the Far East, though it would also make some voyages only as far as Bombay. *Naldera* did make one further sailing to Australia, in June 1934, but the remainder of its career would be spent on the Indian and Far East routes.

In 1938 *Naldera* was withdrawn from service, and laid up. However, the Munich crisis arose at that time, and *Naldera* was hurriedly reactivated to carry troops from Britain to supervise the plebiscite to be held in Czechoslovakia. The ship had actually left Tilbury with

Naldera

Narkunda

the troops aboard when the plebiscite was abandoned, so *Naldera* returned to the Thames, where the troops disembarked and the vessel was laid up again. During November 1938 *Naldera* was sold to P. & W. McLellan, a British firm of shipbreakers with a yard at Bo'ness.

Narkunda remained on the Australian trade, and in 1938 was taken out of service to have the boilers converted to oil firing. At the same time the first class accommodation was reduced to 350, but *Narkunda* looked very old when compared to the latest of the Strath liners, which had been given white hulls and yellow funnels while *Narkunda* still carried its original colours.

When war broke out in September 1939 all the P&O liners on the Australian trade were requisitioned for war service within a matter of months, except *Narkunda*, which had made its last sailing on the regular schedule from Tilbury on 23 June 1939. All future voyages to Australia were made in convoys and at irregular intervals, but in May 1940 *Narkunda* was requisitioned for service as a troopship.

On its final voyage from Australia *Narkunda* arrived at Marseilles on 21 May 1940, then passed through the Straits of Gibraltar four days later on the way back to Britain. While crossing the Bay of Biscay an unknown vessel began to chase *Narkunda*, firing several shots,

but the captain turned his ship west and brought it up to full speed, shaking off the pursuer and continuing the voyage to reach Southampton safely on 30 May, as London was considered too dangerous by that time. As soon as the passengers and cargo were off loaded, the ship was converted for its new role.

For over two years the old vessel carried troops as required, and in October 1942 was one of the huge fleet of troopships gathered at various British ports to carry soldiers for the planned invasion of North Africa. *Narkunda* was deployed in the follow-up convoy to the initial strike force, and on 14 November 1942 arrived at Bougie and landed troops in the harbour within a few hours.

With enemy bombers active in the area, the captain was anxious to get his stationary ship moving as soon as possible, and in the afternoon *Narkunda* steamed out of the harbour, and headed west for Algiers. The sky was cloudy, and suddenly bombs began to fall around the ship. A near miss on the port side wrecked the bridge and chartroom, and as avoiding action was being taken a second stick of bombs struck the stern of the vessel, which began to sink immediately. Boats were lowered as the stern settled, and shortly afterwards the bow rose high in the air, and *Narkunda* slid to the bottom. Thirty-one persons lost their lives in the action.

ORMONDE

Built: 1918 by John Brown, Clydebank
Gross tonnage: 14,853
Dimensions: 600 x 66 ft/182.9 x 20.3 m
Service speed: 18 knots
Propulsion: Geared turbines/twin propellers

Being laid down in May 1914, the Orient Line planned to have *Ormonde* in service two years later, but when war broke out in August 1914 construction work ceased. *Ormonde* remained idle on the stocks until late in 1916, when orders were received to complete the ship as a troop transport.

Ormonde was launched without ceremony on 10 February 1917, being completed in November 1917. Departing Glasgow on 13 November, the vessel arrived in Sydney for the first time on 14 February 1918, departing on 2 March with troops bound for Egypt, and spent the rest of the war in this role.

In May 1919 *Ormonde* was released from military duty. Fitted out with accommodation for 278 first class ,195 second class and 1,000 third class passengers, on 15 November 1919 *Ormonde* sailed from Tilbury on its maiden commercial voyage to Australia.

On its second voyage to Australia, on 2 April 1920 the stern hit the bank of the Suez Canal, damaging the port propeller. The liner limped into Colombo to have a new propeller fitted, then continued to Australia several days behind schedule. On the return voyage engine trouble

developed when *Ormonde* was between Melbourne and Adelaide, where the ship was held up again while repairs were completed.

In July 1923 the boilers were converted from coal to burn oil, and at the same time the accommodation was reconfigured to carry first and third class passengers only. *Ormonde* was not needed all year on the mail run, and was taken off the route for cruises from Britain during the northern summer months. In 1933, *Ormonde* was refitted to carry 777 tourist class passengers only, mostly migrants.

On 23 September 1936, *Ormonde* was bound from Melbourne to Sydney when a fire broke out in No. 4 hold, and the ship diverted into Twofold Bay where the blaze was extinguished. Only minor damage was incurred.

3 September 1939 found *Ormonde* in the Indian Ocean en route to Australia. After one more round trip, *Ormonde* became a troopship once again, being handed back to Orient Line in 1946. Refitted to carry British 1,052 migrants in one class, *Ormonde* left London on 10 October 1947, and over the next five years made seventeen round trips, carrying 17,500 migrants. On 21 August 1952 *Ormonde* left Tilbury on its final voyage to Australia, returning to Britain in October and being sold the following month to shipbreakers. On 1 December 1952 the old ship left London for the last time, going to Dalmuir, where it was scrapped.

Ormonde at Hobart.

MEGANTIC

Built: 1909 by Harland & Wolff, Belfast
Gross tonnage: 14,878
Dimensions: 565 x 67 ft/172.2 x 20.5 m
Service speed: 16 knots
Propulsion: Quadruple expansion/twin propellers

The White Star liner *Megantic* made only one voyage to Australia, in 1920, with returning troops, their dependents, and some migrants. Unlike the vessels White Star Line used regularly on the Australian trade, *Megantic* was primarily a passenger liner with some cargo capacity.

The vessel had originally been ordered for the Dominion Line, and was to have been named *Albany*, but it was transferred within the International Merchant Marine group of companies to White Star Line while still under construction. Launched on 10 December 1908, *Megantic* was delivered in June 1909, and placed on the Canadian trade, leaving Liverpool for the first time on 17 June for Montreal.

Megantic provided accommodation for 260 first class, 430 in second class and about 1,000 third class passengers, the latter being mainly allocated to migrants on the westbound voyages.

In 1914, *Megantic* was requisitioned as a troopship, serving until 1917. The vessel then began operating regular voyages across the North Atlantic between Liverpool and New York, though the accommodation was controlled by the Government. Returned to White Star in 1919,

Megantic was refitted with accommodation for 325 first class, 260 second class and 550 third class passengers and resumed its place on the Canadian trade until being sent to Australia.

Megantic departed Liverpool on 9 January 1920, reaching Melbourne on 24 February, then continuing to Sydney, arriving on the afternoon of 26 February. For the return trip, *Megantic* boarded fare-paying passengers, departing on 12 March on a voyage across the Pacific and through the Panama Canal to New York and then on to Liverpool.

On returning from this trip, *Megantic* went back to the Canadian trade. In 1924 the first class accommodation was altered to carry 452 cabin class passengers, with second and third class remaining as before. In 1927 the vessel made one trip to China carrying British troops, and in 1928 began operating to Canada and New York from London.

The late 1920s were marred by two outbreaks of fire on board, the first occurring on 6 July 1928, when the ship diverted to Southampton with a fire burning in No. 2 hold, though damage was slight. On 1 March 1929 a fire broke out when the ship was berthed in London, again in No. 2 hold, which had to be flooded as it contained rolls of paper and straw. Again damage was slight.

In 1931 *Megantic* again began operating from Liverpool to Quebec and Montreal, but in July that year was laid up in Rothesay Bay, and sold to Japanese shipbreakers in February 1933.

Megantic in Sydney.

EARLY ITALIAN VESSELS

CARIGNANO
Built: 1918 by Ropner & Sons, Stockton
Gross tonnage: 5,359
Dimensions: 412 x 52 ft/117.3 x 15.8 m
Service speed: 11 knots
Propulsion: Triple expansion/single propeller

MONCALIERI
Built: 1918 by Craig, Taylor & Co. Ltd, Stockton
Gross tonnage: 5,359
Dimensions: 412 x 52 ft/117.3 x 15.8 m
Service speed: 11 knots
Propulsion: Triple expansion/single propeller

CAPODIMONTE
Built: 1917 by Kawasaki Dockyard Co., Japan
Gross tonnage: 5,875
Dimensions: 385 x 51 ft/117.3 x 15.5 m
Service speed: 12 knots
Propulsion: Triple expansion/single propeller

CAPRERA
Built: 1917 by Union Iron Works, Almeda, California
Gross tonnage: 8,244
Dimensions: 410 x 56ft/125 x 17.1 m
Service speed: 12 knots
Propulsion: Triple expansion/single propeller

In the years immediately following World War I, Italian shipping companies were able to purchase a number of surplus cargo ships that had been built during the war for the British Government, and operated by the Shipping Controller. Four of these vessels were refitted to carry passengers in very basic quarters on a service to Australia, being operated jointly by Lloyd Sabaudo and NGI.

The first of these vessels to enter the trade which had been named *War Pigeon* when launched in the middle of 1918. It was handed over to the Shipping Controller in September, being placed under the management of Bell, Symondson & Co. The vessel had barely entered service when the war ended.

Early in 1920 *War Pigeon* was sold to Lloyd Sabaudo, and renamed *Carignano*. It was fitted out with very austere accommodation for several hundred migrants, and placed in service between Italy and Australia. On 23 May 1920 *Carignano* departed Antwerp for Genoa, departing there on 21 June on its first voyage to Australia, via the Suez Canal and Colombo, arriving in Fremantle on 4 August, Adelaide three days later, Melbourne on 18 August and Sydney on 21 August.

The second vessel to be placed on the Australian service was *Moncalieri*, which had been named *War Linnet* when launched on 18 October 1918. It was not completed by the time the war ended the following month, being handed over to the British Shipping

Carignano (Martin Navarro collection)

Controller in December 1918. It is likely the vessel saw very little, if any service in the role for which it had been built, and in June 1919 it was sold to Lloyd Sabaudo, being renamed *Moncalieri*. It was fitted out with basic quarters for migrants, and placed on the trade to Australia.

Moncalieri departed Antwerp on 23 August 1920, going to Genoa, from where the vessel sailed on 16 September, arriving in Fremantle for the first time on 4 November 1920. *Moncalieri* then went directly to Melbourne, berthing on 16 November, and arrived in Sydney on 19 November, remaining there until 1 December, when the voyage back to Europe commenced.

Carignanao and *Moncalieri* were soon joined by *Capodimonti*, which had a rather unusual background. While it is well known that during the war a large number of standard design cargo ships were built in both the United States and Great Britain to replace lost vessels, several Japanese shipyards also delivered a number of ships built to British standard designs.

During 1917 the Kawasaki Dockyard Co. delivered nine identical ships, all of which were given War names, the seventh vessel, delivered in October 1917, being named *War Tiger*. Unfortunately I know nothing of its war service, but in 1920 *War Tiger* was bought by Lloyd Sabaudo, and renamed *Capodimonte*.

Capodimonte was fitted out with very basic quarters for several hundred passengers, and on 24 October 1920 departed Genoa on its first voyage to Australia, the first port of call being Catania, leaving there on 2 November. Voyaging by way of the Suez Canal and Colombo, the vessel arrived in Fremantle on 11 December, spending five days in port. On 18 December *Capodimonte* arrived in Adelaide, and Melbourne on 23 December, the voyage terminating in Sydney on 27 December.

The fourth ship, *Caprera*, had been under construction in an American shipyard in 1917 when, ten days after the United States declared war on Germany on 6 April 1917, the Emergency Fleet Corporation came into being, leading to the establishment of the United States Shipping Board. On 3 August 1917, the USSB requisitioned all merchant ships then under construction around the United States, including a number of standard design vessels that were being built in America for the British Shipping Controller. One of these vessels was named *War Sword*, being completed in September 1917 and handed over to the British as originally planned.

War Sword served under the British flag through the rest of the war, being managed for the British Government by the Cunard Steam Ship Co. The vessel was bought by Navigazione Generale Italiana in 1920, and renamed *Caprera*. In 1921 *Caprera* entered the Australian trade, having been refitted with basic quarters for about four hundred migrants, mostly temporary accommodation located in the holds. When the migrants disembarked in Australia, the temporary fittings were taken down so that a full cargo could be loaded for the voyage back to Italy.

These four ships traded to Australia through the 1920s, though migrants were not carried on all voyages, and the number of passengers varied considerably from voyage to voyage. When proper passenger liners began operating on the Australian service, these vessels reverted to carrying cargo only.

Capidimonte was transferred to another Italian shipping company, Marittima Italiana, in 1926, but not renamed, and served in their fleet until arriving on 2 August 1933 at La Spezia, where it was broken up.

In February 1929 *Carignano* made a visit to Hobart to load cargo for Italy. In 1932 *Carignano* was transferred to Italia Line, but not renamed, nor did that happen when the vessel was transferred in 1934 to another Italian company, Lloyd Triestino.

After reverting to cargo ship status, *Caprera* mainly operated between Italy and South America, and on 1 June 1932 ran aground in Guanabara Bay, 15 miles (25 km) from Rio de Janeiro. After being refloated in August, the vessel was towed to Rio, but on inspection was declared to be a total loss, and sold for scrapping. Instead of this happening the vessel was bought by Pedro Luis Correa & Castro, of Rio de Janeiro, but sold again in 1933 to Pedro Brandao. It is reported that the vessel was laid up for the next seven years, but in 1940 work began on rebuilding it at the shipyard of Lage & Irmaos (Henrique Lage Org.) on Ilha do Viana, near Rio de Janeiro, and it returned to service in 1941, under the name *Arabutan*, being managed by Lloyd Nacional.

On the night of 7 March 1942, a torpedo fired by *U155* hit the *Arabutan* when the vessel was about 80 miles off Cape Hattaras, on a voyage from New York to Brazil with a cargo of coal. *Arabutan* sank thirteen minutes after the torpedo hit, with the loss of one life. The survivors escaped in four lifeboats that were sighted soon after dawn the next day by the United States Coast guard cutter *Calypso*, which picked them up, and landed them at Little Creek, Virginia, after sinking the lifeboats as a potential navigation hazard.

Of the other two ships, *Moncalieri* took refuge in Masawa in Africa when Italy came into the war, but was located by British aircraft and damaged by bombs on 13 February 1941. The ship was scuttled at Masawa by its crew in April 1941 to prevent it being captured and used by the Allies. The British managed to refloat the vessel, which was seized as a war prize, but the damage from the bombing was so extensive it was broken up.

In September 1943 *Carignano* was seized by the Japanese at Osaka, and renamed *Teiyo Maru*. It was used as a transport, and may have carried troops, but on 13 November 1944 it was sunk in Manila Bay during an attack by American aircraft.

THE FRENCH VILLES

VILLE DE METZ   VILLE DE STRASBOURG
VILLE DE VERDUN   VILLE D'AMIENS
Built: 1920/20/21/24 by North of Ireland Shipbuilding Co.,
Londonderry
Gross Tonnage: 7,007/7,138/7,007/7,143
Dimensions: 411 x 53 ft /125.3 x 16.4 m
Service speed: 13 knots
Propulsion: Triple expansion/single propeller

This quartet was built for the French company, Cie Havraise Peninsulaire, as passenger/cargo ships for a service from Le Havre to Madagascar via numerous European and Mediterranean ports and the Suez Canal. The first was launched on 20 April 1920 as *Ville de Metz*, being completed three months later. On 13 August 1920 the second vessel was launched under the name *Ville de Lyon*, but this had been changed to *Ville de Strasbourg* by the time it was completed two months later. *Ville de Verdun* was launched on 13 November 1920, entering service in May 1921. As completed they provided accommodation for 54 passengers in one class.

During 1922 these three vessels were chartered to Messageries Maritimes for their Australian service. The first sailing of the trio was taken by *Ville de Metz* from Marseilles in July 1922, arriving in Australian ports during September, then continuing to Noumea.

It was followed by *Ville de Strasbourg* from Marseilles on 23 September 1922, arriving in Fremantle on 30 October, Melbourne on 8 November and Sydney three days later.

Ville de Verdun departed Marseilles on 22 December 1922, arriving in Fremantle on 27 January, Melbourne on 5 February and Sydney three days later. The vessel then continued on to Noumea. On its next voyage to Australia, *Ville de Strasbourg* departed Le Havre in late March 1923, berthing in Fremantle on 15 May, reaching Melbourne on 21 May and arriving in Sydney on 25 May, leaving three days later for Noumea.

A fourth vessel of the class was named *Ville d'Amiens* when launched on 9 April 1924, being completed in November 1924. In March 1925 this vessel was also chartered to Messageries Maritimes for four years for their service from Marseilles via the Suez Canal to Australia and Noumea.

At this time *Ville de Strasbourg*, *Ville de Verdun* and *Ville d'Amiens* were fitted with an additional promenade deck, providing accommodation for 36 first class, 50 second class and 478 steerage passengers. *Ville de Metz* was not altered, but continued to operate to Australia.

In 1928 Messageries Maritimes purchased all four ships outright, and they remained on the Australian trade until 1935, when they made their final appearances in

Ville de Strasbourg

146

Ville d'Amiens passing by Sydney Harbour Bridge.

Australia. All four were then transferred to the route from Marseilles via the Panama Canal to Tahiti and Noumea, on which they remained after war broke out in 1939.

Following the fall of France, on 4 August 1940 *Ville de Metz* was seized by the Germans at Bordeaux, and became a German naval transport under the management of Hamburg South America Line, being renamed *Othmarschen*. On 1 February 1943 the vessel was torpedoed and sunk by the Russian submarine *L-20* in the Varangerfjord in northern Norway.

In July 1940 *Ville d'Amiens* was at Papeete on its way back to France, and remained there until being taken over by the British on 20 September 1940, then handed over to the Ministry of War Transport and managed for them by the Clan Line. Initially the vessel was primarily involved in transporting Free French troops, and later carried American troops to Europe.

Late in 1944 *Ville d'Amiens* was handed back to the French, and began making voyages to Noumea via the Panama Canal again. In August 1947 *Ville d'Amiens* was awarded the Croix de Guerre by the French Government in recognition of the service the vessel gave during the war.

Ville de Strasbourg was captured by British naval forces off the Cape of Good Hope in March 1941 and also handed over to the British Ministry of War Transport, for whom it was managed by the Union Castle Line.

On 7 January 1943 *Ville de Strasbourg* was torpedoed off Bougie, but remained afloat and was towed into Algiers, where it was further damaged during a German air attack. Nevertheless, *Ville de Strasbourg* survived the war, and was handed back in April 1945 to the French Government, who returned it to Messageries Maritimes.

Ville de Verdun continued to serve under the French flag in eastern waters, but on 19 April 1942 was seized by the Japanese, being renamed *Ateison Maru*. On 14 October 1942 the vessel was torpedoed and sunk by the American submarine USS *Finback* off the coast of Formosa.

In the late 1940s both *Ville de Strasbourg* and *Ville d'Amiens* were used primarily on the route from Marseilles to French possessions in Indochina, frequently transporting troops and their dependants to and from the region.

In 1951 the passenger accommodation on both vessels was removed, and they subsequently operated purely as cargo ships on services from France to French possessions in the Indian Ocean.

In September 1952 *Ville de Strasbourg* was taken out of service, and soon after sold to British shipbreakers, arriving at Faslane in Scotland on 6 December 1952. *Ville d'Amiens* survived only a few months longer before being sold to shipbreakers in France, arriving at their La Seyne yard on 27 February 1953.

MAHANA

Built: 1917 by Workman, Clark & Co., Belfast
Tonnage: 10,951 gross
Dimensions: 500 x 63 ft/152.4 x 19.2 m
Service speed: 14 knots
Propulsion: Geared turbines/twin propellers

A slightly enlarged version of the *Rangatira* quartet, *Mahana* was the first turbine steamer to be built for Shaw Savill Line, and the largest cargo vessel in their fleet for several years. A smaller sister ship from the same builders, *Mahia*, was fitted with quadruple expansion engines, and completed in August 1917.

Launched on 11 January 1917, *Mahana* was taken over by the British Government under the Liner Requisition Scheme in April 1917, three months before it was completed in July the same year.

Primarily designed as a large, fast cargo ship, after the war ended *Mahana* was fitted out with cabin accommodation for 12 first class passengers, and dormitories for 450 third class passengers, while temporary accommodation for an additional 1,000 migrants could be installed in the holds on the voyage from Britain to New Zealand.

Mahana was placed on a service from Liverpool or London to New Zealand ports via the Panama Canal. Sister vessel *Mahia* also served on this route, but was not fitted with passenger quarters.

Mahana became known as the Brides' Boat when it sailed from Liverpool on 27 May 1920, as it was carrying a large number of war brides as well as single English women on their way to marry New Zealand soldiers. Among the passengers were three sisters who had lived at Hornchurch, the site of a New Zealand convalescent hospital in Britain, all of whom were engaged to New Zealanders. *Mahana* arrived in New Zealand on 16 July 1920.

Mahana continued to carry passengers until 1926, when the accommodation was removed. Subsequently the vessel operated as a cargo ship between Britain and New Zealand.

During World War II *Mahana* was not taken over for military duty, but did operate under Government control, remaining on the trade between Britain and New Zealand.

In 1949 *Mahana* was chartered by the British Ministry of Food for use as a cold storage unit, serving in this static role until being scrapped in 1953, arriving at Dalmuir on 31 May, but then being moved on to Troon on 15 July, where the actual demolition took place.

Sister ship *Mahia* also survived the war, but was badly damaged by a fire in 1947 when berthed in Melbourne. Following repairs *Mahia* resumed trading from Britain to New Zealand until it arrived at Faslane on 16 July 1953 to be broken up, being the last coal-fired vessel to be operated by Shaw Savill Line.

Mahana

THE SECOND P&O B CLASS

BALLARAT BALRANALD BENDIGO
Built: 1921/1922/1922 by Harland & Wolff, Greenock
Gross tonnage: 13,065/13,039/13,039
Dimensions: 537 x 64 ft/163.7 x 19.6 m
Service speed: 14 knots
Propulsion: Quadruple expansion/twin propellers

BARADINE BARRABOOL
Built: 1921/1922 by Harland & Wolff, Belfast
Gross tonnage: 13,144/13,148
Dimensions: 537 x 64 ft/163.7 x 19.6 m
Service speed: 14 knots
Propulsion: Quadruple expansion/twin propellers

The P&O Line became involved in the migrant trade to Australia in 1910 when they purchased the Blue Anchor Line service and five of their ships, which they renamed the P&O Branch Line. The company built five new ships for the service, all given names starting with B. During the war one of these B ships was sunk.

When the war ended there were four 'B' ships and one former Blue Anchor Line vessel surviving, and these five ships were able to re-establish the Branch Line service by 1920, though only offering one departure every four weeks. P&O anticipated there would be a boom in the migrant trade to Australia in the post-war period, and ordered a new series of five B liners for the service.

The order for all five ships was placed with Harland & Wolff, and three of the ships were assigned to their yard at Greenock with the other two built in Belfast. In general design the new ships would be similar to the original series, and also coal-fired, at a time when almost all new passenger vessels were being fitted with oil fired engines. The most noticeable difference between the old and new series would be the inclusion of a forecastle and a longer superstructure extending right to the stern.

When the first of the new ships was launched on 14 September 1920 it was named *Ballarat*, reviving the name given to the first ship of the first group, which had been lost in the war. On 27 November 1920 the second ship was named *Baradine* when launched. It was the first to be completed, being handed over to the P&O on 18 August 1921, and leaving London on 22 September for Australia. It was not until December 1921 that *Ballarat* was completed, leaving London in January 1922 on its maiden voyage.

By that time, the three other units of the group had all been launched, *Balranald* on 24 February 1921, followed by *Barrabool* on 3 November 1921, and the last, *Bendigo*, on 26 January 1922. Once again the ships did not enter service in the order of their launchings, as *Barrabool* was completed in only four months, and left London in March 1922 on its maiden voyage, while *Balranald* took a year to be completed at Greenock, and did not leave London until April 1922. On 9 August 1922 P&O took delivery of *Bendigo*, the last

Ballarat

Baradine

of the ships. When it entered service later that month, the Branch Line was able to operate a schedule of two-weekly departures from London, using nine ships all with names commencing with B.

The new ships carried third class passengers only, with permanent berths for 490 persons, but there were also temporary berths that could be erected in the holds if required for up to 685 additional passengers. The standard of the permanent accommodation was more comfortable that any previous migrant ship had offered, and this helped make the ships popular in their early years of service. As with the earlier vessels, the new ships had a large cargo capacity, as there was limited demand for passenger accommodation of their type on the return voyage from Australia, and they had to pay their way with cargo.

At the same time the last of the B ships were entering service the Australian Government was placing five new emigrant ships of their own on the route, the famous 'Bay' ships, which were oil-fired and gave the P&O ships considerable competition.

For a couple of years it appeared that the forward thinking of P&O with regard to the emigrant trade had been correct, as the ships were carrying good passenger numbers on their voyages, but by 1925 it was beginning to decrease rather than increase as had been anticipated, and by 1926 the situation was looking very serious for the service.

Demand for migrant and third class passages had all but disappeared, and those people who were travelling preferred the shorter journey offered by other companies through the Mediterranean and the

Suez Canal. In an attempt to attract more passengers P&O began routing some of their Branch Line ships on this route as well, introducing calls at ports in the Mediterranean, in particular Malta, in the hope ogf picking up additional passengers.

This system of using the B ships on both the Cape route and through Suez continued until July 1929, when the service around South Africa was abandoned completely, which also spelled the end of the P&O Branch Line as a separate operation. The four pre-war B ships were withdrawn, and all were sold soon afterwards to Japanese interests and broken up.

The five post-war B ships were taken out of service to be converted to oil-firing, and a Bauer-Wach exhaust turbine was installed in their engine rooms, which increased their service speed to 15 knots, making them more competitive with the Bay ships. The accommodation was also altered, with permanent berths being provided for 586 passengers and the temporary quarters removed. The ships were then placed on a secondary service between Britain and Australia via Suez.

The first sailing on the new secondary service was taken by *Baradine*, which left London on 12 April 1929, calling at Malta and Colombo before proceeding direct to Melbourne and then Sydney. *Balranald* followed on 10 May, then *Ballarat* on 7 June, and *Bendigo* on 5 July. When *Baradine* returned from its first voyage, the vessel went to Liverpool to inaugurate a program of occasional sailings from that port, departing on 10 August 1929, and on 3 September *Barrabool* made its first sailing

150

from London on the new route, thus allowing the introduction of regular four weekly sailings from either London or Liverpool.

The full route worked by these ships from that time took them from Britain to Malta, Port Said, Aden, Colombo, Fremantle, Adelaide, Melbourne and Sydney. On occasion *Bendigo* and *Barrabool* made voyages on the main mail service after two of the C class liners were transferred to the Far East trade and before the new Strath liners (page 190) were completed.

The first two Strath liners was placed on the mail service in 1931, with a third being completed in 1935, and they introduced a new practice P&O dividing their accommodation between first and tourist classes. As the tourist class on the new ships was far superior to the facilities offered by the B ships, though the fares charged were little different, the demand for passages on the B ships began to decline, until it reached the point where *Ballarat* was withdrawn, making its final departure from London on 22 December 1934, was offered for sale in 1935. The only persons to show an interest were scrappers, and later in 1935 the vessel was broken up at Briton Ferry.

By 1936 the secondary service was incurring enormous losses, so P&O decided to abandon it. On 17 January 1936 *Bendigo* made its final departure from London, followed by *Balranald* on 14 February and *Baradine* on 13 March. *Barrabool* that took the final sailing of the B ships, leaving London on 9 April 1936.

As each ship arrived back in Britain it was laid up, and offered for sale. With the world in the midst of the depression, demand for second-hand tonnage for further trading was almost non-existent. Three of the vessels were quickly sold to British shipbreakers in 1936, with *Baradine* ending her days at Dalmuir, *Balranald* at Troon and *Bendigo* at Barrow.

At first it appeared that *Barrabool* might escape, as it was bought by the British Government with the intention of being converted into a troopship, but this did not eventuate, and later in 1936 the vessel was sold to be broken up at Bo'ness.

These five ships were only fifteen years old and still in excellent condition when they were disposed of, the economic conditions of the time brining about their early demise.

Balranald

ORCADES

Built: 1906 by A G Vulkan, Stettin
Gross tonnage: 9,764
Dimensions: 492 x 58 ft/149.9 x 17.7 m
Service speed: 15 knots
Propulsion: Quadruple expansion/twin propellers

This vessel served only three years in the Orient Line fleet just after World War I. It was built for North German Lloyd as *Prinz Ludwig*, being launched on 12 May 1906 and completed in August. It had accommodation for 100 first, 160 second and 80 third class passengers, and was placed on the Far East trade.

Prinz Ludwig was at Bremerhaven when the war started in August 1914, and remained there throughout the conflict. It was seized in 1919 by the Allies as a prize of war, handed over to Britain, and placed under the management of the P&O Line. *Prinz Ludwig* made several voyages to Australia with returning troops, arriving in Melbourne for the first time on 5 September 1919 and Sydney on 8 September.

Early in 1921 *Prinz Ludwig* was purchased from the Government by the Orient Line, and renamed *Orcades*, being given an extensive refit, with accommodation for 123 first and 476 third class passengers, considerably less than the other ships in the company's fleet could carry.

On 8 October 1921 *Orcades* left London on its first voyage to Australia for the Orient Line. The speed required for the mail service was 18 knots, but *Orcades*

could manage only 15 knots. As a result, Orient Line had to operate *Orcades* and another ex-German liner, *Omar*, on an independent schedule from the mail steamers, and they were classed as intermediates. It was not a satisfactory arrangement, but the best the Orient Line could manage until the new ships they had ordered in 1922 could be delivered.

In the off-season *Orcades* spent periods laid up off Southend. *Orcades* was in lay up when, on 8 March 1922, it came adrift during a storm and grounded on mud flats close to Southend Pier. Three days later the vessel was refloated with the assistance of six tugs, having suffered no damage, but remained laid up for another six months, until departing for Australia on 22 September.

The first of the new vessels being built for the Orient Line was due in service in November 1924, and the second would follow in February 1925, so in anticipation of these arrivals the Orient Line lost no time in divesting itself of *Orcades* during 1924. On 20 September 1924 the vessel left London on its final voyage to Australia and on returning to Britain was withdrawn.

By this time most of the shipping companies had been able to rebuild their fleets, and there was not much of a demand for second-hand tonnage, especially over twenty years old, so *Orcades* was sold to shipbreakers in Germany, arriving at Bremerhaven on 5 April 1925 to be broken up.

Orcades

ORMUZ

Built: 1915 by Bremer Vulkan, Vegesack
Gross tonnage: 14,167
Dimensions: 570 x 67 ft/173.7 x 20.5 m
Service speed: 15 knots
Propulsion: Quadruple expansion/twin propellers

This vessel was built for North German Lloyd, and launched on 9 June 1914 as *Zeppelin*, intended to have accommodation for 319 first, 156 second and 342 third class passengers. Its maiden voyage was scheduled to depart Bremen in January 1915 for Australia, but when completed, though not to the original specifications, the vessel was taken over by the German Government for war service. In the end the vessel was not used, remaining laid up throughout the conflict.

After the German surrender *Zeppelin* was handed over to Britain, and on 28 March 1919 left the Weser for England, where it was taken over by the Shipping Controller, and placed under the management of White Star Line, which was not interested in keeping the ship.

The Orient Line purchased *Zeppelin* from the Government in 1920 and renamed it *Ormuz*. The accommodation was changed to carry 293 first and 882 third class passengers, but externally the ship was not altered apart from a reduction in the number of lifeboats carried.

Ormuz operated six 13-day cruises to Norway from June to September 1921, the first such trips to be operated by the Orient Line after the war, then on 12 November 1921 left London on its maiden voyage to Australia, going as far as Brisbane. *Ormuz* was not ideal for the service, its speed being two knots slower than the regular Orient Line ships, but the company had no alternative than to use it on the mail service until new ships then under construction entered service.

Ormuz remained on the Australian route until the end of 1926, making its final sailing from London on 27 November. Having made fourteen round trips to Australia, *Ormuz* was laid up on arrival back in London, and on 22 April 1927 was sold to Norddeutscher Lloyd, the original owners.

Renamed *Dresden*, the vessel was refitted with accommodation for 399 cabin class, 288 tourist and 284 third class passengers and on 5 August 1927 entered service from Bremerhaven to New York. Within a short time the first effects of the depression were being felt, and *Dresden* was used for some cruises in the off-season for several years, then laid up in Bremerhaven in October 1933.

In the summer of 1934 *Dresden* was scheduled to make a series of cruises. On 20 June, on a Norwegian fjords cruise with 1,000 passengers aboard the vessel struck an uncharted rock at Klepp on Boku Island, near Haugesund, causing much bottom damage and flooding. As the ship began to list, and the furnaces were extinguished by inrushing water, the passengers and some crew were put into lifeboats, with the loss of four lives when one capsized during launching, and then *Dresden* was run aground.

Next day the vessel capsized, lying on its port side, with the stern under water. A total loss, the wreck was sold to a firm in Stavanger for scrapping where it lay.

Ormuz

THE BAYS

MORETON BAY   HOBSONS BAY/ESPERANCE BAY   JERVIS BAY
Built: 1921/1922/1922 by Vickers Ltd, Barrow
Gross tonnage: 13,850/13,387/13,839
Dimensions: 549 x 68 ft/167.2 x 20.8 m
Service speed: 15 knots
Propulsion: Geared turbines/twin propellers

LARGS BAY   ESPERANCE BAY/ARAWA
Built: 1921/1922 by Wm Beardmore & Co., Dalmuir
Gross tonnage: 13,851/13,853
Dimensions: 552 x 68 ft/168.3 x 20.8 m
Service speed: 15 knots
Propulsion: Geared turbines/twin propellers

The Commonwealth Government Line of Steamers was formed by the Australian Government in 1916, and when the war ended the Government decided to become involved in the migrant trade by having five passenger ships built.

The keel for the first ship was laid down on 4 September 1919, and it was launched on 23 April 1921, being named *Moreton Bay*. Within nine months the other four had all entered the water, *Largs Bay* being launched on 20 June, *Hobsons Bay* on 4 October, then *Esperance Bay* on 15 December, and finally *Jervis Bay* on 17 January 1922. Fitting out of the accommodation was in accordance with the *Navigation Act* passed in Australia in 1921, which provided far superior quarters for the crew than in vessels on the British register. Accommodation was provided for 723 passengers in third class, with two, four and six berth cabins being available. There were also six two berth cabins of superior grade, which were intended to be used solely by Government officials, but these were soon dispensed with.

Moreton Bay departed from London on 7 December 1921, travelling through the Suez Canal to Aden and Colombo, then directly to Fremantle and on around the coast, calling at Adelaide and Melbourne before arriving at Sydney on 16 January 1922, the voyage terminating in Brisbane. On 17 January the *Sydney Morning Herald* reported:

At dawn yesterday there entered Sydney Harbour, on her maiden voyage, the new Commonwealth Government liner *Moreton Bay*. Her voyage marks the inauguration of a new passenger service designed to provide more rapid transit between Australia and Britain. The *Moreton Bay* is the first of a number of passenger ships specially built for the new service.

With accommodation for 720 cabin passengers, and 12 additional special suites, the public rooms on the ship are tastefully decorated, and in regard to subdivision and life-saving and safety appliances, the vessel fulfils the most modern requirements. A special feature of the ship is the large capacity of insulated holds set apart for carriage of perishable cargo from Australia to the United Kingdom.

The main propelling machinery comprises two sets of double reduction geared turbines of Parsons' type, capable of developing a total of 9,000 shaft horse-power, with the propellers turning at about 90 revolutions per minute. The boilers are of the cylindrical type, two single-ended and three double-ended, and are arranged for 220 lb working pressure. The vessel may be operated on either oil or coal, as desired. All the deck auxiliaries are of a powerful pattern, and steam driven.

The *Moreton Bay* left London on December 7, and the voyage occupied 31 days to Fremantle, of which two days were taken in loading tea at Colombo. On her speed trials the vessel achieved 16.3 knots, but the designed service speed in loaded condition was 15 knots. The voyage as far as Port Said was accomplished at a speed of 16 knots. Through the Bay of Biscay the ship had a fine passage, and Gibraltar was passed after three and a half days steaming. The speed was reduced to 14¾ knots on the way to Adelaide, but the ship was still well up to programme.

One of the most striking features of the equipment of the ship is the new davits which operate the lifeboats. The lifeboats are nested, one small lifeboat resting inside another larger craft. The davits, which are an Australian invention, and have been fitted for the first time on an Australian ship in the *Moreton Bay*, are lattice beams surmounting two arms which swing outward at an angle of 5 degrees on being operated. One member of the crew can launch two lifeboats, whereas under other conditions it is the work of four men. In practice it takes only two and a half minutes to launch two lifeboats. The lifeboats include two motor boats equipped with wireless.

Under the command of Captain J. Avern, RNR, the ship is manned with officers and crew largely made up of Australians. Eight Australian apprentices are included among the ship's company, and seven of the firemen are Australians, while the others have served in Australian waters. The crew is paid Australian wages, and is employed under Australian articles.

The other liners joined the service over the next nine months, *Largs Bay* departing London for the first time on 4 January 1922, with *Hobsons Bay* following on 28 February. There was then a gap of six months before *Esperance Bay* entered service on 1 August, while *Jervis Bay* left London on its maiden voyage on 26 September 1922.

The vessels were named after bays in each of the five mainland states of Australia, and each ship was registered on their first arrival at the major port of the state from whose bay their name derived. Thus *Moreton Bay* was registered at Brisbane on 20 January

Hobsons Bay, later renamed Esperance Bay.

1922, *Largs Bay* at Adelaide on 7 March, *Hobsons Bay* at Melbourne on 12 April, *Esperance Bay* at Fremantle on 27 September, and finally *Jervis Bay* at Sydney on 6 November.

The Commonwealth Government Line had planned to provide monthly sailings from Britain, but due to constant industrial troubles this schedule was hardly ever maintained. In 1923 the service was renamed the Australian Commonwealth Line, but industrial problems continued as before. Each of the ships spent periods laid up because of crewing problems, and huge losses were incurred each year.

During 1923 *Moreton Bay* was involved in two separate accidents, the first being a collision with the steamer *Margit Siemers* in the River Thames in June, with *Moreton Bay* being held responsible, then on 27 August the vessel collided with the Ellerman Wilson cargo ship *Chemnitz*, again in the lower reaches of the Thames.

Early in 1928 the Australian Government decided to sell all five ships. This decision sparked even more union trouble, as the seamen who had done so much to cause the downfall of the service realised that their jobs were now in jeopardy, but it was too late for them to retrieve the situation.

The five liners were sold to the Kylsant group of shipping companies for less than £2 million, a fraction of their original building cost, reputed to have been about £1.3 million per ship. Delivery to the new owners was scheduled for May 1928, and as each vessel completed their voyages from Australia to Britain they were transferred to the British flag, and their crews returned to Australia.

The final voyage was that of *Jervis Bay*, which was delayed at every Australian port by strikes and other union action. The vessel left Melbourne on 6 June, and after calling at Fremantle headed across the Indian Ocean towards Colombo.

On 21 June the radio station in Colombo received a call for help from Captain Daniel of *Jervis Bay*, stating there had been a mutiny on board, and a threat made to set fire to the ship. The message finished with a request for immediate assistance. The only Royal Navy ship available in Colombo at that time was the fleet auxiliary, HMS *Slavol*, which took on board 20 Marines and sailed from Colombo on 24 June to rendezvous with *Jervis Bay*. The ships met the next day and the Marines duly boarded the liner.

Then the true story was revealed, to the embarrassment of all concerned. The trouble had been caused by eight stowaways, assisted by a few dissident crew members. The stowaways had been caught several days out from Fremantle, and placed in a locked cabin, which they set on fire and so had to be released, but were immediately locked up in separate quarters, where they were safely under control when the marines came aboard.

On arrival in London *Jervis Bay* was handed over to the new owners, thus completing the transfer of the liners from the Australian flag. The five liners were placed under the management of George Thompson & Co., which operated ships to Australia as the Aberdeen Line, and was now also part of the Kylsant Group, and the new operation was called the Aberdeen & Commonwealth Line. Apart from a reduction in their passenger capacity to 635 in tourist class only,

Jervis Bay

repainting the hulls in the dark green colours of the Aberdeen Line, and having British crews, the five liners were little affected by the change of ownership.

In 1931 all five vessels were extensively refitted, with their accommodation being reduced to 550 tourist class only, while their gross tonnage rose by about 500 tons each. It appeared that at last the troubles of the five liners were over and they would now be able to operate without any problems, but it was also in 1931 that the Kylsant shipping empire collapsed. The ships continued to operate, however, and in April 1933 a new company was formed, the Aberdeen & Commonwealth Line Limited, being jointly owned by the P&O Line and Shaw, Savill & Albion Co., with the latter firm appointed to manage the ships as it was the major shareholder. Despite these changes the ships continued to operate their own schedule and retained the Aberdeen Line colours.

For the next five years the five ships brought thousands of migrants to Australia. Then, in 1936, Shaw Savill decided to transfer *Esperance Bay* to their fleet. During a refit at the Glasgow yard of Harland & Wolff the accommodation was altered to cater for only 292 tourist class passengers. Renamed *Arawa*, the vessel left Southampton on 22 January 1937 on its first voyage to New Zealand, going out via the Panama Canal and returning round the Cape of Good Hope.

Once the transfer of *Esperance Bay* had been completed, the Aberdeen & Commonwealth Line decided to rename *Hobsons Bay*, which was known for the rest of its career as *Esperance Bay*.

From 1936 the Aberdeen & Commonwealth Line service was reduced to four vessels, with sailings at six-weekly intervals. Their route took them from London, where cargo was loaded, to Southampton to board passengers, Malta, the Suez Canal, Aden and Colombo before calling at Fremantle, Adelaide, Melbourne and Sydney, terminating in Brisbane.

In late August 1939, *Moreton Bay* and *Esperance Bay*, both in Australian waters, were requisitioned by the British Admiralty and quickly converted into armed merchant cruisers. *Moreton Bay* arrived at Cockatoo Dockyard on 31 August, and was commissioned on 19 October 1939, being given pennant number F11, and sent to the China Station. *Esperance Bay* was commissioned on 28 November, its pennant number being F67.

Jervis Bay was requisitioned in London, and sent to Newcastle for conversion into an armed merchant cruiser, being fitted with eight 6 inch guns and commissioned in September 1939. *Largs Bay* was not taken over at this time, but *Arawa* was requisitioned on its arrival in Wellington in September 1939. It was sent to Sydney for conversion into an armed merchant cruiser, and after commissioning on 17 October was also sent to the China Station. In mid-1940 *Arawa* was transferred to convoy escort duty in the North Atlantic, operating between Freetown and Britain.

Jervis Bay had been allocated to convoy escort work in the North Atlantic from the end of 1939, and was the sole escort of convoy HX84, consisting of 38 merchant ships bound for Britain. On the afternoon of 5 November 1940 the German pocket battleship *Admiral Scheer* was sighted. Captain Fegan on *Jervis Bay* ordered the convoy to scatter and turned his ship, though heavily outgunned, towards the warship. Within an hour *Jervis Bay* was a blazing wreck with all guns out of action. About 8 pm that night *Jervis Bay* sank, taking with it some 180 officers and crew, while 65 others were later rescued from lifeboats. This gallant action earned Captain Fegan a posthumous Victoria Cross, and was one of the most notable naval episodes of the entire war, as the time won by *Jervis Bay* allowed all but six of the ships in the convoy to escape the German warship.

In August 1941 *Largs Bay*, which had remained in commercial service to Australia, was taken over and converted into a troopship. It was also during 1941 that *Moreton Bay, Esperance Bay* and *Arawa* were converted into troopships, serving in this capacity until the end of the war.

The conversion work on *Arawa* was done at Birkenhead, and when completed it had accommodation for 1,700 officers and men. *Arawa* made several trips from Britain to South Africa and back before taking part in the landings in North Africa, and after this went onto the Atlantic run, bringing many thousands of American soldiers to the European theatre of war.

On 2 January 1944 *Largs Bay* struck a mine near Naples, but was able to return to service several months later.

The first of the four survivors to be released after the war ended was *Arawa*, which had spent part of 1945 repatriating released prisoners of war from Black Sea ports and Istanbul to Marseilles. Refitted at Newcastle to carry 274 passengers in tourist class only, *Arawa*

left London on 7 February 1946 on its first post-war voyage to New Zealand via Panama. From August 1947 the route was altered so that both outward and return voyages took the vessel around the Cape of Good Hope, and included calls at Fremantle and Melbourne, which was to remain its regular route apart from occasional voyages via the Suez Canal.

In 1947 the three remaining Bay liners were released from Government duty, and refitted to carry 514 tourist class passengers only, returning to service for the Aberdeen & Commonwealth Line during 1948.

Arawa left London on 3 December 1954 on its final trip to New Zealand. Leaving Wellington in March 1955, *Arawa* returned to Britain two months later, and was then sold to J. Cashmore, shipbreakers of Newport in Wales, being delivered to their yard on 21 May.

By then *Esperance Bay*, the original *Hobsons Bay*, had left London on its final voyage to Australia in April 1955, and on returning was withdrawn from service and sold to Shipbreaking Industries, arriving at their Faslane yard on 6 July.

The two remaining liners continued to operate for another two years, but then *Moreton Bay* made its final departure from London on 30 November 1956, and on returning to Britain was sold to T. W. Ward, being delivered to them at Barrow on 13 April 1957.

Largs Bay left London on the final Aberdeen & Commonwealth Line voyage on 11 January 1957. On returning to Britain the vessel was also sold to T. W. Ward, and arrived at their Barrow yard on 22 August 1957.

Largs Bay (John Bennett collection)

RE D'ITALIA and REGINA D'ITALIA

Built: 1907 by Sir James Laing & Sons, Sunderland
Gross tonnage: 6,237/6,560
Dimensions: 430 x 53 ft/131 x 16 m
Service speed: 14 knots
Propulsion: Triple expansion/twin propellers

Lloyd Sabaudo was founded in June 1906, and was able to commence operations between Italy and New York quite quickly by purchasing two cargo/passenger ships being built for a British company, the Prince Line. The vessel that was originally to have been named *Piedmontese Prince* was the first to be launched, on 22 December 1906, as *Re d'Italia*, while the second vessel, which was to have been *Sardinian Prince*, was launched as *Regina d'Italia* on 20 January 1907.

An autographed portrait of Vittorio Emmanual, the King of Italy, was hung in the main saloon of *Re d'Italia*, which departed Genoa on 6 April 1907 on its maiden voyage to New York, with calls at Naples and Palermo. On 15 May 1907 *Regina d'Italia* departed Genoa on its maiden voyage on the same route. They were joined the following month by a third sister, *Principe di Piemonte*.

When completed these vessels measured 5,204 gross tons, but after only a few months in service their superstructure was enlarged, increasing their size to 6,560 gross tons. They were given accommodation for only 120 passengers in first class, and rather basic quarters for 1,700 passengers in third class, soon increased to 1,900.

Lloyd Sabaudo had also ordered two new ships to operate a service to South America, but on 6 October 1907 *Regina d'Italia* left Genoa on the first Lloyd Sabaudo voyage to South America, visiting Rio de Janeiro, Montevideo and Buenos Aires, followed by a second trip on the route before the vessel returned to the New York trade.

Re d'Italia was in Italian waters when a severe earthquake followed by a tsunami decimated the region around Messina, in Sicily, early in the morning of 28 December 1908. The vessel arrived at Reggio on 29 December, and then went to Palermo, taking on board about 1,400 survivors of the disaster. The vessel had been scheduled to depart Genoa on 19 January for New York, but instead remained at Messina as a hospital ship.

Lloyd Sabaudo encountered financial difficulties after a few years, and on 26 September 1911 *Re d'Italia* began a 14-month spell as a hospital ship during the Italo-Turkish War. With 13 medical staff and accommodation for 116 patients the vessel served between Italy and Libya, evacuating 36,983 sick and wounded, and in 1912 made a single voyage to Constantinople.

In 1913, *Principe di Piemonte* was sold, leaving *Re d'Italia* and *Regina d'Italia* to look after the North Atlantic trade. It was at this time that Guglielmo Marconi, the inventor of wireless telegraphy, became chairman of Lloyd Sabaudo, a post he held until 1922.

Both ships continued on their regular trade to New York until 1915, when *Regina d'Italia* became a hospital ship, and later was used to transport American troops to Europe. *Re d'Italia* was fitted with a pair of 3-inch guns aft on either side of the upper deck, and used to transport horses and munitions from New York to Italy, returning with general cargo.

On Saturday, 22 July 1916, *Re d'Italia* departed Genoa for New York carrying a large amount of cargo and three American passengers who had made the trip over from New York to look after the horses. At 9.45 the next morning lookouts sighted the periscopes of three submarines converging on the vessel, two from one side and one from the other. The guns on *Re d'Italia* were brought into action, and when the third shell exploded it was thought to be exactly where one of the periscopes had been located. A column of black smoke rose into the air, leading those on board the ship to claim the submarine had been sunk.

Subsequently only two periscopes were sighted, and the submarines followed *Re d'Italia* at a safe distance astern for a while. One of the American passengers later stated that the ship's lifeboats had been swung out as soon as they left Genoa, and they were not been brought in until the ship was safely past Gibraltar.

After the war *Re d'Italia* and *Regina d'Italia* remained on the North Atlantic route until 1922, when they were replaced by two new, larger liners. *Regina d'Italia* was transferred to the South American trade, but on 12 November 1922 *Re d'Italia*, under the command of Captain Zeletti, departed Genoa on its first voyage to Australia, via the Suez Canal. Unfortunately the timing of the voyage resulted in major problems when the vessel reached Australia, and numerous stories appeared in local newspapers. *Re d'Italia* arrived in Fremantle on 18 December, and the *West Australian* reported:

The largest contingent of Italian migrants that has been brought to Australia arrived at Fremantle yesterday on the ss *Re d'Italia*, a unit of the Lloyd Sabaudo Line, which is inaugurating a passenger service from Genoa to Australian ports. The *Re d'Italia* berthed shortly after noon yesterday.

Inquiries on the vessel yesterday elicited the information that some 655 Italians were passengers on the vessel. Of that number 41 landed at Fremantle. Of those in transit, 37 were to disembark in Adelaide, 171 at Melbourne and the remaining 406 at Sydney.

The majority of the new settlers are trained artisans, but have no definite employment to take up in Australia. It was stated aboard that the reason for the sudden influx of such a large number of Italians was that as the American Immigration regulations had been tightened up few Italians were going from Italy to the United States and Australia was now being regarded as the most likely place to make their future. Some few of the *Re d'Italia* quota were men who had been in the United States but had been forced out of that country through unemployment difficulties.

A number of the Italians on board the vessel met Mr H. W. D. Shallard, the Consular representative in the State, and informed him they intended landing in Western Australia. Fourteen of the Italians possessed tickets to Fremantle, and 270 others optional tickets which permitted them landing in Fremantle if they so desired, and which after hearing of conditions in Australia they decided to do. It is understood Mr Shallard communicated with the main body of the Italians, and informed them that no responsibility for their future welfare could be accepted if they came ashore here.

The vessel continued its voyage to Adelaide, where it arrived on Saturday, 23 December. Several hundred men had been due to leave the ship here and go by train to Port Pirie or Broken Hill, but there was no space for them, so they returned to the ship. *Re d'Italia* left the next day for Melbourne, berthing there on 26 December. The passengers found the city was virtually shut down at the start of the Christmas holidays, and this had a major effect on those who were due to disembark at the port, as they could not find anywhere to stay, and also had to return to the ship. The Consul-General for Italy in Australia, Commendatore A Grossardi, was quoted in the *Sydney Morning Herald* on 8 January as follows:

Unluckily, the *Re d'Italia* reached Adelaide on the Saturday before Christmas, and it was, therefore, impossible to carry out the arrangements which had been previously made to disembark at that port all the miners who had to proceed to Broken Hill and Port Pirie. The Italians could not consequently run the risk of disembarking there, and

all proceeded to Melbourne, where the boat arrived on Boxing Day. The 500 immigrants wandered about the city and suburbs. This was the reason why so many Italians were to be seen in the streets. It was impossible for them to find sleeping accommodation in the hotels and boarding houses, as every place was full up with holiday makers.

Commendatore Grossardi pointed out that in Australia seven out of every 10 Italians were primary producers, and were living in the country. The majority of them were sugar farming in North Queensland, and a great number were employed in the mines at Kalgoorlie and Broken Hill. All those who had arrived in the last few months from Italy had accepted farm work.

Re d'Italia arrived in Sydney on 1 January 1923, and initially dropped anchor in Athol Bight. Next day the *Sydney Morning Herald* reported:

On the decks of the Italian liner *Re d'Italia*, which arrived in Sydney yesterday morning, were 257 immigrants from Italy, whose destination is either Sydney or Brisbane. What they are going to do when they land, however, is a matter which very few of the Italian farmers and artisans on board can tell with any certainty.

Already at other Australian ports visited large numbers of the new settlers have received employment. At Melbourne 250 went ashore, and, according to the captain, found employment. The bulk of the 257 emigrants now on board the vessel are classed as farmers, but actually many of them state that they are first-class tradesmen. Some have friends and relatives here who they can meet, and who may help to place them in employment.

On 2 January, *Re d'Italia* was able to dock at Woolloomooloo, as the *Sydney Morning Herald* reported on 3 January:

The Italian liner *Re d'Italia*, with her company of 257 immigrants on board, berthed at Woolloomooloo Bay yesterday morning, and the quest for employment for the big party has commenced. The whole number passed the health and education tests of the Immigration Acts, and were free to come ashore.

A party of 48 were leaving for Brisbane last night and these had definite employment in the northern state.

Many land-owners in New South Wales had displayed interest, and a number of men had been engaged to go inland in this state. As for the rest, they are being absorbed, and in the meantime are free to remain

Re d'Italia arriving in Hobart. (Martin Navarro collection)

for a few days on the steamer. A great deal of help is being received by the Consulate from Italian residents in Australia, who are doing their best to find places for the new arrivals.

It is pointed out that the present shipment of immigrants from Italy is not singular. For some time Italians have been arriving by almost every mail steamer. Within the past fortnight about 200 immigrants were brought from Italy by a mail steamer. Employment has been found for all these people, and there is every prospect of the present contingent being speedily placed in employment.

Re d'Italia departed Sydney on 19 January, calling at Melbourne, Adelaide and Fremantle on its way back to Italy. Although the news reported it was the first voyage of a regular service, *Re d'Italia* did not return to Australia for two years, instead joining *Regina d'Italia* on the service to South America until the second half of 1924, when they were both transferred to the Australian trade.

Regina d'Italia departed Genoa in August 1924 on its first voyage to Australia, berthing in Fremantle on 14 September. It was reported the ship was carrying 505 passengers, with 79 disembarking at Fremantle. The vessel stopped at Melbourne on 22 September, arriving on 25 September in Sydney, where about 180 passengers disembarked, then went on to Brisbane and back to Sydney, remaining in port until 18 October, when it departed for Italy.

On 20 December 1924 *Re d'Italia* arrived in Fremantle on its second voyage to Australia, and the *West Australian* reported the ship was 'carrying 1,131 passengers, comprising Italians, Greeks, Jugo Slavs and other Southern Europeans.' It was noted there were only 42 passengers in first and second class and they included several 'cultured foreigners on holiday'. Over 200 third class passengers disembarked in Fremantle, and the newspaper reported:

They appeared to be of a better average type than most of the migrants who arrived recently from Southern Europe, and superior to those whom the *Re d'Italia* brought to Australia on a previous trip.

Re d'Italia called at Adelaide on Christmas Day, and berthed in Melbourne on 27 December. The vessel arrived in Sydney on 29 December, then continued north to Brisbane. On the return voyage *Re d'Italia* went to Hobart, arriving on 22 January 1925 for its only visit there, to load wool.

During 1925 each of the ships made two round trips to Australia, *Regina d'Italia* arriving in Fremantle on 14 February and 3 October, while *Re d'Italia* reached the same port on 17 May and 20 November.

However, within two years the onset of the world depression caused passenger numbers to fall dramatically. Towards the end of 1928 *Regina d'Italia* was withdrawn from the Australian trade, and sold to shipbreakers in Italy.

The accommodation on *Re d'Italia* was regraded as cabin class, and the vessel continued to voyage to Australia until the end of 1929, then it too was withdrawn and also sold to Italian shipbreakers.

Regina d'Italia

CÉPHÉE and ANTINOUS

CÉPHÉE
Built: 1912 by Bremer Vulkan, Vegesack
Gross tonnage: 9,680
Dimensions: 491 x 59 ft/149.6 x 18 m
Service speed: 11 knots
Propulsion: Triple expansion/single propeller

ANTINOUS
Built: 1913 by Flensburger Schiffsbau, Flensburg
Gross tonnage: 7,133
Dimensions: 419 x 56 ft 127.7 x 17.1 m
Service speed: 11 knots
Propulsion: Triple expansion/single propeller

Although not sister ships, this pair had a similar background, having been built for German companies, ceded to France in 1919, and bought by Messageries Maritimes for their service from Marseilles to Australia and New Caledonia.

The first of these vessels was launched on 2 April 1912 as the passenger/cargo ship *Buenos Aires* for Hamburg South America Line. It entered service six months later, but operated to South America for only two years before the war brought a halt to the service. In 1919 *Buenos Aires* was handed over to the French Government, and in 1922 it was bought by Messageries Maritimes, who renamed the ship *Céphée*.

Refitted with accommodation for 70 first class, 56 second class and 108 third class passengers, *Céphée*

left Marseilles on 30 August 1922 on its first voyage to New Caledonia via Colombo and Australian ports, terminating in Noumea.

Antinous had an interesting history, being launched on 8 March 1913 as *Wachtefels* for the Hansa Line, and converted in 1916 into the commerce raider *Wolf*, under the command of Count Luckner. A mine laid by the *Wolf* sank the P&O liner *Mongolia* off Bombay in June 1917.

Handed over to the French Government as a war prize in 1919, in 1923 the vessel was purchased by Messageries Maritimes, renamed *Antinous*, and refitted to provide accommodation for 70 first class and 50 third class passengers. *Antinous* was then placed on the service to Australia and New Caledonia, but really was nothing more than a temporary stop-gap until better ships were available. In 1925 the vessel was transferred to a service from Marseilles through the Panama Canal to Tahiti and Noumea.

By the mid-1930s the number of ships required for the Australian trade had been reduced greatly, and Messageries Maritimes began to dispose of some of its older tonnage. *Antinous* was withdrawn from service in May 1931 and sold to shipbreakers in Italy, arriving at Savona on 24 July.

Céphée survived a further five years, but late in 1935 made its final voyage to Australia, and in January 1936 was sold to British shipbreakers, arriving at Blyth on 15 February.

Céphée

THE LAST ABERDEEN LINERS

SOPHOCLES/TAMAROA   DIOGENES/MATAROA
Built: 1922 by Harland & Wolff, Belfast
Gross tonnage: 12,361/12,341
Dimensions: 519 x 63 ft/158.1 x 19.3 m
Service speed: 14 knots
Propulsion: Geared turbines/Twin propellers

These two ships were built for the Aberdeen Line service to Australia. The first to be launched was *Sophocles*, on 22 September 1921, being completed on 2 February 1922. On 1 March, *Sophocles* departed London on its maiden voyage to Australia via Cape Town. *Sophocles* arrived in Sydney for the first time on Saturday, 15 April, and on the Monday morning the *Sydney Morning Herald* carried a short item about the vessel:

The arrival of the Aberdeen liner *Sophocles* in Sydney on Saturday on her maiden voyage marked the inauguration of a regular monthly service by the line between England and Australia, via the Cape, providing a sort of endless chain designed primarily for the carrying of thousands of new settlers to our shores, and the taking back of Australian produce to the old country.

The *Sophocles* is fitted to carry about 130 first class passengers and 425 third class. Looking over the accommodation provided for the latter, one could not but be struck with the resemblance between travelling third class by the *Sophocles* today and first class by many other vessels not so many years ago. The cabins are roomy and well ventilated, and excellently fitted up, and the dining saloon is one of the most commodious that has been seen in these waters.

Most of the passengers were disembarked in Melbourne. When the ship berthed at Miller's Point there were 100 passengers on board, 83 being in the third class. The new settlers seemed delighted with the weather which they had so far experienced in Australia, and spoke highly of the comfort aboard the ship. Captain Ogilvie, the master, reported that the voyage had been without incident, and the new liner had behaved splendidly throughout.

Sophocles continued its voyage north to Brisbane, from where the return trip commenced, calling at the same ports on the way back to Britain.

Meanwhile, *Diogenes* had been launched on 2 March 1922, being delivered to the Aberdeen Line on 4 July. *Diogenes* departed London on 16 August on its maiden voyage to Australia, arriving in Sydney on 2 October. While both liners had permanent berths for 131 first class and 422 third class passengers, the latter number could be considerably increased by the use of temporary berths for migrants on the outward voyage.

For the next four years the two liners operated a regular schedule between Britain and Australia, but by 1926 there had been an enormous reduction in the

Sophocles

number of migrants travelling to Australia, especially on the route via Cape Town. However, it was at this time that the New Zealand Government came to an agreement with the British Government to provide subsidised fares for migrants to New Zealand, which brought about an increase in that trade.

One of the companies that traded primarily with New Zealand was Shaw Savill Line, and in 1926 they arranged to charter both *Sophocles* and *Diogenes* for a service from London to Wellington via the Panama Canal, for which they were given new names, *Sophocles* becoming *Tamaroa*, while *Diogenes* was renamed *Mataroa*. Before entering service the two ships were converted from coal to oil firing, the accommodation was enlarged to carry 135 first class and 570 third class passengers, and they were repainted in Shaw Savill colours.

The first voyage to New Zealand was taken by *Tamaroa*, departing London on 10 September 1926, followed by *Mataroa* on 5 November. Over the next three years they were the best ships on the New Zealand trade, until *Rangitiki*, *Rangitata* and *Rangitane* entered service in 1929 for the New Zealand Shipping Company. In 1931 the accommodation on both *Tamaroa* and *Mataroa* was reduced to just 130 in cabin class only.

In 1932 the Aberdeen Line was purchased outright by Shaw Savill & Albion, who took over ownership of *Tamaroa* and *Mataroa*. Shortly afterwards the accommodation was increased to 158 cabin class passengers, and a verandah café was added at the after end of the boat deck. Through the 1930s *Tamaroa* and *Mataroa* continued to operate a regular service to New Zealand, and this continued for over a year after war broke out in 1939.

In November 1940 *Tamaroa* was requisitioned as a troopship, with *Mataroa* being taken over for similar duty the following month. They were refitted to carry 1,916 men, and spent the rest of the war moving troops to many parts of the world without incident.

During 1947 both vessels were returned to their owner, *Tamaroa* being reconditioned at Liverpool, while the work on *Mataroa* was done at Glasgow, with each vessel having accommodation installed for 372 passengers in tourist class only.

Mataroa was the first to return to commercial service, departing London on 30 April 1948 for Wellington; on 27 August 1948 that *Tamaroa* left London for New Zealand again. The pair gave steady service on the route, the only incident to mar their careers being a serious fire in the forward hold of *Mataroa* when bound for Britain in January 1949. The blaze was extinguished by the crew, but not before it had done some serious damage.

In January 1957 it was announced that both *Mataroa* and *Tamaroa* were to be withdrawn and sold at the end of their current voyages. *Tamaroa* returned to London in early February, and was sold to shipbreakers at Blyth, arriving there on 5 March. *Mataroa* arrived in London for the last time on 19 February, and on 29 March arrived at Faslane to be broken up.

Mataroa

MOLDAVIA and MONGOLIA

MOLDAVIA
Built: 1922 by Cammell Laird & Co., Birkenhead
Gross tonnage: 16,277
Dimensions: 573 x 71 ft/174.6 x 21.8 m
Service speed: 16 knots
Propulsion: Geared turbines/twin propellers

MONGOLIA/RIMUTAKA
Built: 1923 by Armstrong Whitworth, Newcastle
Gross tonnage: 16,385
Dimensions: 568 x 72 ft/173.2 x 21.9 m
Service speed: 16 knots
Propulsion: Geared turbines/twin propellers

During World War I P&O suffered the loss of many of their liners, so as soon as possible after the war orders were placed for new ships. The design for the first pair of post-war liners was a mixture of old and new, since the vessels had only one funnel and old-fashioned counter sterns, but the latest in machinery, with geared turbines driving twin propellers.

The first ship was named *Moldavia* when launched on 1 October 1921. Trials were run on 22 September 1922, following which it was handed over to P&O, briefly becoming the largest vessel in their fleet. On 13 October *Moldavia* left Tilbury on its maiden voyage, reaching Fremantle on 18 November, Adelaide on 22 November, Melbourne two days later, and Sydney on 28 November.

The second vessel was launched on 24 August 1922 as *Mongolia* and handed over to P&O on 25 April 1923, supplanting *Moldavia* as the largest member of the fleet, only to be superseded by *Mooltan* a few months

later. On 11 May *Mongolia* left Tilbury on its maiden voyage to Australia.

Both ships could accommodate about 230 first-class and 180 second class passengers, a very small number considering their size, but they did have a large cargo capacity. There were several minor differences between the two, *Mongolia* having a thicker funnel and plating along the open decks which made it appear more powerful and larger.

In 1928 *Mongolia* was given a refit, during which the second class accommodation was re-graded third cabin. *Mongolia* then operated on a separate schedule catering to the migrant trade from Britain and non-luxury travellers from Australia. *Moldavia* remained on the main service until April 1930, at which time it was also refitted to carry third cabin passengers.

In an extraordinary move, a dummy second funnel was fitted to *Moldavia*, which completely altered the appearance of the vessel. The white band around the hull was painted a deck lower, and the stone colour of the superstructure extended to include the forecastle.

In 1931 both *Mongolia* and *Moldavia* had their accommodation altered again, to 830 passengers in tourist class only, this being a first for P&O. They continued to operate to Australia, usually via Bombay, but on a separate schedule from the mail steamers. In 1934 both liners had super-heaters added to their engines and new propellers fitted to improve their speed and economy of operation.

In 1936 P&O decided to abandon the Indian service as a separate entity, routing their Australian vessels by way of Bombay. On 20 August 1937 *Mongolia* left London on its final voyage to Australia and on returning

Mongolia in Sydney Harbour.

to Britain was laid up. *Moldavia* left London on its final voyage on 17 September, then was also laid up.

Moldavia was sold to shipbreakers during 1938, but *Mongolia* was transferred within the P&O Group to the New Zealand Shipping Company and renamed *Rimutaka*. Still providing accommodation for 830 tourist-class passengers, the vessel left London on 8 December 1938 on its first voyage to New Zealand, passing through the Panama Canal in each direction.

Less than ten months later war broke out, and soon after *Rimutaka* was requisitioned for service as an armed merchant cruiser. Before conversion work started, however, it was decided that the vessel would be more valuable in a commercial role, carrying meat and dairy foods from New Zealand to Britain, so it spent the war years operating on its regular route. The accommodation was controlled by the Ministry of War Transport, and in 1942 *Rimutaka* made a trooping voyage to West Africa. In April 1943 the vessel was narrowly missed by a torpedo while travelling in a convoy.

It was 1948 before the Government released *Rimutaka*, and following a quick refit it was rushed back into service, as the New Zealand Shipping Company was very short of tonnage, and until September 1948 *Rimutaka* was their only ship.

With the arrival of the last of three new ships in 1950 *Rimutaka* was no longer required, making its final departure from London for New Zealand on 11 October 1949.

Despite being nearly thirty years old, *Rimutaka* was to be idle for only a brief period, as early in 1950 it was sold to Compania de Navigacion Incres, a Panama-registered concern. Following a refit in Genoa the vessel was renamed *Europa* and, with a capacity of 614 tourist class passengers only, entered the Atlantic trade with a sailing from New York on 5 July 1950 to Antwerp.

In October 1951 the accommodation was rebuilt to cater for 617 first-class passengers. Renamed *Nassau*, the vessel began a program of regular weekly cruises from New York to Nassau in January 1952, which was to last almost ten years.

In October 1961 the vessel was sold yet again, to Naviera Turistica Mexicana, being renamed *Acapulco*, and becoming the largest vessel under the Mexican flag. Refitted and modernised in Glasgow for the cruise trade from American west coast ports to Mexico, *Acapulco* failed to pass the United States Coastguard safety standards. Instead it was sent to Seattle to act as a floating hotel during the World Fair there in 1962, and later laid up at Manzanillo until being sold to Japanese shipbreakers in 1964 to end a 40-year career.

Moldavia with two funnels.

MOOLTAN and MALOJA

Built: 1923 by Harland & Wolff, Belfast
Gross tonnage: 20,847/20,837
Dimensions: 625 x 73 ft/190.5 x 22.3 m
Service speed: 16 knots
Propulsion: Quadruple expansion/twin propellers

This was the second pair of post-war liners to be built by P&O for their Australian service. *Mooltan* was launched on 15 February 1923 and handed over to P&O on 21 September. Its maiden voyage the following month was to Bombay and return, and on 21 December 1923 *Mooltan* left Tilbury on her first voyage to Australia. *Maloja* was launched on 19 April 1923, and in November made its maiden voyage to Bombay and return, leaving London on 18 January 1924 for its first voyage to Australia.

Accommodation was provided for 327 first class and 329 second class passengers, with first class being located in the forward areas of the ships. When P&O introduced an accelerated mail service in 1929 combining the Indian and Australian routes, it required a higher service speed, so *Mooltan* and *Maloja* had exhaust turbines fitted to their engines, which increased their speed by one knot. During the 1930s both ships had their accommodation altered to cater for 346 in first class and 336 in tourist class, the new popular name for second class.

When war broke out on 3 September 1939 both *Mooltan* and *Maloja* were converted first into armed merchant cruisers, and during 1941 were both altered to serve as troop transports.

In 1947 both ships were handed back to P&O, but by then they were over twenty years old and not worth the huge cost of restoration to their pre-war glory. It was decided instead to use them as migrant ships under charter to the Ministry of Transport, and both were fitted out to carry 1,034 passengers in tourist class only.

The work on *Mooltan* was done by Harland &Wolff in Belfast. *Maloja* was also refitted by Harland & Wolff, but in London. As part of this work extra lifeboats had to be added, but the mainmast was not restored, so the ships lost their balanced profiles. They were also repainted in their pre-war colours, with light stone upperworks and black hulls and funnels, which gave them a very dated appearance.

Maloja was the first to return to service with a departure from London on 10 June 1948, while *Mooltan* made its first departure in August.

On 30 September 1953 *Mooltan* left London on its last voyage to Australia, returning to Tilbury on 7 January 1954. By then the old liner had been sold to British Iron & Steel Corp., and *Mooltan* left Tilbury on 19 January on its last short journey to Faslane.

Maloja departed Tilbury on its final voyage on 5 November 1953, arriving back in Tilbury on 18 March. *Maloja* was also sold to British Iron & Steel, and broken up at their Inverkeithing yard during 1954.

Mooltan

PRINCIPESSA GIOVANNA and PRINCIPESSA MARIA

Built: 1923 by Cant. Nav. Franco Tosi, Taranto
Gross tonnage: 8,389/8,329
Dimensions: 460 x 59 ft/140.2 x 18 m
Service speed: 14 knots
Propulsion: Geared turbine/twin propellers

This pair was designed for Lloyd Sabaudo as large cargo ships with basic accommodation in the upper 'tween decks and deckhouse to carry about 400 third class passengers on the services from Italian ports to Australia or South America.

Principessa Giovanna was launched on 29 April 1923, and departed Genoa in August 1923 on its maiden voyage, to Australia, arriving in Fremantle on 5 October 1923, where only three passengers disembarked, and continuing to east coast ports.

Principessa Maria was not completed until November 1923, leaving the next month on its maiden voyage to Australia, arriving in Fremantle on 16 January 1924, where 219 passengers disembarked, then going on to the east coast. This was the only voyage to Australia by *Principessa Maria*, which was transferred to the South American trade.

Principessa Giovanna made a second voyage to Australia, departing Genoa and other Italian ports in February 1924, and passing through Fremantle on 18 March on its way to east coast ports. *Principessa Giovanna* then joined its sister on the South American trade, with an occasional voyage to New York when required.

In 1932 *Principessa Giovanna* was rebuilt, emerging with a more extensive superstructure and accommodation for 640 third class passengers, a second, dummy funnel, and a white hull. In 1935 *Principessa Giovanna* was briefly used as a troopship for the Abyssinian campaign.

Principessa Giovanna became a troopship again in 1940, and the same year *Principessa Maria* was damaged by fire when off the French coast. After repairs the vessel went to Argentina, and when Italy came into the war it was seized by the Argentine Government, and renamed *Rio de la Plata*. On 18 August 1944 the vessel caught fire when in the Pacific Ocean off AcapulCo., and sank.

After the Italian surrender, *Principessa Giovanna* was taken over by the British, and served as a hospital ship, and later as a troopship. In 1946 *Principessa Giovanna* was returned to the Italians, and refitted at Genoa. Renamed *San Giorgio,* it joined the Italia Line trade to South America with a departure from Genoa on 20 January 1947. *San Giorgio* remained on this route until 1952, when the vessel was transferred to Lloyd Triestino.

San Giorgio departed Trieste on 17 February 1952 for Australia, arriving in Fremantle on 25 March and Melbourne on 1 April, berthing in Sydney on 6 April.

A second voyage departed on 18 June, and a third on 10 October. A fourth voyage, scheduled to depart on 27 January 1953, was cancelled, and *San Giorgio* was laid up. After remaining idle through the year, in December the vessel was sold to Italian shipbreakers, arriving on 30 December at their Savona yard.

Principessa Maria (WSS Victoria)

THE P&O C CLASS

CATHAY   COMORIN
Built: 1925 by Barclay, Curle & Co., Glasgow
Gross tonnage: 15,104/15,116
Dimensions: 545 x 70 ft/166.1 x 21.4 m
Service speed: 16 knots
Propulsion: Quadruple expansion/twin propellers

CHITRAL
Built: 1925 by A. Stephen & Co., Glasgow
Gross tonnage: 15,248
Dimensions: 548 x 70 ft/167 x 21.4 m
Service speed: 16 knots
Propulsion: Quadruple expansion/twin propellers

In 1923 P&O placed orders for three liners for use on either the Australian or Indian trades from two Glasgow shipyards. *Cathay* and *Comorin* were launched at separate ceremonies on the same day, 31 October 1924, while the third ship was named *Chitral* when launched on 27 January 1925.

Cathay departed London on 27 March on its maiden voyage to Australia. *Comorin* made its maiden departure from Tilbury for Australia on 24 April, while *Chitral* left on 3 July.

There was a slight difference in accommodation between the three ships, *Chitral* carrying 199 first-class and 135 second class passengers, while the other two catered for 203 first class and 103 second class passengers.

The ships were employed permanently on the Australian trade until 1931, when *Chitral* and *Comorin* were transferred to operate to Bombay or the Far East as required, with an occasional trip to Australia.

On 15 December 1933 *Cathay* was crossing the Indian Ocean when the port propeller fell off, causing the speed of the ship to be greatly reduced. *Cathay* did not arrive in Sydney until the afternoon of Monday, 1 January 1934, and had to remain there while a new propeller and tailshaft were sent out from Britain.

On 4 August 1939 *Cathay* departed Tilbury on a voyage to Australia, but on arrival at Bombay on 24 August the ship was requisitioned and converted into an armed merchant cruiser. *Chitral* and *Comorin* were converted into armed merchant cruisers in Britain.

On 6 April 1941 a fire broke out in the engine room of *Comorin* and spread through the ship, which was deliberately sunk the next day.

Cathay was included in the North African landings, and arrived at Bougie on 11 November 1942. Unable to offload troops due to a heavy swell, the vessel lay off the port and was attacked by German aircraft, being hit by a stick of three bombs and set on fire. Shortly after daybreak on 12 November depth charges stored aft exploded and blew off the stern. *Cathay* rolled over and sank, with the port side still above the water.

Chitral was returned to P&O in September 1947, and refitted to carry 738 passengers in one class. On 30 December 1948 *Chitral* left Tilbury on its first post-war voyage to Australia. It left London on its final voyage on 19 December 1952, arriving back at Tilbury on 18 March, and was sold to W.H. Arnott Young Ltd, arriving at their Dalmuir shipbreaking yard on 1 April 1953.

Comorin

PALERMO

Built: 1907 by Laing, Sunderland
Gross tonnage: 6,592
Dimensions: 430 x 53 ft/131.1 x 16 m
Service speed: 14 knots
Propulsion: Triple expansion/twin propellers

This vessel was originally named *San Giovanni*, being the second of a pair built for Sicula Americana Societa di Navigazione for a service from Naples and ports in Sicily to New York.

The first vessel was launched on 10 April 1907 as *San Giorgio*, departing Naples on 19 July on its maiden voyage. *San Giovanni* was launched on 27 June 1907, making its maiden departure from Naples on 14 October. Both ships were fitted with accommodation for 30 first class, 60 second class and 1,800 steerage passengers.

On 2 October 1912 *San Giovanni* left Naples on a voyage to Buenos Aires. Over the next two years the vessel made another four trips to the River Plate port, the last after war broke out in 1914. *San Giovanni* remained on the New York trade through the early war years, then, in August 1917, Sicula Americana was bought out by Navigazione Generale Italiana. They merged the Sicula Americana fleet with that of another Italian company they owned to form Transoceanica Societa Italiana di Navigazione, but the ships were not renamed and for the next few years they continued to operate to New York.

In August 1921 the vessels operated by the Transoceanica company were absorbed into the main fleet of Navigazione Generale Italiana, and at the same time *San Giovanni* was renamed *Palermo*. The vessel continued to operate to New York until 1925, when it was transferred to the Australian trade, with the accommodation altered to carry 1,500 passengers in third class only.

Palermo departed Genoa in March 1925 on its first voyage to Australia, reaching Fremantle on 22 April and Adelaide on 27 April, remaining there several days before continuing to Melbourne, where it berthed on 3 May. The vessel then went on to Sydney, arriving on 7 May, with the voyage terminating at Brisbane a week later.

Palermo departed Genoa on its second voyage to Australia in early August 1925, following the same route as before, arriving in Melbourne on 21 September, Sydney four days later, and Brisbane on 28 September.

A third voyage left Genoa in late December 1925, passing through Adelaide on 8 February, arriving in Melbourne on 11 February and Sydney on 15 February.

It was not until March 1927 that *Palermo* departed Genoa on its fourth voyage to Australia, reaching Melbourne on 19 May and Sydney on 23 May, departing Sydney on 6 June on its way back to Italy.

This would be the final voyage this vessel would make to Australia, as later in 1927 *Palermo* was withdrawn from service, and sold to shipbreakers at Genoa, arriving there on 11 January 1928.

Palermo (WSS Victoria)

VEDIC

Built: 1918 by Harland & Wolff, Govan and Belfast
Gross tonnage: 9,332
Dimensions: 460 x 58 ft/140.4 x 17.8 m
Service speed: 14 knots
Propulsion: Geared turbine/twin propellers

Harland & Wolff built a large number of ships for the White Star Line in the early years of the twentieth century, but only two of them were given geared turbine machinery, *Vedic* and the much larger *Doric* in 1923. *Vedic* was designed as a large cargo steamer for trans-Atlantic service, but could also be used to transport migrants in temporary quarters installed in the holds.

At times it was the practice of Harland & Wolff to have the hulls of vessels built at their Govan yard, on the River Clyde, from where they were towed to Belfast to be completed. *Vedic* was on the slip at Govan when war broke out in 1914, and all work ceased on commercial shipping until orders were given to complete all the ships sitting on the stocks unfinished.

Vedic was launched on Tuesday, 18 December 1917 without any ceremony, and towed to Belfast, where the vessel was completed on 10 July 1918. The next day *Vedic* left Belfast for the Clyde, where it was taken over by the British Government for service as a troopship, its first voyage being across the Atlantic to Boston.

In December 1918 *Vedic* was handed over to White Star Line, and left Glasgow on its first commercial voyage for them on 28 December, going to Boston. In September 1919 *Vedic* was again placed under Government control, being sent to Archangel in Russia to embark British troops and return them home. On 20 September, with over 1,000 troops on board, *Vedic* ran ashore in the Orkney Islands, north of Scotland. Several nearby warships were soon on the scene, followed by tugs, and between them they were able to pull *Vedic* free. The vessel then continued its voyage.

On being handed back to White Star Line, *Vedic* went to a shipyard at Middlesborough to undergo a refit, during which more permanent accommodation was installed for up to 1,250 third class passengers. On returning to service in 1920, *Vedic* was placed on the migrant trade between Liverpool and Canada.

In the 1920s White Star was operating a service to Australia requiring five ships, but in 1925 one of those ships, *Runic*, was forced to miss one round trip. As a replacement, *Vedic* departed Liverpool on 31 October 1925 on its first trip to Australia, voyaging by way of Cape Town to arrive in Melbourne on 16 December, and Sydney on 22 December, then continuing north to Brisbane.

The *Sydney Morning Herald* reported on 23 December that the vessel was carrying several hundred migrants, the principal groups being twelve families brought out by the Presbyterian Church, and forty-two boys sponsored by the Salvation Army. The newspaper report later stated:

Many of the migrants had bitter complaints to make about the food and accommodation on the vessel. One said, 'There was nothing for children to eat sometimes but undercooked meat. Husbands were separated from their families, so that in a cabin holding eight people the mother had to look after six sick children unaided and suffer the presence of some strange woman. The lower parts of the ship were shockingly ventilated, and we had hardly any deck room for exercise. About 400 of the passengers joined in signing a protest and sending it to the Home Office in London.'

Major G. Davies, who acted as welfare officer on the voyage, said that as far as he could make out the complaints about the food were unfounded. It seemed reasonably good during the whole trip. Parts of the steamer, however, were certainly under-ventilated, and the deck accommodation was cramped.

On returning to Britain, *Vedic* was again refitted, and returned to the Canadian trade, but also began making occasional voyages to Australia. *Vedic* arrived in Melbourne on 27 July 1926 on its second voyage, continuing to Sydney. The next voyage to Australia did not depart Liverpool until December 1926, and was made under the auspices of the Aberdeen Line, reaching Melbourne on 30 January 1927, and Sydney on 4 February.

Vedic operated one more voyage to Australia in 1927, under charter to the Salvation Army, who sponsored all 644 migrants aboard the ship when it departed Liverpool on 15 October. Among the passengers were several hundred unaccompanied young boys ranging upward in age from ten, and a smaller number of girls.

Vedic arrived in Albany on 22 November, where it was reported that 201 migrants landed, including 84 youths. The vessel continued to Melbourne, where it berthed on 28 November, at which time Australian ports were coming to a standstill due to an overtime ban by dock workers. *Vedic* was held up for several days, but then was able to continue its voyage, arriving in Sydney on 5 December. Next day a story appeared in the *Sydney Morning Herald*, which included these comments on the youths on board:

'They overran the ship. I'd have liked to lock the young scamps up,' said the skipper. No wonder. Here were several hundred eager boys, full of life, hungry for any sort of adventure, suddenly come into an inheritance that measured up to their dreams. A ship to themselves — a ship on the high seas.

True this was not an ideal ship. It was a cargo vessel, temporarily converted. Many a tourist on the 'first class only' liners would have faced a voyage in it with dire forebodings. But it was a ship — and, as far as romance is concerned, it was all the better for not being 'first class only. If it had been, they might not have been able to invade the cookhouse, and peel vegetables, and stir stews. They might not have been able to go down into the stokehold and shovel coal. They might not have gone up into the crow's nest and kept watch. But even with these avenues open there was never enough for them to do. Concerts and swimming baths and other things were arranged to keep them out of mischief. They played all the customary games of youth upon the decks. But still there was never enough.

They became restive. One or two of them had to be slightly disciplined. And what Mrs Grundy would complain about that? It showed spirit, life, resilience, youth. And what youth! Despite the conditions, the heat, and other trying circumstances, there was no sickness among them. One child died in the Red Sea, and was buried there, but that child was frail and weak before it left England, and sending it on the voyage was an attempt to save its life. But among the others there was no illness, and they start out in their adopted country strong and healthy.

This experiment in migration is the first of its kind to be made. The Salvation Army has sent chartered ships to Canada with its migrants, but Australia has not been so honoured before. The *Vedic* has been a dry ship, and gambling has been taboo. All old enough to work, including the parents of the younger ones, had work arranged for them here before they left England. More than a hundred disembarked at Albany, and another two hundred at Melbourne. The rest disembarked yesterday, and about 50 of these will go on to Queensland. Most of the lads have undergone a course in agriculture at Hadleigh, the Salvation Army farm near London. Many of the girls are domestics, all with situations ready for them.

Apart from those who met the ship, there was no life about the wharf at the arrival. All the men who would ordinarily have been there to unload the 2,900 tons of cargo on board were absent on strike, and after youth had carried its belongings ashore the vessel lay temporarily idle.

Two more voyages were made to Australia by *Vedic* during 1928, both sponsored by the Salvation Army, the first departing Liverpool in March, being in Melbourne on 24 April. In October *Vedic* again left Liverpool for Australia, arriving in Melbourne on 23 November.

On 19 October 1929 *Vedic* left Liverpool, again sponsored by the Salvation Army, and a passenger on that voyage who disembarked at Fremantle later wrote:

There were 147 emigrants bound for Fremantle (I don't know how many were bound for other ports) on board in October 1929, a mixture of migrants (with a total capital of £200) and 'nominees'. Migrants were classified as either 'learners' or 'domestics'. The 'selected' civilians, travelling alone, were as young as 14, some destined for the Salvation Army 'training Colony' in Brisbane. Most however were being brought out to be servants (many had been servants, labourers, porters and the like), and the public was advised 'farmers etc requiring farm workers or married couples for both branches of work — domestic and farm - should apply at once to the officer in charge of immigration.' There were also the 'nominated' families, destined for the various Group Settlement schemes, many of whom had been miners in England.

This was the last voyage the vessel made to Australia. *Vedic* returned permanently to the Canadian trade, on which it spent the rest of its career. In 1934 *Vedic* was withdrawn from service, and sold to shipbreakers at Rosyth, on the Firth of Forth, arriving there on 3 February 1934.

Vedic

THE ORIENT LINE ORAMA CLASS

ORAMA OTRANTO ORFORD
Built: 1924/25/28 by Vickers Armstrong, Barrow
Gross tonnage: 19,777/20,032/19,941
Dimensions: 659 x 75 ft/200.6 x 22.9 m
Service speed: 20 knots
Propulsion: Geared turbines/twin propellers

ORONSAY
Built: 1925 by John Brown, Clydebank
Gross tonnage: 20,001
Dimensions: 659 x 75 ft/200.6 x 22.9 m
Service speed: 20 knots
Propulsion: Geared turbines/twin propellers

ORONTES
Built: 1929 by Vickers Armstrong, Barrow
Gross tonnage: 19,970
Dimensions: 664 x 75 ft/202.3 x 22.9 m
Service speed: 20 knots
Propulsion: Geared turbines/twin propellers

At the end of World War I the Orient Line placed orders for three new liners, to be enlarged and improved versions of *Ormonde* (page 142), with two more being ordered in 1926. The first was launched at Barrow on 20 May 1924 as *Orama*, leaving London on 15 November on her maiden voyage to Australia. On 14 August 1924 *Oronsay* was launched, entering service on 7 February 1925.

Orama and *Oronsay* accommodated 592 first-class and 1,244 third class passengers. They were the first British mail steamers not to have second class.

Otranto was launched on 9 June 1925, and joined its sisters with a departure from Tilbury on 9 January 1926. *Otranto* had berths for 572 in first class and 1,114 in third class.

After one trip to Australia, *Otranto* was diverted to cruising from Britain for several months. On 11 May 1926 the vessel struck rocks off Cape Matapan in the Greek Peloponnese, incurring serious bow damage, and limped back to Britain for repairs. *Otranto* would continue to operate seasonal cruises from Britain for several years.

Otranto was involved in another incident during its 1928 cruise season. Just two hours after leaving Immingham on 11 August at the start of a cruise to Norway with 520 passengers on board, *Otranto* collided almost head-on with the Japanese steamer *Kitano Maru*, the impact causing the Japanese vessel to swing round and crash into *Otranto* again

Orford

amidships. *Otranto* again suffered severe bow damage as well as being holed amidships, and had to limp back to port for repairs. An inquiry later blamed the Japanese vessel for the accident.

Meanwhile, *Orford* had been launched on 29 September 1927, being completed six months later, and having accommodation for 550 first and 1,150 third class passengers. *Orford* first made a series of cruises to Norway and the Mediterranean, so it was not until 13 October 1927 that the vessel left Tilbury on its first voyage to Australia.

As soon as *Orford* had left the builders' yard, work started on the next vessel, which was named *Orontes* when launched on 26 February 1929. Completed during July, *Orontes* differed from the other vessels in being given a raked bow, and having accommodation for 460 first class and 1,112 third class passengers. *Orontes* was sent cruising for several months, then on 26 October 1929 left Tilbury on its first voyage to Australia.

Both *Orford* and *Orontes* were regularly used for cruising from Britain during the northern summer, carrying 550 passengers in a single class. This was so successful that Orient Line decided to try cruising from Australia, and on 24 December 1932 *Oronsay* left Sydney on a cruise to Noumea, the largest ship to have called there up to that time.

The company then scheduled several cruises each year from Australia as well as Britain, adding extra ports of call. In 1934 *Orontes* grounded off Gallipoli while on a cruise, but was quickly refloated without damage. In 1935 *Orford* and *Orontes* had their third class accommodation upgraded to tourist class for about 500 passengers.

In 1935 *Orama* was repainted with a corn-coloured hull and made two voyages to Australia to test reaction, which was favourable. *Orama* was then repainted black, but when the new liner *Orion* was completed later that year it was given the new hull colour.

In the northern summer of 1936 *Otranto* was sent on a cruise to the Mediterranean and Black Sea, and ran aground on the Gallipoli Peninsula but was soon refloated without sustaining damage.

From November 1938 the Orient Line, in conjunction with P&O, began extending some voyages from Australia to New Zealand, the first of these being made by *Orford*. During 1939 *Orontes* made one trip across the Tasman and *Orford* made its second such trip. *Orama* and *Oronsay* made only one trip each across the Tasman, while *Otranto* made two.

Within weeks of the outbreak of war in September 1939 all five ships were under Government control as troopships, with *Orford* and *Otranto* being in the first convoy to carry Australian troops overseas in January 1940.

Orford was sent to the Mediterranean in May 1940 to assist in the evacuation of British troops from the south of France. On 1 June the vessel was attacked by German bombers off Toulon, set on fire, run ashore and then abandoned, but not before fourteen

Orama with corn-coloured hull.

Oronsay

men had been killed and a further twenty-five wounded. Left to burn out, *Orford* became a total loss.

Orama was one of several troopships sent urgently to Norway early in June 1940 in an attempt to rescue thousands of British troops surrounded by Germans along the coastline. *Orama* sailed independently for Narvik, but was sighted by the German cruiser *Admiral Hipper* on 8 June. The British ship had no chance of escape as it was hit by heavy shells, and sunk. The Germans rescued 280 survivors, but twenty men were killed.

Also in June 1940 *Oronsay* came under heavy attack from German aircraft while boarding troops at St Nazaire. *Oronsay* suffered serious damage in the attacks, but was able to reach England safely. Later in 1940 *Oronsay* was attacked a second time by German bombers off the coast of Ireland, but again survived.

On 9 October 1942 *Oronsay* was 500 miles (800 km) off Freetown when it was struck by a torpedo fired by the Italian submarine *Archimede*, and after a second torpedo hit the order to abandon ship was given. Five persons were killed, but the survivors managed to get away in lifeboats; *Archimede* then put two more torpedoes into *Oronsay,* which sank soon after. Over the next eight days the lifeboats kept together and sailed toward Freetown, until they were eventually sighted by a British naval vessel.

Otranto had an active war, including assisting in the evacuation of British troops from France during 1940. The vessel then made several trips to the Middle East and India, often unescorted. Late in 1942 *Otranto* was converted into a landing ship, with barges replacing the lifeboats, and took part in the North African campaign, landing troops at Algiers, and the landings at Sicily and Salerno. After this the landing craft were removed and the vessel reverted to transporting troops.

In 1945 she carried New Zealand troops back home, then went to the Far East to board British troops and take them home, and was also used to transport released prisoners of war.

Orontes was also included in the invasion of North Africa, and later took part in the landings on Sicily, putting ashore the first wave of troops on Avola Beach. As *Orontes* withdrew it was attacked by a German bomber and straddled by five bombs, but escaped unscathed. Later *Orontes* took part in the landings at Salerno before going on to the Atlantic route, bringing thousands of American troops to Italy until late in 1943, then was transferred to long-distance trooping.

Orontes was returned to the Orient Line in 1947, refitted for 502 first-class and 618 tourist class passengers, and on 17 June 1948 left Tilbury on its first post-war commercial voyage to Australia. In 1953 *Orontes* was converted to carry 1,410 passengers in tourist class only.

Otranto remained under Government control until August 1948, then was rebuilt to carry 1,416 tourist class passengers only, and on 14 July 1949 left Tilbury on its first commercial voyage to Australia since the war.

On 13 February 1957 *Otranto* left Tilbury on its sixty-fourth round trip to Australia in peacetime, and shortly after was sold to British Iron & Steel Corp., being allocated to Shipbreaking Industries at Faslane. On 12 June *Otranto* left Tilbury for the last time, arriving at Faslane two days later.

On 25 November 1961 *Otranto* left Tilbury for Australia for the last time, and was sold to Ordaz & Co., shipbreakers of Valencia, arriving at their yard on 3 March 1962.

TAORMINA

Built: 1908 by D. & W. Henderson & Co., Glasgow.
Tonnage: 8,298 gross
Dimensions: 482 x 58 ft/146.9 x 17.6 m
Service speed: 16 knots
Propulsion: Triple expansion/twin propellers

Taormina was operated by three Italian companies at various times, always under the same name, and began making voyages to Australia only toward the end of its career. The vessel, along with two sister ships, *Ancona* and *Verona*, was built for Italia Societa Anonima di Navigazione, a company in which a major interest was held by Navigazione Generale Italiana,

The last of the three ships to be completed, *Taormina* was launched on 15 February 1908, and left Genoa on 3 September that year on its maiden voyage, calling at Naples and Palermo on the way to New York and Philadelphia, joining her two sisters. Accommodation was provided for 60 first class and 2,500 third class passengers, the latter being used by migrants wishing to start a new life in North America. In 1910 accommodation for 120 second class passengers was added.

This service was operated in conjunction with three other Italian lines, NGI, La Veloce and Lloyd Italiano. At various times ships were interchanged between these companies, and on 16 December 1911 *Taormina*

arrived in Genoa at the end of her final voyage for Italia, and was transferred to Lloyd Italiano.

Taormina departed Genoa on 23 January 1912, and then Naples, on her first voyage for the new owners, going only as far as New York. *Taormina* remained on this trade through World War I, but both her sisters were sunk.

On 1 June 1918 Lloyd Italiana was absorbed into the NGI fleet, though the official name of the company was Navigazione Generale Italiana - Flotte Riunite Florio-Rubattino & Lloyd Italiano. *Taormina* remained on the Genoa –Marseilles–New York service for the NGI until the mid-1920s, by which time the company had taken delivery of a number of newer and larger liners.

The NGI had become involved in the Australian trade in the years following the First World War, and during the 1920s demand for migrant berths from Italy to Australia began to increase. In 1926 *Taormina* was refitted to accommodate 93 first class and 542 third class passengers, and on 7 May 1926 departed Genoa on its first voyage to Australia, calling at Fremantle, Melbourne, Sydney and Brisbane.

Taormina did not return to Australia until early in 1928, arriving in Sydney on 25 February. The vessel continued to trade to Australia over the next year, but in 1929 was withdrawn from service, and broken up at Savona.

Taormina (Martin Navarro collection)

COMMISSAIRE RAMEL

Built: 1920 by Soc. Provencale de Cons. Nav., La Ciotat
Gross tonnage: 10,061
Dimensions: 500 x 59 ft/152.5 x 18 m
Service speed: 14 knots
Propulsion: Triple expansion/single propeller

Built for Messageries Maritimes, *Commissaire Ramel* was launched on 20 March 1920, and completed as an 8,308 gross ton cargo ship, but had been designed so that it would be possible to alter it to carry passengers as well. The vessel traded to China until 1926, then returned to the builder's yard at La Ciotat to be converted into a passenger liner.

The superstructure was greatly enlarged and accommodation installed for 58 first class, 78 second class and 416 third class passengers, the latter intended for the use of emigrants, and extra berths could be added when required. The machinery was converted from coal to oil firing and an extra boiler added to raise speed from 11 to 14 knots.

Commissaire Ramel left Marseilles on 19 January 1927 on its first voyage via the Suez Canal to Australian ports and Noumea, arriving in Fremantle on 21 February. On board were 47 first class, 55 second class, and 550 third class passengers, of whom 125 disembarked in Fremantle. The vessel went on to Melbourne, arriving on 2 March, and then to Sydney two days later.

In 1935 the extension to Noumea was abandoned, and the route terminated in Sydney. Over the next few years Messageries Maritimes reduced their Suez service, and shortly before the war started they withdrew from the route altogether.

Commissaire Ramel made some further trips to Australia and the South Pacific islands, and was in Suva in July 1940. Following the fall of France, the ship was seized by the Governor of Fiji on behalf of the Ministry of War Transport in Britain, and sent to Sydney, where a British crew was signed on and the vessel placed under the management of Shaw Savill & Albion, but not renamed. After loading general cargo and wool, *Commissaire Ramel* left Sydney on a voyage to Britain, and was crossing the Indian Ocean when, on 20 September 1940, a seemingly innocent cargo ship was sighted.

The other ship closed on *Commissaire Ramel*, then suddenly dropped its innocent disguise and ordered the French vessel to stop. It was the German auxiliary cruiser *Atlantis*. The French ship obeyed the command to stop, but then tried to send out a raider message. *Atlantis* began firing its guns into the radio shack, and soon *Commissaire Ramel* was on fire. During the barrage the port side lifeboats were destroyed, and three men in the engine room killed. The rest of the crew was taken on board *Atlantis*, which then sank *Commissaire Ramel*.

The crew from *Commissaire Ramel* was transferred to another vessel that had been captured, and taken to a location near Mogadishu in the Sudan, where they were liberated by British forces in February 1941.

Commissaire Ramel

MARIA CRISTINA

Built: 1908 by Germania Werft, Kiel
Tonnage: 8,512 gross
Dimensions: 448 x 55 ft/136.6 x 16.8 m
Service speed: 13 knots
Propulsion: Quadruple expansion/twin propellers

This vessel was built for Hamburg America Line, being named *Corcovado* when launched on 21 December 1907, and departing Hamburg in April 1908 on its maiden voyage to ports in Brazil. At that time accommodation was provided for 136 first class and 1,126 third class passengers. In 1911 *Corcovado* was transferred to a shorter route, from Hamburg to Cuba and Mexican ports.

On 19 October 1912, *Corcovado* departed Hamburg on its first voyage to New York, and in April 1914 was placed on a service from New York to the Mediterranean and the Black Sea, terminating at Odessa. When war broke out in August 1914, *Corcovado* sought shelter at Constantinople, where it became an accommodation ship.

In 1915 *Corcovado* was transferred to Turkish ownership, being renamed *Sueh*. When the war ended the vessel was surrendered to France, by whom it was renamed *Corcovado*. In May 1920 it was sold to an Italian company, Sicula Americana, otherwise known as the Sicilian American Line, which was based at Messina until the 1908 earthquake virtually destroyed that city, at which time the company moved to Naples. They renamed the vessel *Guglielmo Pierce*, after one of the two brothers who founded the firm, the other one, Giorgio, having been killed in the earthquake.

Sicula Americana initially placed *Guglielmo Pierce* on a service from Naples to South America, but on 9 December 1920 it left Naples on the first voyage to New York, remaining on this trade until late in 1923, then reverted to the South American route.

It was the only passenger liner to be operated by the company, which encountered financial problems in the mid-1920s, and in 1926 *Guglielmo Pierce* was chartered to another Italian company, Cosulich Line, for their South American service.

In 1927, *Guglielmo Pierce* was sold to Lloyd Sabaudo, and renamed *Maria Cristina*. In April 1928, the vessel departed Genoa on its first voyage to Australia, berthing in Fremantle on 20 May, and continuing to east coast ports, arriving in Sydney on 1 June.

Maria Cristina was back in Fremantle from Genoa on 24 September 1928, and made two more voyages to Australia in 1929, arriving in Fremantle on 16 February and 21 August. This would be the last time the vessel was seen in local waters.

In 1930 *Maria Cristina* was sold to a Portuguese company, Cia Colonial, being renamed *Mouzinho*. The vessel was placed on a service from Lisbon to the Portuguese African colonies of Angola and Mozambique, on which it remained for the rest of its career, apart from two voyages between Lisbon and New York during 1941. In 1954 *Mouzinho* was withdrawn from service, and sold to shipbreakers at Savona, in Italy.

Maria Cristina

RANGITIKI, RANGITATA and RANGITANE

Built: 1929 by John Brown & Co., Clydebank
Gross tonnage: 16,698/16,737/16,737
Dimensions: 553 x 70 ft/168.5 x 21.4 m
Service speed: 15 knots
Propulsion: Sulzer diesels/twin propellers

The order for these ships was placed in the mid-1920s, but before any work commenced the New Zealand Shipping Company decided to defer construction due to the worsening world economic conditions. It was not until 1927 that the order to proceed was given, with the first vessel being launched on 29 August 1928, and named *Rangitiki*. After running trials on 26 January 1929, *Rangitiki* was handed over to the NZSC, and after loading cargo in London, departed Southampton on 15 February on its maiden voyage to New Zealand, via the Panama Canal.

On 26 February 1929 *Rangitata* was launched, followed on 27 May by *Rangitane*. *Rangitata* departed Southampton for the first time on 22 November, and *Rangitane* completed the trio's departures from Southampton on 20 December. *Rangitata* was actually registered under the ownership of the Federal Steam Navigation Company, a subsidiary of the NZSC, but always operated as a unit of the NZSC fleet.

These three vessels were the first motor ships to be built for the NZSC, and also their first liners in to have two funnels. Each ship provided accommodation for 100 first class, 85 second class and 410 third class passengers. In 1933 the second and third class accommodation was reclassified as Tourist A and Tourist B.

Initially the vessels loaded cargo in London, and went to Southampton to embark passengers, but from November 1932 the call at Southampton was eliminated, and both passengers and cargo were taken on in London, though on the return voyage passengers continued to disembark at Southampton.

In January 1940, *Rangitata* was requisitioned to embark troops in Wellington, the first New Zealand troops to be sent overseas in the war. *Rangitata* also loaded up her extensive refrigerated cargo holds with New Zealand meat and dairy produce, while wool was packed in the other holds, all destined for England. The ship departed Wellington on 6 January and travelled in a convoy to Sydney where they were joined by ships carrying Australian troops, and the convoy then proceeded to Egypt. Once the troops had disembarked, *Rangitata* continued to Britain, where the cargo was unloaded.

Rangitata resumed its place on the New Zealand trade, and in November 1940 had a narrow escape from destruction in the North Atlantic. *Rangitata* was one of thirty-eight merchant ships in convoy HX48 bound

Rangitane (Ian Farquhar collection)

for Britain when, on the afternoon of 5 November, the German warship *Admiral Scheer* was sighted. The escort ship, the armed merchant cruiser *Jervis Bay*, ordered the convoy to scatter, then turned to face the German battleship. Within a short time *Jervis Bay* had been sunk, but the heroic action allowed all but six ships of the convoy to escape, among them *Rangitata*.

On the afternoon of 24 November 1940, *Rangitane* left Auckland carrying 111 passengers and 200 crew as well as a full cargo. For safety reasons she anchored overnight in the Rangitoto Channel and at dawn continued her voyage to Britain via the Panama Canal. At 3.40 on the morning of 27 November the officers on watch were blinded by a searchlight, followed by an order to stop and not use the radio. Instead the radio officer on *Rangitane* began sending a message that the liner had been stopped by a raider. The enemy ship opened fire on *Rangitane*, but the radio officer sent a message that there were women on board, and the firing ceased.

By then *Rangitane* was on fire and ten persons had been killed—five passengers including three women, three engine room crew and two stewardesses—with many others wounded. The attackers were the German commerce raiders *Orion* and *Komet*, accompanied by the supply ship *Kulmerland*. The survivors were taken on board the raiders, after which a German boarding party opened the sea cocks to sink the liner. To speed up proceedings, *Komet* also fired a torpedo into the ship, and several shells along the waterline.

The loss of *Rangitane* was quickly followed by the requisitioning of *Rangitiki* during December 1940, and of *Rangitata* in February 1941. Both were converted into troopships, with facilities for 2,600 men being installed. Neither liner suffered any damage during their war careers, and as soon as peace came they were returned to the New Zealand trade, though still in their troopship guise.

Rangitiki was the first to resume service, during April 1945, followed by *Rangitata* the next month. Both ships were used to repatriate New Zealand soldiers from Europe on their southbound voyages, and carry Government sponsored passengers and cargoes of meat and dairy produce northbound. They continued to operate in this manner for almost three years, until being released by the Ministry of Transport early in 1948, and sent to the John Brown shipyard for a much-needed refit. At the same time their original Sulzer diesel engines were replaced by more powerful Doxford diesels, which increased their service speed to 16 knots. Following their refits, the liners had accommodation for 123 first class and 288 tourist class passengers.

Rangitiki departed London on 24 September 1948, while *Rangitata* returned to service with a departure London on 23 September 1949. *Rangitata* left London on her last trip to New Zealand on 12 January 1962, while *Rangitiki* left London for the last time on 16 March. On their return both vessels were laid up pending disposal, with *Rangitata* being sold to a Dutch company, N. V. Holland, in May 1962, and then being resold to Brodospas, a Yugoslav firm of shipbreakers who took delivery of the vessel at their Split yard on 21 July 1962. *Rangitiki* was sold to Spanish shipbreakers, and on 26 July 1962 arrived at Santander.

Rangitiki

PRINCIPE DI UDINE

Built: 1908 by Barclay, Curle & Co., Glasgow
Gross tonnage: 7,785
Dimensions: 451 x 55 ft/137.5 x 16.7 m
Service speed: 16 knots
Propulsion: Quadruple expansion/twin propellers

Operated by the Italian company Lloyd Sabaudo, this vessel spent the final years of its career on the Australian trade, commencing in 1928. The second of a pair, the first to be launched was *Tomaso di Savoie*, on 15 September 1907, which departed Genoa on 11 November on its maiden voyage to Rio de Janeiro, Montevideo and Buenos Aires. *Principe di Udine* was launched on 19 December 1907, its maiden departure for South America from Genoa was on 31 March 1908.

Both ships were given cabin accommodation for 114 passengers in first class, and 147 second class, while 1,012 passengers could also be carried in third class. The latter accommodation was very basic, mostly consisting of large dormitories in the holds which were removed for the voyage back to Italy, when a large amount of cargo was carried.

Principe di Udine and *Tomaso di Savoie* remained on the South American trade until 1915, when they were transferred to the North Atlantic service from Genoa to New York. By 1919 they were back on the South American route once again, on which *Principe di Udine* remained until 1928, when it was placed on the Australian trade.

The ship relied on the migrant trade for most of the outbound passengers from Genoa to Fremantle, Melbourne and Sydney, providing accommodation for about 1,700 passengers in third class only.

In February 1928 *Principe di Udine* departed Genoa and other Italian ports on its first voyage to Australia, reaching Fremantle on 17 March, Melbourne on 23 March, and Sydney two days later. A second voyage from Italy arrived in Fremantle on 15 July, and Melbourne on 24 July. Next day *The Argus* reported:

> The Italian liner *Principe di Udine*...brought 290 foreign settlers, only three of whom could speak English. They were mostly sturdy young Italians, who intend to go on the land.

Among the passengers to disembark was Luigi Grollo, aged nineteen, who was able to circumvent Mussolini's edict of the previous year which restricted Italian emigration, as he was sponsored by his brother Giuseppe, already in Australia.

The vessel continued to Sydney, arriving on 27 July. This was the final voyage made by *Principe di Udine* to Australia, as on returning to Italy it was withdrawn from service, and sold to shipbreakers in Italy. Sister ship *Tomaso di Savoie* continued in service to South America until the end of 1929, when it was also withdrawn and sold to Italian shipbreakers.

Principe di Udine

RANPURA and RANCHI

Built: 1925 by Hawthorn, Leslie & Co., Newcastle
Gross tonnage: 16,601
Dimensions: 570 x 71 ft/173.7 x 21.7 m
Service speed: 17 knots
Propulsion: Quadruple expansion/twin propellers

Ranpura made only one voyage to Australia, in 1929. It was the first completed of four liners built for P&O Line for their Indian service, and was named after a small princely state in Orissa. *Ranpura* was launched on 13 September 1924, delivered to P&O on 8 April 1925, and departed London on 3 April 1925 on its maiden voyage to Bombay.

The vessel was fitted with accommodation for 305 first class and 282 second class passengers. Over the next year *Ranpura* was joined by three sister ships, *Ranchi*, *Rawalpindi* and *Rajputana*, which became the prime ships on the P&O service to India.

In May 1929 *Ranpura* was hurriedly placed on the Australian service to replace *Mongolia* for one round trip. Departing London on 17 May, *Ranpura* called at Bombay and Colombo before arriving in Fremantle on 20 June, then continued to Adelaide, where it berthed on 23 June. The liner arrived in Melbourne on 24 June, and the voyage terminated at Sydney on 27 June. This was the only time one of the R ships made a voyage to Australia before 1939.

In 1930 *Ranpura* and her sisters were placed on the Far East service to Hong Kong and Shanghai, on which they served for the next nine years. In September 1937 *Ranpura* was fortunate to survive one of the worst typhoons ever to strike Hong Kong, in which more than 30 ships were lost.

On 6 September 1939, five days after World War II began, *Ranpura* arrived at Colombo on an outward voyage, but was immediately requisitioned and sent to Calcutta to be converted into an armed merchant cruiser.

All three sister ships also became armed merchant cruisers, and on 23 November 1940 *Rawalpindi* was sunk by the German battleships *Gneisenau* and *Scharnhorst* off Iceland. On 13 April 1941, *Rajputana* was torpedoed and sunk by the German submarine U108 west of Ireland.

In December 1944 *Ranpura* was bought by the British Admiralty, and converted into a fleet repair ship, being commissioned in this role in April 1946.

Ranchi also survived the war, and on 17 June 1948 left London on its first voyage to Australia as a migrant ship, a role it served in until 1953, when the vessel was sold to shipbreakers.

Ranpura served in the Royal Navy until November 1958, when it was laid up at Devonport. The vessel was sold to shipbreakers in Italy in April 1961, arriving at La Spezia on 25 May 1961 to be scrapped.

Ranpura

ESQUILINO, VIMINALE, ROMOLO and REMO

ESQUILINO VIMINALE
Built: 1925 by San RocCo., Trieste
Gross tonnage: 8,657
Dimensions: 462 X 57ft/140.8 x 17.3 m
Service speed: 13 knots
Propulsion: Diesel/twin propellers

ROMOLO REMO
Built: 1926/1927 by Stablimento TecniCo., Trieste
Gross tonnage: 9,780
Dimensions: 506 x 62 ft/154.2 x 18.9 m
Service speed: 13 knots
Propulsion: Diesel/twin propellers

Lloyd Triestino came into existence in 1919 as a result of Trieste becoming a part of Italy after World War I. The company was originally an Austrian concern known as Lloyd AustriaCo., which had been based in Trieste since 1836, but lost its entire fleet at the end of the war. Over the next few years Lloyd Triestino developed a network of services within the Mediterranean, and also to India and the Far East. For the latter service the company ordered two new motor ships, the first being launched in January 1925 and named *Esquilino*.

The first ocean-going passenger and cargo ship to be built in Italy, *Esquilino* entered service in June 1925. *Viminale* was launched on 9 May 1925 and departed Trieste on 25 October on a voyage to Shanghai and Yokohama. They were the first new ships built for Lloyd Triestino, and the first motor ships in their fleet.

Neither vessel was given a conventional funnel, instead having a small stovepipe for the engine exhaust. They had a small central superstructure with accommodation for 42 passengers in first class only, and black hulls.

Soon after *Esquilino* and *Viminale* entered service, Lloyd Triestino ordered two cargo liners for the Far East trade which would carry only three passengers. They were still under construction when it was decided to add extra accommodation due to the success of the first pair. The keel of the first ship was laid on 30 June 1925, and it was named *Romolo* when launched on 29 May 1926, being completed on 21 November, and entering service the following month. Construction of the second vessel commenced on 1 September 1925, and when launched on 14 August 1926 it was named *Remo*, being completed on 15 December and joining *Romolo* on the Far East trade in January 1927. As they were larger than the first pair, *Romolo* and *Remo* had supercharged diesel engines, and accommodation for 66 first class passengers.

In 1930 all four ships were chartered from Lloyd Triestino to operate on a combined Lloyd Sabaudo-NGI service between Italy and Australia. *Esquilino* and *Viminale* were altered to carry 60 first class and 200 third class passengers, while *Romolo* and *Remo* could accommodate 68 first class and 190 third class passengers. This entailed reducing the cargo capacity by constructing extra cabins in these areas, with additional superstructure and lifeboats.

The new service began during the second half of

Esquilino (WSS Victoria)

1930, the route being from Genoa, Naples and Messina to Port Said, Aden and Colombo, thence to Fremantle, Adelaide, Melbourne, Sydney and Brisbane. The first departure was taken in early June 1930 by *Remo*, but no passengers were carried. *Remo* arrived in Melbourne on 7 July and Sydney on 9 July, and the next day the *Sydney Morning Herald* reported:

Under command of Captain G. Camelli, the Italian motorship *Remo*, which is inaugurating a new monthly service between Genoa and Australian ports, arrived at Sydney yesterday afternoon. The service will be maintained by four motor vessels, chartered by Lloyd Sabaudo and Navigazione Generale Italiana lines in conjunction, and the *Remo* will be followed by the *Romolo*, *Esquilino*, and *Viminale*.

Built in 1927, the *Remo* is of 9,779 tons gross, and was formerly engaged in the Trieste-Japan trade. She has accommodation for 68 first-class passengers, and a limited number of third-class passengers, but on the present voyage is carrying only general cargo. The passenger service of the new line will be opened by the *Romolo*.

The amount of fuel carried gives the *Remo* a cruising radius of 12,000 miles. Whilst she was engaged on the Trieste-Japan run it was customary to take in fuel at Singapore on the outward voyage only, and this enabled her to run the round trip without refuelling at any other stage.

From Genoa the *Remo* brought a general cargo of 1,500 tons, 700 of which was brought to Sydney. For the return voyage her cargo will be mainly flour.

The first passenger voyage was taken by *Romolo*, which departed Genoa in August 1930, arriving in Sydney on 11 September. There was a very brief report

in the local press, which stated that 3 first class and 50 third class passengers disembarked in Sydney. Next came *Esquilino*, which arrived in Melbourne for the first time on 1 October 1930, and berthed in Sydney two days later. *Viminale* arrived in Melbourne on 28 October and Sydney two days later. *Remo* departed Genoa in October on its second voyage to Australia, but the first with passengers, arriving in Sydney on 28 November. A regular schedule of monthly departures was established, *Esquilino* being back in Melbourne on 30 January 1931, and *Viminale* making its second arrival on 4 March.

On 2 January 1932 Lloyd Sabaudo, NGI and a third Italian shipping company, the Cosulich Line, were merged by the Italian Government into a single company, Italia Flotte Riunite, better known as Italia Line, and from that date the Australian service was known as Italia & Cosulich Lines. At this time Italy was involved in a military operation in Ethiopa, and *Viminale* was taken off the Australian trade to make four trips with troops to Mogadishu, with a stop at Massawa en route.

In a booklet produced by Italia Line at this time there was a description of the first class accommodation on board the four ships:

The cabins are so commodious, with windows instead of portholes, a large mahogany wardrobe and mirror, modern bedsteads, electric fans, and an unlimited supply of fresh, running water. There is no sense of living in cramped quarters, and no part of the ship is overcrowded. You are very soon quite at your ease in the perfectly appointed Dining, Smoking, Reading and Music Rooms, and pick out your favourite corners in the comfortable Lounges and spacious Verandahs.

Romolo (WSS Victoria)

Remo with white hull

During the 1930s the number of Italian migrants coming to Australia increased considerably, but the vast majority were fathers and their older sons, the wives and other children following later. As there were few single women of Italian background in Australia, couples who had either never met, or not seen each other since they were children, would become engaged by proxy, then the fiancée would travel to Australia to meet up with her future husband on the dock, and marry him within a few days of arriving. This system was occasionally commented on in the local press. In 1935 the *Esquilino* made a special stop at Port Pirie to load cargo and disembark some passengers from Italy, and the local newspaper reported:

There were emotional scenes when the 18 for Port Pirie landed, and husbands and wives who had been separated for years met. Anxiety was depicted in the faces of both the men on the wharf and the women on the ship, who had been engaged by proxy, and had never seen each other before. There were numerous children, including babies in arms, among the passengers. All looked happy and hearty. They were particularly well dressed, not excepting those who had travelled third class.

In 1936 the Italian Government decided on a further rationalisation of the nation's shipping services, with Italia only operating services across the Atlantic, while Lloyd Triestino operated routes to the Far East, Africa, and Australia.

The arrangement came into force on 1 January 1937, when *Remo*, *Romolo*, *Esquilino* and *Viminale* reverted to Lloyd Triestino. Their hulls were repainted white, and the third class accommodation was increased to cater for up to 330 migrants.

In late August 1939, *Romolo* was on a voyage to Australia, but instead of entering Fremantle as planned stayed out at sea until it was known whether Italy would come into the war. When this did not happen, *Romolo* berthed in Fremantle, on 11 September. With Italy remaining nominally neutral, the four ships continued to operate to Australia.

Romolo arrived in Sydney on 9 May 1940, and was due to load 14,000 bales of wool, but as it was thought Italy was then about to enter war, the loading was delayed as much as possible. Eventually the cargo was loaded, and *Romolo* went on to Brisbane to load a further 5,000 bales of wool. Again the loading was held up as long as possible, but *Romolo* was allowed to depart on 5 June, supposedly for Genoa, but in reality bound for Yokohama. On board were 21 passengers and a crew of 115.

Romolo was shadowed by the Australian armed merchant cruiser *Manoora*, until on 9 June *Manoora* was ordered to return to Brisbane. Hours later Italy declared war, and *Manoora* was ordered to find *Romolo* and seize her. During the morning of 12 June she came upon *Romolo*, but a rain squall temporarily obscured the Italian vessel from her pursuer. By the time the storm passed the crew had set *Romolo* on fire and taken to the lifeboats. *Manoora* put some men on board *Romolo* to try and quell the blaze, but during the afternoon they were withdrawn. *Manoora* then fired several rounds into *Romolo* along the waterline, causing the vessel to sink. Her crew was taken back to Brisbane, and interned for the duration of hostilities.

Remo arrived at Fremantle on 5 June 1940 from Italy, and was due to land a small amount of cargo and continue its voyage to eastern Australia. The Australian Government insisted that all the cargo be unloaded at Fremantle, so the vessel was still there when Italy came into the war on 10 June. *Remo* was seized by the Australian Government. The crew and all 226 passengers on board were interned.

The ship was renamed *Reynella* and the passenger accommodation was removed to increase cargo capacity. Over the next five years *Reynella* made voyages from Australia to Liverpool, Colombo and Bombay, with occasional calls at Karachi, Cochin and Calcutta. However, the vessel suffered from endless machinery problems, and spent considerable periods laid up being repaired.

Of the other pair of ships, *Esquilino* was in Aden on 10 June 1940, the day Italy entered the war, and was seized by British military forces stationed there. She was renamed *Empire Governor*, and managed by the P&O Steam Navigation Co. for the Ministry of War Transport, serving the Allies for the remainder of the war. *Empire Governor* survived the war, but was then sold to ship-breakers, arriving at Dalmuir in March 1946.

Viminale was able to get back to Italy and on 6 September 1940 was taken over by the Italian Navy as a troop transport, mostly going to Albania and Greece. From November 1942 the vessel was engaged in transporting Italian troops across the Mediterranean to Tunis.

On the night of January 2–3 1943 *Viminale* was damaged during a raid on the port of Palermo by three British two-man mini-subs, known as 'chariots', launched from the British submarine, HMS *Trooper*, a short distance off the port. Chariot XVI was assigned *Viminale* as its primary target. The chariots had to get through an anti-torpedo net to get into the harbour, and only two actually succeeded. Rodney Dove, one of the crew from Chariot XVI, later described his attack:

After working our way hand over hand up the inner side of the net to the surface, I steered the chariot across the harbour to where our target, the 8,500-ton transport *Viminale*, was moored alongside the quay. The ship had a huge overhanging stern, with the rudder post coming down vertically into the water. It happened that, before leaving *Trooper*, I had picked up and fastened to my belt a coiled length of rope, about 15 feet, on the general grounds that it might well come in handy. It certainly did. I lashed the chariot's warhead to the ship's rudder post, on the seaward side so it wouldn't be seen from the quay, released the warhead from the chariot, and set the detonation time clock for one hour — or so I thought; in fact I must have set it for two hours. We then proceeded on the chariot (minus warhead) back to the anti-torpedo net at the harbour entrance, where I scuttled the chariot, and we made our way to the end of the mole, discarded our suits etc, and in due course made our way on foot out of the harbour.

The explosion of the warhead blew the stern off *Viminale*, and the damage was so extensive the ship needed to be moved to a mainland drydock for major repairs. On 23 January 1943 *Viminale* was off Capo d'Armi, being towed by a tug to Taranto, when both were hit by torpedoes fired by a British submarine. The tug was sunk, but *Viminale* was able to get back to Messina.

On 25 July 1943, when under tow off Cape Vaticano in the Straits of Messina, bound for Naples, *Viminale* was hit by torpedoes fired from two boats from American PT Squadron 15. This time the damage was mortal, and *Viminale* sank. The wreck is now a popular dive site, sitting upright on the bottom in clear water 100 metres down.

When the war ended, *Reynella* was placed under the control of the Australian Shipping Board, being managed by McDonald, Hamilton & Co., and operated mainly on a service to New Guinea. On 18 August 1947 on a voyage from Lae to Sydney, *Reynella* stranded on Jamard Island, near Finschhafen, when she was carrying a cargo of earthmoving equipment, and also 31 passengers. Initial attempts to refloat her, including one by the coastal liner *Duntroon*, proved unsuccessful, and eventually part of the reef on which she was sitting had to be blasted away. On 12 September *Reynella* was finally hauled free by HMS *Tancred*, and had to be towed stern first to Sydney, where she arrived on 18 October, and was laid up for several months.

On 13 February 1948 *Reynella* was towed out of Sydney to Newcastle and placed in the State Dockyard drydock for repairs. When the work was completed she was offered for sale, and on 1 July 1949 Lloyd Triestino purchased *Reynella*, giving her back the name *Remo*.

The ship still needed considerable refitting, and it was not until 21 November 1949 that *Remo* left Sydney for Italy. It had been the intention of Lloyd Triestino to return her to the Australian passenger trade again, but the vessel was damaged in a collision, and then further affected by a fire, so that eventually she was laid up and offered for sale.

In 1951 *Remo* was sold to Società Triestina Impresi Marittimi, another Italian concern, who removed much of her superstructure, installed new engines and added a normal funnel. The vessel was mainly intended for trade between Italy and Germany carrying ore and coal, but in November 1951 she loaded a cargo of 150 prefabricated houses constructed in Austria, and carried them to Australia, arriving in Newcastle on 30 December 1951. The vessel also went to Melbourne, being in port from 31 January to 22 February 1952 to load flour, then continued to Wallaroo to load wheat before returning to Italy.

This was her last visit to Australia, as later in 1952 *Remo* was sold again, to another Italian company, Nav. Triestina. Renamed *San Sergio*, she continued to operate as a cargo ship and in 1956 was transferred to the ownership of Marigensa Maritima Genovese SpA, of Genoa, but not renamed. On 22 August 1959 the vessel arrived at Kure, Japan, having been sold to shipbreakers there.

ERIDAN

Built: 1929 by Soc. Provencale de Cons. Nav., La Ciotat
Gross tonnage: 9,928
Dimensions: 475 x 61 ft/144.7 x 18.6 m
Service speed: 14.5 knots
Propulsion: Sulzer diesels/twin propellers

Designed to operate from Marseilles to the Far East, *Eridan* was launched on 3 June 1928. Completed eighteen months later she was the largest motor ship built in France up to that time. Accommodation was provided for 60 first class, 90 second class and 420 third class passengers, the latter aimed at the migrant trade from France. Third class was housed in the forward part of the ship, with the forward well deck covered over to provide a promenade deck.

On 19 November 1929 *Eridan* departed Marseilles on a special shakedown voyage to Alexandria, Haifa and Beirut, and on 10 January 1930 left Marseilles on its first voyage to Australia, arriving in Melbourne on 19 February and Sydney three days later. On 23 February the *Sydney Morning Herald* reported:

The *Eridan* carries three classes of passengers. Even the third class travel in comparative luxury. The first-class accommodation is remarkable for the handsome furnishings, woodwork, and decorative paintings, roomy state-rooms, airy dining rooms and generous deck promenades are noticeable features on this unusual vessel. The *Eridan* has two square funnels, a feature which...has not made its appearance on any other vessel afloat.

The motor ship brought 114 passengers, including British, French, Greeks, Hindoos, Poles, Germans and Americans.

The vessel made one more voyage to Australia in 1930, arriving in July, and left Marseilles again in December on its third trip to Australia. During the next five years, *Eridan* made two trips a year to Australia, the last departing Marseilles in August 1935, passing through Melbourne on 13 September.

Eridan was then used on a route from Marseilles through the Panama Canal to Tahiti and Noumea, and also operated to the Far East. *Eridan* came under Vichy control in 1940 following the fall of France, was captured by Allied ships off North Africa on 8 November 1942, and subsequently was operated as a troopship by the British Government.

After the war *Eridan* operated from Marseilles to Madagascar, Reunion and Mauritius. On 19 November 1948, *Eridan* departed Marseilles on a voyage to Australia, and on returning to France resumed trading to the Indian Ocean islands.

In 1951 the two square funnels were replaced by a single conventional funnel, which quite changed the appearance of the vessel. After a further spell on the Indian Ocean trade, *Eridan* made several more trips from Marseilles to Noumea via the Panama Canal. Its last voyage ended in Marseilles in January 1956, and in March *Eridan* was sold to local shipbreakers

Eridan

STRATHNAVER and STRATHAIRD

Built: 1931/1932 by Vickers Armstrong, Barrow
Gross tonnage: 22,547/22,544
Dimensions: 664 x 80 ft/202.4 x 24.4 m
Service speed: 20 knots
Propulsion: Turbo-electric/twin propellers

The design of this pair revolutionised the appearance of the P&O fleet, with their totally new colours and new name theme. On 5 February 1931 *Strathnaver* was launched, the second being named *Strathaird* when launched on 18 July 1931. The two ships provided berths for 498 first-class and 668 tourist class passengers.

On trials both ships managed 23 knots, and could maintain 21 knots for lengthy periods with ease. Their three funnels were just for appearance as only the centre one worked, the other two being dummies.

Handed over to P&O on 2 September 1931 *Strathnaver* left Tilbury on her maiden voyage to Australia on 2 October. *Strathaird* was delivered to P&O on 10 January 1932 and left Tilbury on her maiden voyage on 12 February.

On 23 December 1932 *Strathaird* left Sydney on the first P&O cruise from Australia, a five-day jaunt to Norfolk Island. Throughout the 1930s both ships operated cruises at irregular intervals.

Within weeks of the declaration of war in September 1939, *Strathnaver* and *Strathaird* were taken over by the British Government as troopships. Both loaded troops in Australia and New Zealand in January 1940 and sailed in the first convoy to Egypt. *Strathaird* returned to Australia to carry troops in the second convoy, leaving Melbourne for the Middle East on 15 April 1940.

Both ships were involved in the invasion of North Africa in November 1942, *Strathnaver* being in the first convoy. *Strathnaver* also took part in the Italian landings, then both ships returned to general trooping duties until the end of the war.

Strathaird was returned to P&O in 1946 and refitted by Harland & Wolff at Belfast. The two dummy funnels were removed, the remaining funnel raised in height, and accommodation was installed for 573 first-class and 496 tourist class passengers. On 22 January 1948 she left Tilbury bound for Australia.

Strathnaver was not released until October 1948, then was refitted in identical manner. She was the last of the P&O liners to return to service, leaving Tilbury on 5 January 1950.

In 1954 both vessels were converted to carry 1,252 tourist class passengers only. On 28 March 1961 *Strathaird* left Tilbury on her final voyage to Australia, then was sold to Shun Fung Iron Works of Hong Kong, where she arrived on 24 July for breaking up.

Strathnaver left on her final voyage to Australia from Tilbury on 7 December 1961. Sold to the same breakers as *Strathaird*, she arrived in Hong Kong in April 1962.

Strathnaver

CARTHAGE and CORFU

Built: 1931 by A. Stephen & Co., Glasgow
Gross tonnage: 14,304/14,293
Dimensions: 540 x 71 ft/164.5 x 21.7 m
Service speed: 17.5 knots
Propulsion: Geared turbines/twin propellers

This pair was designed for the P&O service from London to the Far East. The first to be launched was *Corfu*, on 20 May 1931, being handed over to P&O on 24 September, and departing London on its maiden voyage on 16 October. *Carthage* was launched on 18 August 1931, and completed quite quickly, being handed over to P&O on 25 November, and leaving the following month on its maiden voyage to the Far East.

Corfu was fitted out to carry 178 first and 200 second class passengers, while *Carthage* had berths for 175 first class and 196 second class.

In 1932 both liners made voyages to Australia while *Strathaird* and *Strathnaver* were cruising from Britain. The first departure was taken by *Carthage* from London on 22 April 1932, going to Bombay and Colombo before reaching Melbourne on 30 May and Sydney on 2 June.

Corfu departed London on 20 May 1932 on its first trip to Australia, arriving in Melbourne on 27 June, Sydney three days later, and Brisbane on 3 July. *Corfu* went back to the Far East trade until departing London on 20 April 1933 on its second voyage to Australia, arriving in Melbourne on 29 May, Sydney on 1 June and Brisbane on 5 June.

On 14 June 1935, *Corfu* left London on its final trip to Australia, via Bombay, Colombo, Fremantle and Adelaide, reaching Melbourne on 22 July, Sydney three days later, and Brisbane on 28 July.

On 12 June 1936, *Carthage* departed London on its second voyage to Australia, passing through Fremantle on 14 July, Adelaide on 18 July, Melbourne two days later, arriving in Sydney on 23 July and Brisbane on 26 July.

Soon after the war started both liners were requisitioned and converted for service as armed merchant cruisers. On 10 July 1940, *Corfu* collided with the aircraft carrier HMS *Hermes* off Freetown, with both ships sustaining considerable damage which had them out of action for several months. Later in the war *Carthage* and *Corfu* were used as troop transports.

Handed back to P&O in 1947, both vessels underwent lengthy refits, during which they were fitted with accommodation for 181 first class and 213 tourist class passengers, the dummy after funnel was removed, and they were given white hulls and a single tall yellow funnel.

In 1948 *Carthage* and *Corfu* returned to the Far East trade, on which they served until 1961, when both were sold to shipbreakers in Japan, being renamed *Carthage Maru* and *Corfu Maru* for their final voyages from Britain. *Carthage* arrived in Osaka during May 1961, while *Corfu* arrived at Niihama in August the same year.

Carthage

ORION and ORCADES

Built: 1935/1937 by Vickers Armstrong, Barrow
Gross tonnage: 23,371/23,456
Dimensions: 665 x 82 ft/202.7 x 25 m
Service speed: 20 knots
Propulsion: Geared turbines/twin propellers

The launching of *Orion* on 7 December 1934 in Barrow was performed by remote control by wireless by the Duke of Gloucester in Brisbane, when he pressed a button that sent an electric signal to the shipyard, triggering the launching mechanism.

Orion was the first British ship to be fitted with air conditioning, though this was confined to the dining rooms. Her full passenger complement was 486 in first class and 653 in tourist class, with a crew of 466, but she was also intended for cruises, carrying a maximum of 600 passengers in one class. On delivery in August 1935 *Orion* made a series of cruises, the first leaving Tilbury on 14 August for Norway. On 29 September the vessel left Tilbury on her maiden voyage to Australia. The only problem encountered was smuts from the funnel falling on the after decks, but this was rectified when the funnel was increased in height.

Orcades was launched on 1 December 1936, and handed overe on 10 July 1937. *Orcades* could carry 463 first class and 605 tourist class passengers. Her first voyage was a Mediterranean cruise, which left Southampton on 21 August. On 9 October 1937 *Orcades* left Tilbury on its first voyage to Australia.

Orion and *Orchades* alternated line voyages to Australia with cruises until war broke out in September 1939, when they were converted into troopships. Both were included in the first convoy to carry Australian troops overseas in January 1940.

On 15 September 1941 *Orion* was following the battleship HMS *Revenge* in a convoy in the South Atlantic when the steering gear on the warship jammed. *Orion* rammed *Revenge* and the impact tore a large hole in her bow, but she was able to continue to Cape Town where temporary repairs were made. Then she stayed with the convoy to Singapore, where repairs were completed.

On 10 October 1942 *Orcades* was struck by three torpedoes fired by *U172* some 217 miles out from Cape Town, and the liner was abandoned by all but a handful of crew and officers. Later three more torpedoes hit her and she sank soon afterward.

Orion was released from Government control in April 1946, having steamed over 380,000 miles and carried some 175,000 persons in her war career. Increased passenger accommodation was installed for 546 in first class and 706 in tourist class, and on 25 February 1947 *Orion* left Tilbury, the first Orient liner to return to the Australian trade.

On 28 February 1963 *Orion* left Tilbury on her final voyage to Australia, then was chartered for service as a hotel ship at Hamburg. On 1 October that year she left Hamburg for Antwerp to be scrapped.

Orcades

STRATHMORE, STRATHEDEN and STRATHALLAN

Built: 1935/37/38 by Vickers Armstrong, Barrow
Gross tonnage: 23,428/23,722/23,722
Dimensions: 665 x 82 ft/202.7 x 25 m
Service speed: 20 knots
Propulsion: Geared turbines/twin propellers

Strathmore was launched on 4 April 1935, being completed in September that year. Her first voyage was a cruise, then on 26 October the vessel left Tilbury for Australia. Despite being larger than the original Strath liners (page 187), *Strathmore* carried fewer passengers, 445 first class and 665 tourist class.

Stratheden was launched on 10 June 1937, handed over to P&O on 10 December, and left Tilbury on 24 December 1937 on her maiden voyage. *Strathallan* was launched on 23 September 1937, making her maiden departure from Tilbury on 18 March to Australia. Both vessels could carry 448 first class and 563 tourist class passengers.

All three ships spent part of each year cruising. When war broke out in September 1939 they were taken over for duty as troopships, carrying troops to many parts of the world. All three were involved in the North Africa landings in November 1942.

Early on 21 December 1942, *Strathallan*, carrying 4000 troops and 250 nurses, was torpedoed off Oran. An attempt was made to tow the ship to safety, but a fire started and the ship had to be abandoned. In the early hours of 22 December *Strathallan* sank, only 12 miles (19 km) from Oran.

In 1946 *Stratheden* was handed back to P&O and refitted with berths for 527 first class and 453 tourist-class passengers, leaving Tilbury in June 1947 for Australia.

Strathmore was retained by the Government until 1948, when she was finally returned to her owners. Her refit was scheduled to finish in June 1949 but dragged on several months longer, so it was 26 October 1949 before she left Tilbury on her first voyage to Australia since the war. The accommodation was rebuilt to carry 497 first class and 487 tourist-class passengers. In 1962 both *Strathmore* and *Stratheden* had their accommodation altered for 1,200 tourist class passengers only.

On 20 June 1963 *Strathmore* left Tilbury on her final voyage to Australia. *Stratheden* left Tilbury on 7 August 1963 on her final voyage, and was then chartered to the Travel Savings Association for four cruises.

Both ships were sold to Greek shipowner, John S. Latsis, *Strathmore* being renamed *Marianna Latsi* while *Stratheden* became *Henrietta Latsi*, but in 1964 the liners swapped names. Used occasionally on the pilgrim trade to Jeddah, they spent long periods laid up at Piraeus. Finally both were sold to shipbreakers at La Spezia in 1969, the former *Stratheden* arriving there on 19 May, followed by her sister on 27 May.

Strathallan

DOMINION MONARCH

Built: 1939 by Swan, Hunter & Wigham Richardson Ltd,
Newcastle
Gross tonnage: 26,463 gross
Dimensions: 682 x 84 ft /207.8 x 25.8 m
Service speed: 19 knots
Propulsion: Doxford diesel /quadruple screws

Dominion Monarch was built for Shaw Savill Line, being launched on 27 July 1938. The vessel departed London on its maiden voyage on 16 February 1939, calling at Southampton the next day to embark passengers. The voyage went to Cape Town and Durban before arriving in Fremantle on 13 March. Following visits to Melbourne and Sydney, *Dominion Monarch* continued to New Zealand ports, then followed the reverse route back to Britain. The vessel could accommodate 517 passengers, all first class, with six holds capable of carrying a large amount of cargo.

Dominion Monarch remained in commercial operation to Australia and New Zealand until August 1940, then was requisitioned and sent to Liverpool for conversion into a troopship.

In December 1941, *Dominion Monarch* arrived in Singapore, and was put into drydock to have the engines dismantled for overhaul. When it became clear that Singapore was about to be captured by the Japanese, the ship's own engineers were able to rebuild the engines very quickly, and the ship escaped just before the island fell.

By the time the war ended, *Dominion Monarch* had carried over 90,000 troops and 70,000 tons of cargo while travelling some 350,000 miles.

After the war ended, *Dominion Monarch* made several voyages repatriating troops to Australia and New Zealand, then in July 1947 was handed back to its owners, and was given an extensive refit, in which the accommodation was rebuilt for 508 first class passengers. *Dominion Monarch* left London on 17 December 1948, on its first post-war commercial voyage to Australia and New Zealand.

Dominion Monarch carried fare-paying passengers and assisted migrants to both Australia and New Zealand, but relied heavily on cargo to make its operation financially viable. Due to frequent waterfront strikes in both Australia and New Zealand, the schedule was often disrupted, which was unpopular with passengers. In 1955 Shaw Savill introduced *Southern Cross*, which carried no cargo, and such was its success a second ship was ordered to replace *Dominion Monarch*.

Dominion Monarch departed London on 30 December 1961 on its final voyage, departing Wellington on 15 March 1962 to return to Britain. By the time the liner reached London, it had been sold to the Mitsui Group of Japan.

They chartered *Dominion Monarch* to an American consortium for service as a floating hotel in Seattle during the World's Fair held there from June to November 1962.

When the charter ended, the liner was renamed *Dominion Monarch Maru* for the voyage from Seattle to Osaka, where it arrived on 25 November 1962 at the Mitsui shipbreaking yard.

Dominion Monarch

Index